PRAISE FOR *THE HYBRID TIGER*

"A richly rewarding examination of Chinese and American culture and parenting. . . . The rewards promise to transcend the classroom."

—*Publishers Weekly*, starred review

"Huang's thoughtful praise and critically constructive observations of two widely regarded and often-replicated educational systems readily translate into practical applications for improving today's schools. What a pleasure it is to see the personal and familial value assigned to education heralded as critical to a student's success at the primary and secondary level."

—Thomas M. Kelly, PhD
Headmaster, Horace Mann School, New York, NY,
#3 Best Private Day School in the United States (PrepReview.com, 2013)

"Huang lays out before us a very interesting phenomenon as he analyzes the Chinese family's approach to education and the very American approach. . . . Dr. Huang forces us to view the successes of both cultures in the hope of finding the ideal view of education."

—Mark E. Ertel
Principal, Darnell-Cookman Middle/High School of the Medical Arts,
Jacksonville, FL, #7 Most Challenging High School (*Washington Post*, 2013)

"Provides substantial insight into many of the factors that empower Asian and Asian-American students to succeed at much higher levels than their American peers. . . . As Huang explores the spectrum of differences between American and Chinese culture . . . one significant conclusion emerges: both cultures have much to offer, but the real power is in a healthy blend of both so that students and families can achieve balance in pursuit of achievement and joy."

—Tim Gott, EdD
President, National Consortium for Specialized
Secondary Schools of Mathematics, Science, and Technology;
director, Gatton Academy of Mathematics and Science,
Bowling Green, KY, #1 High School in the United States (*Newsweek*, 2013)

"Huang's work illustrates the paramount strengths and glaring weaknesses of our pedagogy and gives commonsense strategies for how to improve and reform. Anyone interested in a real comparative analysis of Chinese and American educational systems will appreciate the new lens that Huang brings into focus."

—Bob Holden
Chairman of the Midwest US–China Association;
former governor of Missouri

"An extraordinary book. . . . I would recommend [it] as an educational tool to understand the differences between the cultures of Asian and American education. More importantly, I believe it will confirm important habits and traits that help lay out critical components to successful parenting with regards to education."

—Dr. Susan Lang
Superintendent, Wyoming City Schools, Wyoming, OH
(Wyoming High School, #2 Best High School in Ohio,
US News & World Report, 2013)

"[Huang's] personal stories and reflections serve to underscore the Chinese 'collectivist sacrificial style of cooperation' with respect to parenting, education, and child development, and to bring the reader to a clearer understanding of the American and Chinese cultural similarities and differences through the personal voice of Quanyu Huang, 'the hybrid tiger.'"

—Judith Peterson
Principal of Academic Magnet High School,
North Charleston, SC, #10 Best High School (*US News & World Report*)

THE HYBRID TIGER

THE
HYBRID
TIGER

Secrets of the Extraordinary Success
of Asian-American Kids

QUANYU HUANG

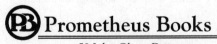

Prometheus Books

59 John Glenn Drive
Amherst, New York 14228

Published 2014 by Prometheus Books

Prometheus Books recognizes the following registered trademarks mentioned within the text: Big Mac®, Coke®, Dairy Queen®, Facebook®, Flintstones®, McDonald's®, Nintendo®, PlayStation®, Popsicle®, Twitter®, Xbox®.

Coverage image © Media Bakery
Cover design by Nicole Sommer-Lecht

Inquiries should be addressed to
Prometheus Books
59 John Glenn Drive
Amherst, New York 14228
VOICE: 716–691–0133
FAX: 716–691–0137
WWW.PROMETHEUSBOOKS.COM

18 17 16 15 14   5 4 3 2 1

Library of Congress Cataloging-in-Publication Data Pending

ISBN 978-1-61614-851-5 (pbk.)
ISBN 978-1-61614-582-2 (ebook)

Printed in the United States of America

CONTENTS

6   CONTENTS

ACKNOWLEDGMENTS

In chapter 5 I mention a sixteen-year-old Olympian stepping out onto a ten-meter diving platform with the weight of the world on her shoulders. While she was the only one on the platform, she did not get there on her own. Countless others worked tirelessly and sacrificed to help her climb onto that platform. Like her, I've been able to get where I am because of the people around me.

One of those people is my father. I came to the United States to pursue a dream that began with him. From the time he first encountered American airmen in China during World War II, my father dreamed of coming to this country. While he himself never had the means or the opportunity, he made sure that I did. That dream was bolstered by my mother, who told me when I was young that *engaging in education is to write history*. It's taken me more than thirty years to understand what she meant—and I'm still today unraveling more of the meaning contained in that single sentence.

This book is a perfect example of how all projects are family projects. From its inception, my wife has helped me in innumerable ways—not just by helping to shape the contents of the book and the underlying theory, but also by raising our son and helping me create the material to fill out its pages. And these acknowledgments would not be complete without thanking my son, who has in many ways inspired this text, bearing witness to the many poignant moments that underpin it and living through this life with my wife and me. This "family project" also depended on the help of my sisters, who took care of my ill father and mother after I left China, and the selfless support my brother provided when I was a poor doctoral student. Each of these people has helped me get to where I am.

In addition, I would like to acknowledge and thank my editors, Steven L. Mitchell, Brian McMahon, and Swapna Lovin, and my agent, Bridget Wagner Matzie. I'd also like to express my gratitude to all those at Random House and Prometheus Books who have made this book possible, especially Jill Maxick, Meghan Quinn, and Melissa Raé Shofner. And of course, I'd like to thank my students, who have also provided assistance, especially Aaron Gilkison, Rachel Wayne, Kexin Li, and Maria Song.

Finally, I would like to give a very special thank you to Rick Wolff, who has believed in and supported me, and has kindly helped me to make this book a reality.

INTRODUCTION
THE BESIEGED CITY

Life is a besieged city girded by high walls. As the struggle continues, the people who live inside dream only of getting out, and the people who live outside want only to get in. This is the way of marriage, and business, and life, and everything in between.[1]
— *The Besieged City*, Qian Zhongshu

JOURNEY TO THE WEST

1

I first encountered American primary education as a professor in the summer of 1989. I had no way of knowing it then, but this experience would have a profound effect on me, haunting me for years to come and ultimately changing the course of my entire life. It also brought out a lot of stories, forcing me to rethink my beliefs about Chinese parenting and American education.

In 1988 York College of Pennsylvania offered me a teaching position. The terms of York's offer were simple: as part of a new exchange program, I would teach Chinese and Chinese culture, and, in return, the university would provide me with free board and lodging as well as what they called a "modest" stipend of $400 per month. At that time, my salary as a lecturer in China was exactly 69 Yuan per month, or about $18. In comparison, $400 per month was a *fortune*. This was my once-in-a-lifetime chance. With little delay, I accepted York College's offer. However, by taking this new position in faraway America, I was leaving behind my wife, my three-year-old son, and nearly everything else I'd ever known in China. I was thirty-six.

On January 23, 1988, I rode on an airplane for the first time, headed for a place called "New York," where my friend, Dr. Peterman, would meet me.

Together, we'd drive to Pennsylvania. I'd originally met Dr. Peterman in China, where I'd taught him Chinese. I was relieved that I'd have a familiar face to meet me upon landing in America. In my pocket, I had $55 in cash: one $50 bill (by far the most valuable thing I'd ever owned) and five $1 bills. I'd been told that I should bring a few single dollar bills because Americans always pay tips. I wasn't sure who these tips were for, but I was certain this was one of those many details I'd figure out along the way.

Though commonplace today, Chinese professors teaching in American universities were a rarity in the 1980s. At that point in my life, I felt every bit the frontiersman. Few in my family had ever even left our home province of Guangxi, let alone the country or continent. Indeed, not a single one of my classmates had ever been to America at that point. On the plane, I remember realizing that, apart from when Deng Xiaoping met Jimmy Carter, I couldn't really think of many other Chinese people who had ever set foot in America. And here I was, headed for Pennsylvania to teach at an American university. This was my age of discovery. I was Vasco da Gama. I was Ponce de León. And York, Pennsylvania, was the new world.

And what a bizarre world it was! From the big to the small, everything in America seemed to operate by a different set of rules. The colors, the sounds, and even the smells seemed to be drawn from a different palette entirely. In the evenings in particular, when York began to settle down and the cloudless sky grew dark and somber (and that unique, eerie silence of the American Midwest set in), I often felt as though I'd walked through a tear in space and time.

Like any cautious frontiersman, I explored my new surroundings deliberately but carefully. I began by watching hundreds of hours of American television—including two full seasons of *Cheers*. In order to facilitate my assimilation, the friends I made (the Bittners, Glandons, Achtzehns, Kulbickis, and many others) often subjected me to a variety of strange American activities. For whatever reason, these activities usually involved food.

With my stomach as the conduit, I grew more American by the day. Within a few months, I'd eaten my first hamburger, my first basket of French fries, my first hot dog, and my first bucket of fried chicken, and I'd drank my first (and last) cup of coffee. I'd also tried no less than a dozen brands of dry cereals and even more types of ice cream. Then there were the *hundreds* of Cokes I drank to wash it all down. Each of these foods intrigued and delighted me.

But not all American cuisine made sense to me. I found some staples of American food culture to be truly and deeply enigmatic. Consider, for example, the *salad*. Few American customs perplexed me as much as the salad before dinner. I was not alone. I remember having tremendous difficulty describing the basic concept of a salad to my wife.

"Lettuce," I remember stating in exasperation into the phone. "It's mostly lettuce."

"Is that it?"

"There are also very small tomatoes . . . and carrots . . . and white broccoli." The concept of cauliflower was foreign to me.

"I don't get it," my wife said. "They don't cook it?"

"No."

"They don't even steam it? Boil it?"

"I told you already. It's raw."

"How do you eat it?"

"You put some sour oil on it, and then you just eat it cold."

"Just like that?" I remember her asking. "Like . . . like a cow?"

Other oddities I encountered included casseroles, mustard, beer, bourbon, and rare, bloody steaks—tastes that, to this day, I have yet to master. And, finally, there was *cheese*. Few in America truly appreciate just how profoundly odd cheese is. From texture to flavor to concept, cheese remains (for me) a great and ongoing mystery.

2

The most vexing and meaningful American mystery, however, materialized in May 1989. Around that time, a colleague of mine at York College invited me to give a short lecture at his son's private school. His son was only in fifth grade, he told me, but he was in the gifted program and they just happened to be learning about China in their world history class. He asked me whether I would be willing to give a short speech about China or Chinese culture to some of these students.

"It'd be a real treat," he said. "Most of the kids have never even met anyone from China."

Not giving it much thought, I agreed.

To be honest, I was not overly enthusiastic about visiting or lecturing at an American primary school. I'd heard stories about how unruly and disrespectful American students were and felt that I already knew everything there was to know about American primary education. Schools in the United States were vastly different from Chinese schools. American kids cared more about having fun than studying. American pupils simply could not compete with their Chinese peers. These truths seemed evident to me, and I had little interest in exploring them. Nevertheless, I had promised my friend I would go, so there was no backing out.

On the day of the lecture, when I arrived at the school, I was directed to a small classroom. The teacher, a nice middle-aged woman, met me outside and introduced herself before leading me into the room. Several different things caught my eye.

The first thing that struck me was the size of the class. There were no more than fifteen or twenty kids—barely a class at all by Chinese standards, where classes hold at least fifty or sixty students each. A friend of mine who is a principal at a very highly rated Chinese elementary school is fond of telling a joke about the size of the classes at his school: when parents call to beg and plead to have their child admitted to a particular class, the first question he asks is "How fat is your kid?"

The second thing I noticed was that none of the kids greeted me as I entered the classroom. This would have been unthinkable in China, where utter respect for teachers is drilled into children at a young age. Students immediately stand at attention to greet any lecturer in a classroom. Not only did these students not stand up, few bothered to even acknowledge my presence.

After a brief introduction by the teacher, I began the short lecture I'd prepared. I immediately noticed something else: none of the kids were paying attention. Barely a minute had passed and they had already started to lose interest.

To be fair, the lecture I prepared was quite tame. Perhaps even worse than tame. I dare say that by my current standards, the lecture I gave that day was nothing short of *boring*. I discussed such evocative themes as what Chinese people ate for breakfast, how to say a few basic greetings in Chinese, and what the weather was like in my hometown of Liuzhou. Add that to the fact that I spoke little English at the time, and it's understandable that the kids would have been less than enthralled.

As I diligently made my way through my presentation, I watched them as much as they watched me. The kids didn't sit like Chinese students. They slouched and slumped. Their eyes wandered. Some stared into space. What's more, they didn't pay attention like Chinese kids. Most seemed to be following along, but others barely seemed to notice I was there. Two in the back paid no attention at all, whispering back and forth with one another while giggling. A plump red-haired boy in the corner puzzled me the most, nodding his head slowly and rhythmically in such a way that I didn't know if he was following along and agreeing or simply falling asleep.

This is preposterous, I remember thinking to myself. These American kids have no respect! They're not even listening. At least Chinese kids would feel obligated to feign some sort of interest. There must be some merit in that.

At the end of my bumbling lecture, I was relieved to wrap up. When I finally finished, the kids clapped begrudgingly and the teacher had them thank me aloud. Then she did something unexpected.

"All right class, does anyone have any questions for Mr. Huang?" she said. I was shocked. In China, even my college students weren't allowed to question me, their professor. And here I was about to be interrogated by a group of American primary school students!

"What do you think about that stuff that's going on in Ten-ah-men right now?" a boy asked, referring to the Tian'anmen Square protests that had occurred just a few weeks earlier. Slightly pudgy with short brown hair, he had a kind face, I thought to myself. He didn't *look* like a menace. But there he was, standing up and asking me a question with so many repercussions. I knew, as a visiting professor who had just come from China, that I shouldn't even begin to touch on this sensitive topic. Not only did I not have an answer to the question; I couldn't have answered it if I'd had an entire year to prepare.

"Excuse me," I said, scrambling for time. "I did not hear your question."

The boy stood up again and repeated his question once more.

"I was just wondering, like, what you thought of the stuff that's on the TV about China and Ten-ah-men."

I looked at him, stunned and, for a moment, confused. Initially, I had been taken aback. I couldn't believe this child's disrespect and lack of sensitivity. I was sure that the teacher, the kind woman who was sitting at her desk in the corner, would intercede at any moment—jump in, scold him, and apologize to me.

But she did nothing of the sort. Instead, she just looked up at me from her desk with what seemed like avid interest. Was she allowing this? No, worse, she was condoning it—encouraging it even! Perhaps sensing my agitation, *all* of the children suddenly seemed to be alert and listening. Even the fat one with the red hair had awoken from his slumber. All of them looking at me, expecting an answer.

"Well," I began, "this is a very ... this question is not ... I would say that there are many ... uh ... the modern ... you see, it is complicated."

I went on and on. I can't pretend to tell you I gave a competent answer. I highly doubt any of it was even comprehensible. I was so caught off guard by the child's question that I couldn't string together a presentable thought in Chinese, let alone in English!

While I was struggling, the boy laughed. "You said a lot of stuff," he said, perhaps just as confused as I was by my ramblings, "but you really haven't answered my question yet."

Before I had a chance to recover, another hand shot up.

"My daddy goes to Japan sometimes. What is the biggest difference between Chinese people and Japanese people?"

The question came from a little girl in the second row. I looked at her in wonder. In *The Art of War*, Sun Tzu once said, "If you know neither your enemies nor yourself, you will be imperiled in every single battle."[2] Ever since the Sino-Japanese War in 1894, and particularly after World War II, the Chinese have been asking themselves the very question this little girl had just posed to me. *Who are the Japanese? Who are we? How are the Japanese different from us?* These were questions that could have changed the course of history, if anyone in China had bothered to ask them earlier in the century. While I fumbled together an answer for her, more hands shot up.

"What part of American culture do you dislike most?"

"What do you miss most about China?"

"What do you like best about America?"

"What parts of China would you change if you could?"

"What do you think China will be like in ten years?"

3

That night, I couldn't sleep. I lay in the dark, staring at empty space, thinking of what had transpired. I was rattled. My entire world was all of a sudden uncomfortable and strange. I felt bizarrely naïve. It was as though I had been one of Plato's simple cave creatures, staring at the shadows on the wall, and it was this class of ten-year-old children that had led me into the world with all of its brightness and brilliance. And here I was, with the blindness quickly fading from my eyes.

In China, I thought to myself, I'd never seen a child of that age ask questions such as these. And it wasn't just the content of the questions, but the way they were asked! There was a boldness, a direct and unabashed quality that I hadn't seen before. Though they weren't necessarily thinking at an abnormally high level, these kids weren't afraid to think independently. Nor were they afraid to voice their questions and challenge their teachers.

Then came an even more shocking thought. Was this typical of American students? Was this typical of American schools? What kind of primary education system does America have? How did their children learn to be so bold? So confident? So brash yet so reflective?

Nevertheless, where at one time I felt confident that Chinese primary and secondary education was far superior to America's, all of a sudden I had very few answers.

4

I couldn't help but be reminded of something my mother, a teacher, once said to me about education and history.

My mother graduated from Sun Yat-Sen University in China after World War II. At that time, very few women could go to such a school, which was one of the top universities in China. Later, she served as a teacher at an ordinary middle school. I thought that was very unusual, as I'd have expected her to pursue grand opportunities with her illustrious degree.

One day, I asked her, "You went to a prestigious university and majored in history. Why, out of everything you could have chosen, did you decide to teach middle school?"

She smiled and said cryptically, "Son, engaging in education is to write history."

I couldn't understand what she was saying then, but her words stuck with me for many years: "To engage in education is to write history." What did it mean?

Now I realized that the questions those American children asked me had given me fascinating insight into my mother's words: the future of a country did not rest in the hands of its politicians but instead in the forgotten hands of its teachers and parents, who educated and cultivated children. How far a country could go would depend on its education.

CHINESE EDUCATION
VERSUS AMERICAN EDUCATION

1

I once heard a very interesting anecdote about Chinese and American education. It is said that in the late 1970s, after the dust settled from the Cultural Revolution, China suddenly realized that it had been isolated from the outside world for a very long time. In a rare example of outward curiosity, Chinese officials decided that it was high time to see what the rest of the world was up to—especially those old American imperialists across the ocean.

How far ahead were the Americans? What were they teaching their children? How did they run their schools? How far behind had the Chinese fallen? With these questions in mind, a cabal of Chinese educational experts left on a mission to investigate American education.

No one was sure what to expect.

When the Chinese delegation arrived in the United States, they visited a local public school. They were dumbstruck by what they found. These were not classrooms. *They were carnivals!*

From kindergarten to high school, the students seemed to care very little about learning. Most were inattentive and uninterested. Some were even actively disruptive and highly disrespectful. To make matters worse, the teachers seemed to hold little authority, often begging and negotiating with students for their attention. These classes were reminiscent of the chaos of Chinese farmers' markets, the delegates thought, rather than proper educational classrooms.

On top of all this, it was clear that the American kids lagged far behind in terms of ability. None of the children in the second and third grades knew their multiplication or division tables. Even in middle school, many kids failed to grasp these basic concepts. Meanwhile, school administrators and teachers seemed oblivious, prattling on about meaningless subjects such as personal growth, self-esteem, individuality, and creativity.

What use are these lofty concepts, the Chinese delegates laughed, *when the kids still count with their fingers?*

Upon returning to Beijing, the Chinese delegates reported their findings.

There is nothing to fear, they told their comrades. *American education is broken. The students are inept and unmotivated. The schools are little better than circuses. As an institution, American education is sick beyond treatment. In twenty years*, they concluded, *China will most assuredly make unrivaled advances in science and technology and overtake America as the preeminent global superpower. And America, just like the fabled kingdom of Atlantis, will descend into the unknown.*

2

The story doesn't end there. It is also said that America sent a delegation to China that very same year in the late 1970s. Like their Chinese counterparts, the Americans were interested in how the Chinese educated their children.

And just like their Chinese counterparts, they were shocked by what they found.

From kindergarten to high school, Chinese schools were *terrifying* displays of focus, industry, and capability. Every day at dawn, students of all ages sat patiently in massive classrooms across the country in the same unnatural posture: backs straight, feet flat on the floor and shoulder width apart, hands on their desks, and eyes fixed on the teacher. Even the youngest of students held this posture with militaristic diligence. No one spoke out of turn. No one acted out. Every eye stayed carefully trained on the teacher at the front of the class.

On top of that, Chinese students seemed to spend nearly double the amount of time in class and were assigned *many* times the amount of homework as their American peers. Even the youngest among them had homework of a nature and amount that the American delegates had rarely (if ever) seen in America.

Upon returning home, the American delegates presented their findings.

Chinese students are the most diligent in the world, they reported. *Their intensity and abilities cannot be matched by their American peers. The Chinese system reinforces and refines these strengths at every turn. If this continues*, the American delegates concluded (with furrowed brows and subdued voices), *the advances China will make in science and technology will be unfathomable. In a mere twenty years, by the time this generation of super students comes of age, the Chinese will leave the United States far, far behind.*

3

This anecdote is just one version of a more general story that has been told for quite some time now: Chinese education is on the upswing and American education is in decline. Not only has this been a popular nationalist view in

China, it is a recurring tale told more and more frequently in America by Americans.

Indeed, for more than thirty years now, Americans have been decrying their own education system while praising the education systems of foreign nations (and especially the Chinese). In 1983, the Reagan administration produced the ominously titled "A Nation at Risk,"[3] a massive report on the purportedly deteriorating state of American education. Citing ineffective curricula, low student expectations, low amounts of time spent in class and on school work, and a national shortage of qualified teachers, "A Nation at Risk" seemed to arrive at the same conclusion as the Chinese delegates in our story: America's educational system was broken and in dire need of *comprehensive reform*. Coincidentally, American schools seemed to need those very things that the Chinese system had in abundance: "effective" high-test-score-producing curricula, extremely high student expectations and interest, and greatly increased class time and school work.

A more recent example of the delegates' story is the No Child Left Behind Act.[4] The legislative history of this law reads like a sequel to "A Nation at Risk"— picking up right where it left off. The move toward more standardized testing (a central tenet of the Chinese system) demonstrates that the delegates' story is still very much alive and central to modern American education reform.

Not only is it thriving, the delegates' story has grown in popularity and scope. Over the past few years, America's burgeoning obsession with China has fueled an increase of interest in and reverence for Chinese education. Today, I hear the delegates' story from all sides and many different factions. I hear praise and statements of wonderment in regard to Chinese education from friends, colleagues, and even strangers on the news. My students often want to discuss it with me. I read article after article about China this and China that—the common theme with regard to education being that the Chinese are doing something right and the Americans are doing something wrong. Even President Obama couldn't resist the allure of the delegates' story, hinting in his 2011 State of the Union that America should take notes from the Chinese and educate its children "earlier and longer" and "with greater emphasis on math and science."[5]

But is this praise warranted? Is it clear that the delegates, "A Nation at Risk," No Child Left Behind, and standardized testing proponents are correct? Is American education on the decline? Is Chinese education the way to go?

I submit to you that whatever the answer to these questions might be, they are not nearly as straightforward as they may appear.

4

More than thirty years have passed since the delegates' predictions. Were they correct? Has Chinese education left the United States in the dust? Is the American education system broken beyond repair? Has the United States disappeared into the abyss? Has Chinese technology and science overtaken the rest of the world?

No. Not quite. As an initial matter, it must be noted that the delegates' overall predictions were, in fact, *wrong*. American education has not dragged America into anonymity on the world stage. Despite using a "broken" system to educate its children, the United States remains an undisputed global leader in nearly all education-reliant fields (including science, technology, politics, business, academia, and so on). Chinese education, on the other hand, has failed to live up to expectations. While China has made great economic gains in recent years, it is not clear that this is a boon attributable primarily (or even reasonably) to its educational system. In fact, many of these economic gains seem to have been made *in spite of* China's system of education rather than because of it. Moreover, the game-changing advances in Chinese science and technology predicted by both delegations have not yet materialized. And there is little indication they will anytime soon.

As for the delegates' specific assessments of American and Chinese education, the answer is more complicated. A proper and thorough examination of both styles of education reveals two paradoxical patterns. First, if analysis is confined to students at the primary and secondary levels, there is no question that the delegates were correct. Chinese education is undoubtedly "better" during these early phases. In fact, its excellence is peerless in these initial stages of education—rising almost to the level of bizarre.

In the later stages of education, however, there is a surprising, countervailing pattern. At the highest levels of academic and scientific achievement, the very same Chinese-educated students who excelled in the early stages *struggle* to have any impact at all. In fact, in terms of important postgraduate scientific research, researchers at Chinese universities and institutions have almost entirely failed to contribute anything of note. Americans and American-educated students, however, have produced high volumes of important innovative research and scholarship at an unparalleled consistency and profundity for the past hundred years (and counting). Indeed, American (and American-educated) scholars are responsible for more great scientific and academic advancements than the scholars of any other country. In these later stages of education, American education is unquestionably "better."

5

The first pattern is familiar to most Americans. At the primary and secondary level, Chinese and Chinese-American (and Asian-American) students *routinely* and *drastically* outperform their American peers in nearly every measurable way. From grades to standardized test scores, early-stage Chinese education is, quite simply, much better than its American counterpart.

This pattern is especially evident on standardized tests. Take, for example, the test offered by the Program for International Student Assessment (or PISA). Every three years, PISA produces and administers a massive, carefully designed international achievement exam for high-school-aged students. This is no pop quiz. It covers three broad subjects (math, science, and reading) and is designed to be a comprehensive measurement of ability.

Though PISA issues its test in multiple languages in dozens of countries all across the world, China had not officially participated until 2009, when it entered a team from Shanghai. In only their first official crack at the test, the kids from China placed first in *all three subjects*. Not only did they beat every other student from each and every participating country, the Chinese students shattered all the previous records, achieving the highest scores in PISA history in each individual subject. In comparison, the United States turned in a decidedly mediocre performance, placing seventeenth in Reading, twenty-third in Science, and thirty-first in Math.[6]

I've spoken with many Chinese people who were neither surprised nor impressed by these results. In China, performances like these have become a matter of course. It's simply expected.

"Of course," they say. "Of course our kids placed first on that test. So what?"

"Forget Shanghai!" Some of them tell me. "We could have sent kids from any city—even from the countryside—and they would have done just as well or more likely even better!"

For Americans, the sobering reality is that this is not mere puffery. In China's own internal national college examinations, kids from Shanghai were not standouts in any way. While the Shanghai students shattered score records on the PISA, the fact is that they are actually far from the "top students" in China. China could very likely have sent teams from dozens of cities large and small and achieved *better results*. Other international tests tell the same story: Chinese (and other Asian) students simply crush their American peers on big standardized tests.

This pattern of Chinese educational supremacy is not confined to the international arena. Here in the United States, on national tests such as the SAT and the ACT, Asian Americans perennially achieve the highest median score of any racial group.[7] Asian-American students are also more likely than any other demographic to graduate high school and go on to college. Additionally, they do so with the highest average GPAs of any recorded demographic group.

Perhaps nowhere is this pattern more evident domestically than in college admissions. Despite making up only 4.8 percent of the population as of 2010,[8] Asian Americans made up 17 percent of the freshman class enrolled at Harvard University as well as:

- 28 percent at the Massachusetts Institute of Technology (MIT),
- 23 percent at Stanford,
- 18 percent at Columbia,
- 18 percent at the University of Pennsylvania,
- 40 percent at the California Institute of Technology (Caltech), and
- 42 percent at University of California Berkeley.[9]

Of the twenty top-ranked schools, Asian-American enrollment seems to hover at 20 percent of the total student enrollment—a rate nearly *five times* what population stipulates we should be seeing. How has 5 percent of the population managed to occupy 20 percent of the seats in the best schools in this country? Even the elite institution with the lowest Asian matriculation numbers (Princeton, with a comparatively lukewarm 15 percent) admitted Asians at nearly three times their population rate.

The lopsided numbers don't stop at matriculation. Asians attain college and graduate degrees at a disproportionate rate as well. Census data indicates that Asian Americans, as a group, tend to hold the highest percentage of bachelor's degrees of any racial demographic.[10] Graduate degree numbers are just as galling. With chillingly few exceptions,[11] Asians and Asian Americans are overrepresented in nearly every type of master's, professional, and doctoral degree program currently offered. Especially in lucrative areas such as business and engineering, Asians are a substantial and persistent presence.[12] It should come as no surprise then that census data has revealed that Asian men and women have, on average, higher annual incomes than any other racial demographic in the United States.[13]

6

The second pattern, however, makes things even more interesting. Despite their extreme early successes, Chinese-educated students and scholars have not been able to keep up with their American-educated peers in truly world-class postgraduate academia.

The Nobel Prize is a stark example of this trend. Since the Nobel Prize's inception, no researcher at a Chinese university has ever won a Nobel Prize in the sciences. Read that again. Since the first Nobel Prizes in science were awarded in 1901, *not a single person at a Chinese research institution has ever won*. And not for lack of effort. The Nobel and other higher academic prizes are a painful topic in Chinese educational circles. The question of why China has not been able to produce a Nobel laureate in science has been discussed endlessly in the Chinese media.

Despite what seems to be unparalleled academic excellence at the primary and secondary school levels, and hundreds of thousands of disciplined and hardworking Chinese students rising up through the ranks year after year, China falls behind at the highest levels of science and academics. In comparison, as of the year 2012, Americans and American-educated men and women have managed to win a total of 330 merit-based Nobel Prizes: 64 in chemistry, 51 in economics,[14] 88 in physics, 95 in physiology or medicine, and even 11 in literature.[15] No other nation is even close in high-level scientific and academic output. Ironically, the *only* Chinese people to have ever won a scientific Nobel Prize undertook their advanced education in America.[16]

Chinese students are intimidatingly superior in primary and secondary education; there's no doubt about that. But somehow Americans surpass their Chinese peers in research and postgraduate education, securing their dominance of the endgame. As good as Chinese education seems to be at producing high-performing students in the early stages of education, American education excels at creating superstar academics in the later stages. The Chinese are quick out of the gate (and for some time thereafter), but, puzzlingly, they invariably fail to reach the "finish line." Americans, on the other hand, start the race slowly but manage to catch up, overtake, and finally leave the Chinese behind in their dust.

So which education system is better? The real answer depends on the metric used. How do we define and view the purpose of education? Is education simply a tool to allow individuals to do well at discrete tasks? Or is the purpose of education broader in scope: to advance human thought at the highest levels? Does learning involve rote memorization or exploration and independent thought? Is education the final goal in and of itself or is it a means to a greater end?

CHINA'S EDUCATIONAL "EARTHQUAKE"

1

Ten years after I first heard the delegates' story I experienced American primary education in Pennsylvania firsthand, as I've previously discussed. I not only started reevaluating what I knew about Chinese and American education, I also brought my family across the ocean to this strange land. Thus, this comparison became a reality for me, which I lived every single day. While I pursued my doctorate in education, as a parent I also experienced American primary and secondary education through my son's struggles in American schools.

Because of my experience not only teaching but also studying in both China and the United States—because and my access to both educational systems—I have a unique view of the strengths and weaknesses of each country's methods. I realized that the Americans deserved more credit than the delegates' story awarded them, and I was determined to introduce the Chinese to America's educational strengths.

By 1999, long after I'd first heard the story about the American and Chinese delegations both predicting that China would overtake the United States in science and technology, I started publishing books in China comparing Chinese and American education. In those books, I poured out all the questions that I'd been exploring for years by rethinking and reevaluating everything I knew about the concepts, pedagogy, style, and systems of traditional Chinese education. In my first book, *Quality Education in America*, I discussed the strongest virtues of the American system; that is, the aspects of American education that I believe are sorely missing from Chinese traditional education. In that book, and those that would come after, I argued—in stark contrast to the prevailing view then and now—that education was not one of the strongest points of Chinese society. In fact, I believe that traditional Chinese education is actually the weakest link. It is the single strongest factor in holding all of China back from progress.

In *Quality Education*, I raised two main questions for Chinese educators and parents: Why do Chinese elementary and middle school students win virtually every single international academic prize every single year, yet not one single adult at a Chinese university has ever earned a Nobel Prize in science? And why do Chinese kids so handily beat Americans out of the gate but go on to lose to them at the finish line?[17] These questions have been dubbed by some Chinese educators as "Mr. Huang's thorny problems," and they continue to be a source of great disturbance for the unthinking trumpeters of Chinese education.

Quality Education helped open up the educational discussion in China, a debate that had largely been closed for hundreds of years. During this period of educational introspection, many millions of Chinese people became very interested in the parenting and educational methods and philosophy of Americans.

As the famous Chinese novel *The Besieged City* pointed out:

> Life is a besieged city girded by high walls. As the struggle continues, the people who live inside dream only of getting out, and the people who live outside want only to get in. This is the way of marriage, and business, and life, and everything in between.[18]

In America, we would probably say, "The grass is always greener on the other side."

While those inside the city ramparts wanted to get out, the people outside the city walls wanted to get in. Not all of them agreed that America's educational system was the answer, but my book introduced an important debate into Chinese society that is still raging today, and what's more, many supporters of the traditional Chinese methods of education have been forced to take a long, hard look at what the Americans are doing right.

My message caught on quickly. In 2000, *Quality Education in America* rose to be the number-one bestselling nonfiction book in China.[19]

This book was praised as the *Émile* of China, the Chinese answer to Jean-Jacques Rousseau's landmark treatise on education. It shook up what people thought of the Chinese educational system and created a bit of an earthquake when it came to traditional views. More books on the topic followed, and they became a series of bestsellers in China, each discussing strong aspects of the American educational system.

Pirating is a big problem in China. There's a joke among Chinese publishers: the more a book is pirated, the bigger a bestseller it must be. Being pirated is an honor, then? I don't know about that, but I can say I was "lucky" enough to have this "honor." There's no knowing how many pirated copies of my books were sold on street corners! In my personal collection alone I have eight different pirated versions of *Quality Education in America*.

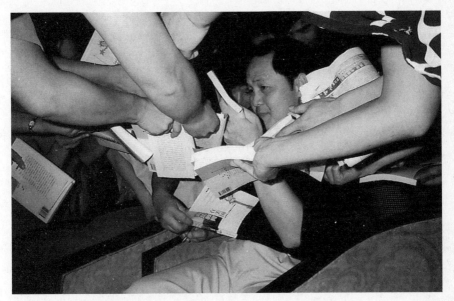

Fans in Nanning, China, asked countless questions about
Sino-American education, then clamored for author Quanyu
Huang's autograph following a presentation on his bestselling book
Quality Education in America. Photo by Tong Chen.

2

In China, discussion of the American system is at the core of any dialogue about Chinese education. So, then, we must ask the question: what's missing on the American side of the debate about education?

My answer: some perspective. I cringe as I see more and more American educators and policymakers blindly praising or adopting elements of Chinese education. I don't mean to say that there aren't any aspects of Chinese education worth replicating in the United States. In fact, there are many *powerful* and *useful* pieces and traditions that could serve both parents and policymakers well in deciding how best to raise a child. But by applying Chinese educational practices to American schools without analyzing what works and what doesn't over the long term, policymakers and educators risk moving backward rather than forward in the quest for an educational system that truly works.

If, indeed, Americans are interested in adopting or mimicking aspects of the Chinese style of education, why don't they look closer to home first? Why should America forego what is within reach while seeking something virtually unreachable? I refer, of course, to the vivid Chinese-American parenting and educational style, which is present and thriving within American culture.

In pursuit of answers to these many questions, I have written this book wearing multiple hats. First, I have approached it as a parent, a father of my own Chinese-American son Yan, who has been in America since the age of five and recently graduated from a top American law school with honors. Noticeably and interestingly, while he was subject to American schooling and society, he was raised in a Chinese household. In many ways, his life has been an ongoing clash of Chinese and American cultures and values. His upbringing has provided us with ample opportunities for reflection upon our own Chinese-American parenting method, or as I call it, *Co-Core Synergy Education*. Indeed, I first encountered many of the issues discussed in this book on a firsthand basis through raising my son. As such, many of the central points contained in this book will be punctuated by true stories from his upbringing.

I have also approached this book as an educational researcher, and, as such, it includes quite a bit of in-depth examination. I explore the Chinese view and approach to education, contrasting it with the American view and approach. Through this comparison, I attempt to explain how the Chinese view the task of educating their young, why they view it that way, and what real-world effect this has. I also discuss how the Chinese approach to education has produced the amazing results we tend to see from Chinese students in primary and secondary school. Specifically, we will look at how Chinese students are able to achieve these results, the origins of the Chinese "study" culture, and how the study culture has perpetuated itself for centuries. I will also examine the ramifications of the Chinese approach with America as a backdrop, including several glaring downsides that have been largely ignored.

Finally, I have also approached the writing of this book as an outside observer of American culture. As such, I hope not only to be able to explain *why* the Chinese approach education the way that they do, but also *how* it differs from the American approach and *what* I believe the American approach is. Sometimes it takes an outsider's perspective to point out the unique aspects of something with which we're familiar, attributes that would otherwise go unnoticed. I also explain what I think are the strongest and weakest points of American education through the eyes of a *Chinese* parent.

America may adopt elements of Chinese education, but let it do so with more perspective and thoughtfulness. What is the Chinese style of parenting and education? Why has it developed the way it has? How is it different from the typical American approach to parenting and education? What are the main tenets of Chinese parenting and education? What are its drawbacks? Before we open the city gates, rush outside, and usher in the besiegers, let us take a long, close look at what we may be getting into first.

3

Take a moment to consider the following questions before reading the main text. You'll want to keep them in mind as you read and revisit them when you're done.

Are you still bothered by the dilemmas of the besieged city and the struggle concerning which is better—Chinese education or American education?

Should Americans adopt the philosophy, methods, and approaches of Chinese and/or Chinese-American parenting and education? Or would the Chinese be better off adopting the American philosophy, methods, and approaches?

After refreshing yourself on the struggles and puzzles of the two systems, are you able to list the strengths of Chinese education? How about American education? Should American parents raise their children the way Chinese or Chinese-American parents do? Or do Chinese and Chinese-American mothers and fathers, in fact, have a few things to learn from American parenting?

More importantly, are we able to synergistically combine the best aspects of the two traditions so as to prepare our children to thrive in the competitive and constantly evolving global landscape in which we now reside?

And how?

CHAPTER 1
"CHINESE-AMERICAN" EDUCATION

*Oranges growing to the south of the Huai River are oranges,
but north of the river, they become* zhi. *The leaves of both are
similar, but their tastes are very different. Why? This must be
because the natural environments and climates of the lands to
the south and to the north of the Huai River are different.*[1]
—Quoted from Yan Tzu

TIGERS WITHOUT A "TIGER MOM"

1

At the end of the most recent Year of the Tiger, in 2011, a self-stylized so-called Tiger Mom named Amy Chua published a book in America titled *Battle Hymn of the Tiger Mother*. Featuring heavily (and, perhaps, grotesquely) in this book was what the author purported to be Chinese parenting. The author of *Battle Hymn* devoted large sections of her memoir to describing her parenting methods and philosophy. But instead of labeling it as her own personal parenting philosophy, a style of parenting that she created, Chua boldly branded it as "Chinese parenting."

Her book created quite the firestorm in the US media; her vitriolic parenting style was foreign to American parents. However, what many don't realize is that the way Chua chose to bring up her daughters is alien to most Chinese families as well. Indeed, her harsh, anachronistic methods are out of date and *far* outside of what is acceptable and encouraged in mainstream society in China today; it should go without saying that it's below the standards of most

Chinese-American parents. The Tiger Mom's misinterpretations and mischaracterizations have led Americans astray in understanding the Chinese style of parenting and education. Consequently, this inaccurate portrayal has served only to deepen social biases against Chinese-American parenting and education.

Amy Chua's decision to refer to herself as the Tiger Mother is a confusing choice. I am no zoologist, but I submit that the behavior of a real female tiger mother (the animal) is quite different from Amy Chua's (the human). Just take a look at an actual tiger mom. You've seen her at the zoo or perhaps on TV. Picture her in your mind, a five-hundred-pound Bengal tiger. While tigers are dangerous and feared apex predators, we aren't talking about their hunting methods. We're talking about family education. Don't imagine a tiger stalking her prey. Instead, try to imagine her with her cubs.

How does she act around them? How does she treat them?

Surprisingly, this calls up a vastly different set of traits. As a parent, a *real* female tiger mother is always unbelievably *nice* to her kids. Indeed, she's a pushover! Real tigers coddle their children, exhibiting infinite patience and understanding. Real tigers protect their young; they play with them; they lick and clean them gently and diligently. When her cubs jump on her broad head, back, and stomach, she doesn't bite or curse at them. She's patient, allowing her children to play as they see fit. The one thing we can say for sure that a real tiger mother does *not* do to her young? She does not hurt them.

A real tiger mother saves her fierceness for the outside world, for the dangers lurking out there that would harm her kids. She doesn't turn it upon her own children. Now think about Amy Chua. Would you say she was hurting her children through her strict parenting and ridiculous demands? I believe that most American parents (and Chinese and Chinese-American parents, for that matter) would.

Many years ago, when I was young, there was a woman in the neighborhood that we called a "tiger mom." Back then, however, it meant something very different for us. The "tiger mom" we knew truly deserved her name—not because she forced her children to abide by a very strict set of parenting rules, but, to the contrary, she always aggressively and priggishly protected her spoiled kids whenever they caused any trouble. This "tiger mom," like the real tigers in the wild, only bared her teeth at outsiders, while spoiling her own kids rotten.

2

Oddly, the outwardly hostile, inwardly protective tiger is generally closer to the real essence of Chinese mothers than Amy Chua's version of the Tiger Mother. Take Ms. Chua's infamous list of ten things her children were "never allowed to do."[2] Her kids weren't allowed to participate in school plays (or complain about missing them), attend play dates, participate in sleepovers, watch TV, play video games, choose the extracurricular activities they participated in, play any instrument other than the piano or violin (and they weren't allowed to *not* play one of these instruments), be anything other than the top student in school for all subjects (except gym and drama, because of course those didn't matter). And, of course, A's were not only expected, they were required.

I've put this list in front of many real Chinese and Chinese-American mothers (including my own wife), and the reaction is almost universally the same: incredulity. While many of Ms. Chua's rules are reflective of the traditional Chinese belief that education is supreme (which we will discuss in great detail in later chapters), Amy Chua has adopted an imprecise, self-centered, and highly distorted version of these values.

While I don't doubt that this list may be true for Ms. Chua, and that some Chinese parents may be as strict as Ms. Chua purports to have been, you may find it surprising to hear that many—if not *most*—Chinese parents in China would find Chua's list disagreeable, even laughable.

Among those Chinese parents are my wife and myself. While it's true that Chinese parents are stricter than American parents in general, the complete suffocation of a child's social life or autonomy is not a true tenet of Chinese parenting. Chua's style of parenting is a particular style of hard-lined, strict parenting popular in certain portions of the Chinese immigrant community in the 1970s. While it may have been the style in which Amy Chua was raised, it is by no means the norm in most parts of China.

It certainly wasn't our parenting style. Ms. Chua's list makes me laugh because it reminds me of situations we dealt with when raising Yan and how differently we approached those situations. To give you a flavor of how another set of Chinese parents approached the same situations, let's go down the list:

- **Play dates and sleepovers.** Very few Chinese parents would advocate isolating their children to the point of not allowing them have any play dates with other children their age. Does Ms. Chua honestly believe that Chinese children aren't allowed to have friends? While we were demanding with Yan about his grades and performance in school, it never even occurred to us to prevent him from playing with any of his friends or attending sleepovers. On the contrary, we openly and actively encouraged Yan's socialization from the beginning, hoping it would help him to learn English quickly, to relate to Americans, and to avoid isolation from American culture.

- **School plays.** To be honest, Yan never had much enthusiasm for school plays. The one time he exhibited some interest in a high school play, we did not have an issue with him trying out. In fact, we supported the endeavor even though he wasn't a talented singer.

- **TV and video games.** One of Yan's favorite pastimes is playing video games. Even as an adult, his girlfriend bought him a PlayStation 3. I blame myself. Indeed, I believe I was the one who first introduced Yan to video games. When he was about four years old and still in China, I excitedly related a story about this new video game I'd played in America. "You control a little fat man," I remember telling him, "and you have to jump on turtles, eat mushrooms to grow, and jump over fireballs!" When we could finally afford it, I proudly bought him a Nintendo to show him the game I'd told him about. While we did limit the amount of time he was allowed to play, I doubt this is that different from what most American parents do.

- **Extracurricular activities.** Yan has *always* chosen his own extracurricular activities. From tennis to soccer to violin, his after-school activities always reflected his interests rather than our preferences. The one exception was the high school wrestling team, which he very much wanted to join but we thought was too dangerous.

- **Grades.** Ms. Chua is not wrong in believing that Chinese parents demand excellence from their children in school, but she goes to extremes. The average Chinese parent does, of course, expect high grades. We were no exception.

- **Violin and piano.** The strange aspect of Chua's insistence on her daughters playing *only* the violin and/or piano and ascribing it to Chinese parenting is that these are not Chinese musical instruments at all. If we're discussing pure and traditional Chinese parenting, why is it that Chua's methods so doggedly insist that her children play Western instruments and exclude traditional Chinese instruments entirely?

To be sure, many of her fanatical rules defy basic reason—what is their purpose?

While Chinese parents have high academic expectations for their children, Amy Chua is not representative of the norm. *Any* type of educational values taken to an extreme are unhealthy. Chinese education is no different.

The idea that *all* Chinese mothers follow a strict set of rules similar to Ms. Chua's is misleading and ridiculous. The biggest problem here is that this is never explained or put forth clearly by Ms. Chua, who often writes in absolutes and makes inaccurately broad generalizations about "Chinese parenting."

It is a stretch to call her approach genuinely Chinese. Consider Chua's own background. Amy Chua was born and raised in the United States, in Illinois and Indiana to be exact. If Amy Chua were the recipient of any Chinese parenting, it would have been the same style of parenting *her* parents received. And therein lies the quandary. While Amy Chua's parents were ethnically Chinese, they grew up and resided in the Philippines. This means that any Chinese parenting her parents received, and used to raise her, was actually from *their* parents. Doing the math, you'll realize we're now talking about a style of Chinese parenting from the late 1920s to 1940s, *at the latest*. Take another look at Ms. Chua's list above. Now think about what an American parent in the 1940s would and would not have allowed. Is this hyper-strict form of parenting genuinely reflective of the Chinese parenting of today? Or is it simply a tragic interpretation of what Ms. Chua *thinks* is Chinese but is simply outdated?

3

Battle Hymn of the Tiger Mother also fails in another fashion. While it describes Ms. Chua's view of *how* Chinese parents try to raise their children, the author largely ignores the more interesting question of *why* Chinese parents choose to do certain things in their own ways. While she doesn't hesitate to make generalizations, her book is surprisingly light on explanation.

In the few instances she does attempt to explain why Chinese parents do the things they do, her explanations fall woefully short of clarity. Take, for example, her description of the "three big differences"[3] between Chinese and Western parents.

> (i)   "Western parents are concerned about their children's psyches. Chinese parents aren't."

In Chua's mind, because of this, Chinese parents do not feel bad demanding more from their children than Western parents do.

(ii)   "Chinese parents believe that their kids owe them everything."

Because of this, Chinese kids "must spend their lives repaying their parents by obeying them and making them proud."

(iii)   "Chinese parents believe that they know what is best for their children and therefore override all of their children's own desires and preferences."

Because of this, "no Chinese kid would ever dare say to their mother, 'I got a part in the school play! I'm Villager Number Six. I'll have to stay after school for rehearsal every day from 3:00 to 7:00, and I'll also need a ride on weekends.'"

I would quarrel with all three of these assertions (in my opinion, they are each overly broad, skewed, or simply incorrect), but I take particular issue with point (i), psychological punishment, which I will address later in this chapter and this book. We must face the fact, however, that there are bigger problems with Chua's arguments. After all three incredibly broad declarations, Ms. Chua declines to explain any further. The reader is left asking why? Her best attempt at an explanation comes after point (ii), where she states, "the reason [Chinese parents believe their kids owe them everything] is *a little unclear*, but it's *probably* a combination of Confucian filial piety and the fact that the parents have sacrificed and done so much for their children."[4]

Unfortunately, after reading Ms. Chua's *Battle Hymn*, one is left with the impression that she simply doesn't know any more than this about Chinese parenting and therefore can't explain it to the reader. In the end, her presentation of Chinese parenting to the American public is both inauthentic and disingenuous. Who is the Tiger Mother? I submit that the Tiger Mother Amy Chua has described is not the average Chinese mother. The Tiger Mother is a creature of confusion. She is a mix of Amy Chua's interpretation of what Chinese mothers do, Western egocentrism, and plain, simple sensationalism.

4

China is not immune from the concept of sensationalism in parenting either. Just as the United States has Amy Chua, the Tiger Mother, China has the "Wolf Dad." The Wolf Dad claimed he'd achieved his dream of sending his children to Peking

University (the best university in China) through his own system of parenting. He simply and systematically beat his children in order to educate them.

As an educational "expert," I was invited to participate in a live debate with the Wolf Dad through *Tencent*, one of the largest microblogs in China (similar to Twitter or Facebook here in the United States) on November 29, 2011. The vast majority of the debate observers and participants—all of whom were Chinese—were openly against the Wolf Dad's brand of family education. By the end of the one-hour debate, it seemed as though I was leading the audience to attack the Wolf Dad because the sentiment was so against his parenting methods.

Though Chua and the Wolf Dad had different parenting styles, it's interesting to compare the two. While the Wolf Dad in China advocates the use of *physical* punishment to educate his children, the Tiger Mother in America employed something I consider even more damaging: *psychological* punishment. Ms. Chua's system of psychological punishment is actually more like the way American parents raise their children than the way Chinese parents do. I will address the differences, and how they affect children, later in this book.

5

Not only are Ms. Chua's ideas not reflective of Chinese parenting, they are even less emulative of Chinese-American parenting. Chinese-American children are subject to a unique set of educational pressures. In particular, Chinese-American children have the potential to receive the best values of both Chinese education and American education. I call this type of cross-cultural education *Co-Core Synergy Education*.

There is a Chinese saying, "A mountain cannot accommodate two tigers," but I believe that in the past few decades, something very unique has been happening here in America. A hybridization, so to speak, of two different kinds of "tigers" into one has occurred and has resulted in many dazzling achievements. As mentioned previously, Asian Americans—just under 5 percent of the nation's population—have managed to occupy 20 percent of the seats in the top twenty universities in the United States,[5] hold the highest percentage of college and graduate degrees, and make a higher annual income than any other racial demographic in the United States.[6] Since most Chinese-American parents do not agree with and do not carry out the type of parenting espoused by Amy Chua, it's clear that the harsh educational styles of thousands of Tiger Mothers are not responsible for these remarkable successes. Instead, Co-Core Synergy Education is responsible.

Many Americans agree that a mountain cannot accommodate two tigers. Consequently, there has been much argument over whether America should adopt some tenets of traditional Chinese education. But here's my question: why should America forgo what is within reach but seek something unreachable? By doing so, Americans are neglecting the demonstrably successful and organic Chinese-American parenting and educational standards, which were developed and reside within America.

At their foundations, Chinese-American parenting and education are very different from traditional Chinese parenting and education. In addition to maintaining some of the core features of Chinese family education, Chinese-American parenting and education have also stemmed from and created two primary characteristics: the internalization of the "American Dream" and the synergizing of Chinese and American education.

Over the course of this book, I include mock dialogues with both American and Chinese parents, presenting questions I believe a typical set of parents from each culture would ask about my arguments. These dialogues should help answer some of the questions you may have, and they should also help provide a prescription for applying Co-Core Synergy Education to your own parenting style.

DIALOGUE

Chinese parents: What are your opinions about the Chinese Wolf Dad?

Huang: I strongly and completely disagree with the Wolf Dad's approach to parenting. It's possible that parents might strike their children when they lose their tempers; this happens relatively often within Chinese families. But the Wolf Dad's physical punishment of his children wasn't due to heightened emotions resulting from his kids' bad behavior. Instead, he calmly beat his children in a methodical, systematic way. As an example, when one of his children failed to recite an article from memory, he checked his plan in order to decide how many strikes (quantity) the child should receive and how heavy (quality) they should be.

Chinese parents: His approach really scared people.

Huang: Yes, his approach wasn't parenting; it was criminal. During our debate, I asked the Wolf Dad, "Did your children rebel as adolescents?" He responded, "They never rebelled." I was surprised by this answer because all children naturally rebel as teenagers. I wondered if he was ignorant about his children or perhaps unaware of common knowledge. The more disturbing answer is that his children were probably warped by his physical abuse.

American parents: Can you explain whether Amy Chua, the Tiger Mom, had a Chinese style of parenting? Why or why not?

Huang: It's evident that Chinese parents tend to have high academic expectations for their children, but Amy Chua isn't representative of the norm. She stopped being a typical Chinese parent when she pushed the supremacy of education to the extreme. As I said in the text, one example of this is how she only allowed her children to play two Western instruments, the violin and the piano. If her approach had been *genuinely* Chinese, she would have expected them to play at least one traditional Chinese instrument as well.

American/Chinese parents: We're curious to see how you'd compare the Wolf Dad in China with the Tiger Mother in America.

Huang: It's very interesting to compare these two parents and their parenting styles. They're both absolute dictators in their families, and they both discourage their children's socialization. They put an emphasis on "book smarts" rather than "street smarts." The major difference between the two is that, while the Wolf Dad used *physical* punishment to discipline and educate his children, the Tiger Mother employed *psychological* punishment. Which is more damaging? I argue later in the book that it's actually the Tiger Mother's psychological approach that hurts children more.

WHO STILL DREAMS THE AMERICAN DREAM?

1

The first characteristic of Chinese-American parenting, the "American Dream," is critical to the way Chinese-American parenting and education has developed over the years. With $55 in my pocket, I came here for my family's American Dream, which even my father had cherished since he, as an interpreter, helped the American Air Force build airports in China during World War II.

A *son* came to America to pursue his *family's* dream, which began almost *a half century* ago by *his father*?

I am not sure whether many Americans today can fully comprehend the depth of this dream.

The American Dream was a uniquely American concept and was once something that all Americans struggled toward and fought for. At one point in history, it was synonymous with the quest for freedom. Today, the American Dream is largely absent in America, at least among those who have resided in the United States for generations. It's difficult to say what prevalence and influence it still has.

My brother-in-law from China went to New York City to visit my son in February 2012.

"What does the Statue of Liberty look like?" he asked my son. "How tall is it? Is it really that color?"

"I don't know," my son said.

"What do you mean, you don't know?" he asked.

"I've never seen it," my son said, shrugging. "Only tourists go see the Statue of Liberty."

This was truly a revelation for me. New Yorkers don't *care* about the Statue of Liberty? It's only for tourists? How was it possible that true New Yorkers didn't bother to give thought to this symbol of freedom? How could this be?

The American Dream is no different than this forgotten symbol in New York Harbor. It has lost its essential meaning in the hearts of many Americans. It's been reduced to a phrase or a concept that exists for historical reference. While it continues to be mentioned in politicians' speeches about the greatness of America, is it actually ever *dreamt* by Americans anymore? Who dreams the American Dream today?

2

It's said that Christopher Columbus was disappointed upon learning that he had discovered the New World. He had always imagined that by sailing west across the open sea he would end up in China, a land of riches. People in China drank tea, he was told. They wore silk. They had priceless spices. This new desolate land had nothing comparable to the wealth of China.

In Chinese, the word *China* literally means "the Middle Kingdom." It was so named because the Chinese considered all their neighbors and surrounding countries to be undeveloped and barbarian. China was the center of the world, and the Chinese were so sure of its preeminence that they felt comfortable ignoring the cultures and languages of others. Because of this attitude, the Chinese turned their backs on many potential positive influences in the outside world for hundreds of years.

China's ignorance and sense of superiority prevented the country from reaching its full potential, so it's surprising to see that Americans today seem to have a similar state of mind. "We are number one!" they say. "We are the center of the world!"

When visiting China, people think it's laughable that the world maps printed in the country place China in the very center, with the rest of the world around it. But if you look at many maps printed in the United States, they do the same! The United States is smack dab in the middle of the map, and poor Russia is split in two. Here's another example: the metric system is the world standard for measurement. The world uses kilograms to measure weight but America, at the "center" of the world, uses its own measurement: the pound. The rest of the world says "one kilometer," but Americans say "0.6214 miles." The entire world measures temperature in degrees Celsius, but Americans use Fahrenheit.

So how does America's self-centeredness affect the conception of the American Dream in this country? Well, it's thought, the American Dream is already here. Americans achieved it long ago. The American Dream and the New World used to be synonymous. However, the state of mind that America is at the top has made the American Dream more meaningful for immigrants because they still dream that dream. They sacrifice everything to come to the New World and achieve the American Dream.

3

Some of the top students in America's best universities are from countries such as Vietnam and Cambodia. Indeed, many of them are from actual refugee families that escaped danger by a hair's breadth and came to the United States by boat in the 1970s. These refugees did not have anything—they had no money; they didn't speak the language; and they had no roots in this country. They had nothing but the American Dream. Despite these shortcomings, the inspiration that came from the American Dream allowed them not only to survive here, but to thrive. They now send their children to the best universities in this country.

I once chatted with a Cambodian restaurant owner who sought asylum in the United States as a refugee. We exchanged old war stories. I told him that when I first came to this country, I had only $55 in my pocket. He laughed and said, "Well, I was much richer than you were!"

"You were? How many dollars did you have?"

"I had millions of. . . ." He was laughing so hard that he was having trouble forming a complete sentence.

"What did you have?" I asked, thinking that he must have been a corrupt official with piles of gold when he fled Cambodia.

His laughter finally subsided, and he said, "Well, I had millions of lice and fleas when I arrived in this land!"

Nonetheless, he sent his daughter off to Princeton a few years ago, paying for her tuition with the money he'd saved from operating his restaurant.

In contrast to the children of families that have been in the United States for generations, the children of immigrant families have stronger pioneering spirits and perseverant attitudes out of necessity. They must overcome various lingual, cultural, economic, and social barriers. With no foundation or support system to fall back on, these families must seek out ways to assimilate into mainstream society quickly, safely, and successfully. The hardships that come with immigrant life provide a type of education that others are unable to replicate through schools and classes.

America, of course, is an immigrant society. Nevertheless, after more than two hundred years, more and more people are content with their lot. The unique spirit of the pioneer has gradually atrophied. The American Dream was once the *core* of American education. Now, though its ubiquity in everyday American society has decreased, it still lives on in the daily lives of immigrants hoping to create a new life for themselves and their families in the United States.

DIALOGUE

American parents: Dreams are crucial to development. They offer hope and help motivate and inspire. They can take you from being a nobody to being a somebody. However, many American children today don't have a dream. How can we nurture dreams in our children?

Huang: There is a Chinese saying, "What a person will dream at night is what he or she has thought most about during the daytime." Applying that to a person's life, you can see that if you don't have a dream in childhood, you will not be able to develop one as an adult. If you cultivate ambition in your children, then you'll be creating a lifelong dream that will inspire them as they grow.

American parents: There's something that bothers us about our children's ambition. We know it's there; we know they want to do something great with their lives. However, they just don't want to work very hard and aren't willing to persevere in the name of that ambition.

Huang: A child has to have more than just general ambition. They have to have a specific, clearly defined goal. Ambition is broad; wanting to do "something" is a great first step, but what exactly is that "something"? Their goal must be clear and specific or it won't be enough to guide them through the more difficult times.

American parents: Interesting! We've never thought of goals and ambition this way.

Huang: Here's an example. Let's say you're a runner and you decide to run "very far" each day. Well, how far is "very far"? It could be a mile. It could be ten miles. Your goal here is neither clear nor specific; therefore, you'll run as far as you feel like running (which probably isn't very far) and then stop. That's not helpful if you want to become a better runner. Likewise, your children saying they want to do "something great" isn't specific enough; they need a clear-cut idea of what it is they're working toward. This is why Chinese-American parents always encourage their children to set definitive goals, such as wanting to be a lawyer, a doctor, or an engineer.

CHINESE-AMERICAN EDUCATION—"CO-CORE SYNERGY EDUCATION"

1

The second characteristic of Chinese-American education (and indeed, Asian-American education in general) is its *synergy*. In other words, it's fundamentally different from Chinese or Asian education. There is an old Chinese story that is meaningful here:

Yan Tzu was a famous and skilled speaker of the Qi State. He would visit the Chu State. The king of the Chu State despised Yan Tzu and wanted to humiliate him. An official suggested to the king, "When Yan Tzu is here, let's tie a man up and parade him about and tell everybody that he is a thief from the Qi State, Yan Tzu's home state." The king agreed this was a good idea.

When Yan Tzu drank with the King of Chu, two soldiers carried the bound man into the room and set him down in front of them.

"This man is a thief from the Qi State!" they announced.

The king looked at Yan Tzu and asked, "Is it custom for people from Qi to steal?"

Yan Tzu smiled, ignored the bound man and guards, and replied, "I've been told that oranges growing to the south of the Huai River are oranges, but north of the river, they become *zhi*. Isn't that odd? The leaves of both are similar, but their tastes are very different. Why? This must be because the natural environments and climates of the lands to the south and to the north of the Huai River are different. Well, this man did not steal in the Qi State, but became a thief in the Chu State. Does this mean that the environments of Chu State make people steal?"

The King of Chu sighed and said, "Joking with a sage is to insult yourself!"[7]

This story about Yan Tzu sounds like a joke, but if you examine it carefully, you will find that profound reason lies within the story: different environments and climates can produce fruit with different flavors.

This Chinese story may be too difficult to apply to American life, in which case, we can use an example from one of the most American institutions there is: McDonald's. McDonald's restaurants are ubiquitous in China, and though they bear the same branding, colors, and corporate parent as their American brethren, they serve vastly different foods. Even the same particular foods, such as the Big Mac, have been altered to suit to the Chinese palate. Though the menu of a McDonald's in China may look familiar to Americans, the flavors are subtly different. Because of the different climate and social and cultural environment in China, a thing that is so American takes on surprisingly altered attributes.

Chinese-American education is no different. Chinese Americans have generated their own particularities resulting from their struggles in the American cultural and educational environment.

Just as the McDonald's in China is different from the McDonald's in America, so Chinese-American parenting and education in America differs from Chinese parenting and education in China. Traditional Chinese education has in America been infiltrated and remolded by various American cultural and educational influences. This is one of the most important reasons why Chinese-American parenting and education is able to excel in America.

Before proceeding further, it should be noted that I make many generalizations about American parenting in this book. This doesn't mean that the generalizations apply to every American parent's behaviors or values. Because of the broad subject matter of this book, it's impossible to compare American parenting to Chinese and Chinese-American parenting without making generalizing about both.

Here are some critical differences between Chinese and American parenting and family education.

Chinese	American
Education is supreme.	Education is important but certainly not supreme.
Emphasizes respect for teachers and proper formalities between the young and old.	Stresses equality and respect for a child's independence.
Pays great attention to filial education and emphasizes obedience of and respect for one's elders.	Relationships between family members tend to be kept at arm's length, where family members prioritize their own needs above those the family unit.
Parents and children become united in joint familial goals and parents are willing to sacrifice themselves for their children.	Parents and children are individuals with individual ends. While young children do rely on their parents, parents have their own individual lives and goals.
Children must set up ambitious goals. Without career achievements, there can be no permanent happiness.	Children are encouraged to pursue their own desires and interests and are not necessarily pushed to be ambitious.
Parents guide or direct children to select their interests or careers.	Parents do not interfere with children's selections for their interests or careers.
Fostering smart, well-behaved, sensible, and thoughtful kids.	Cultivating kids with independence, creativity, and critical thinking.

2

Just as an "orange can become a *zhi* north of Huai River," family education in China is very different from Chinese-American family education in America. The differences are multifold. For example, many Chinese-American parents refrain from reflexively spanking their children, as might have been done to them in China. Many Chinese-American parents try to build authority in their children's minds instead of using their power indiscriminately. Most Chinese-American parents acknowledge or even encourage children's creativity. They guide their children in their interests and career choices but do not dictate to them, allowing children to explore different areas for themselves. I discuss several of these differences in later chapters.

In my view, a child's education is quaternary. This means that it is comprised of four different parts: (1) family education, (2) school education, (3) social education, and (4) self-education. I call this the "tripod theory"—three legs and one head, similar to the structure of a camera tripod. Imagine a tripod with a camera on top. The three "legs" are family education, school education, and social education. Together, they support self-education, which is like the camera (the item that provides meaning to the whole structure).[8]

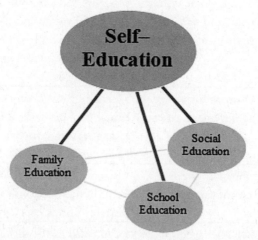

When people talk about a child's education, they generally think solely of *school* education. But that's just one type of education, and how a child accepts and incorporates his or her schooling is also determined by the other "legs" of the tripod: family education and social education. Beyond that, holding everything together is self-education, the starting point and destination of education. If an egg is broken from the outside, you're making breakfast. But if an egg is broken from the *inside*, a life has been created. Whether any form or type of education is effective (regardless of whether it is from one's family, elders, peers, school, or society in general), the outcome ultimately hinges on how the individual will react—how any particular person chooses to accept or reject certain influences. This is self-education. Of course, self-education does not just passively reflect family education, school education, and social education, since an individual is able to initiate his or her self-education as well.

For a child raised in China, the elements are simple: they will receive a Chinese-style family education, school education, and social education. For an American child, whose family has been in the United States for generations, the tripod will look similar: American-style family education, school education, and social education. However, because Chinese-American children are educated in America, yet still have important Chinese family influences, their diagram is as follows:

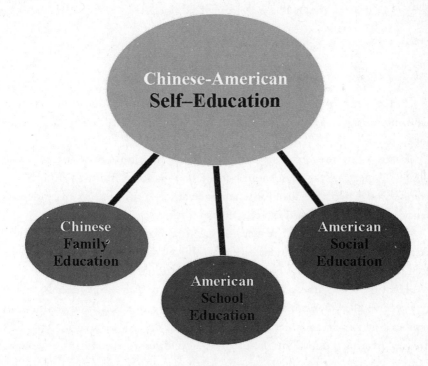

The three supporting points of the tripod for Chinese-American children are *Chinese* family education, *American* school education, and *American* social education. What effects or results will this synergy of educational influences produce? It depends on the recipient and his or her self-education.

A core tenet of Chinese-American family education is the "supremacy of education," with the primary goal of education understood as the acquisition of academic competence. In contrast, American school education and American social education tend to prioritize the cultivation of creativity, independent thinking, self-esteem, and such. The confluence of these educational influences (the two cores melding together) produces something unique. Therefore, this type of Co-Core Synergy Education can merge to push children to be even more outstanding.

All in all, Chinese-American children experience Co-Core Synergy Education in America, which generally keeps the cream of Chinese education and also absorbs the essentials of American education. Will a Chinese-American child end up more Chinese or more American? The answer to this question will ultimately depend on self-education. It's the children, and not the Tiger Mother, who determines where he or she will end up. In other words, it's the Co-Core Synergy Education that makes a child a hybrid tiger.

Dialogue

American/Chinese parents: The Co-Core Synergy Education theory is really interesting and fresh. How can we apply it to our own children and within our own families?

Huang: The key to this style of education is that it has two different *cores*. Chinese-American families should make a conscious effort to absorb the strengths of American education, such as creativity, critical thinking, independence, social skills, physical exercise, and so forth.

American parents: We're glad to hear that our educational system has its strengths. But we need to understand the Chinese side of things as well. Do we need to absorb Chinese strengths into our educational style?

Huang: Yes. Chinese-American children go to American schools, where they receive an American school education. Additionally, Chinese-American families are living in an American cultural climate and social environment. This ends up creating a hybrid model that has a good result. Americans, of course, do not face an analogous situation, where they must study in Chinese schools and live in a Chinese social and cultural climate; instead, they need to make a conscious effort to learn about the strengths of Chinese-American parenting and education.

American parents: What are these Chinese-American strengths?

Huang: If you read further, you'll find that the Chinese style is *very* different from American parenting and education. You should think about whether or not you should

(1) pay much more attention to your children's school education,

(2) sacrifice more for your children's education,

(3) involve yourself in your children's studying (as you likely do in their sports and other extracurricular activities),

(4) turn your power into authority,

(5) guide your children's career selection,

(6) enhance your children's responsibility to your family, and more.

American parents: This would be quite a change from our current parenting style. We can't imagine what would happen if we tried to apply all of these at once!

Huang: It might be difficult, but I can demonstrate the power of this style of education through an example. Chinese children are often called "human calculators" because they can do so much math in their heads, whereas American children tend to need a calculator to solve even the most basic math problems. Despite how much better Chinese students are at math, Chinese science and technology is behind America's. Why is this? Because American mathematicians, Nobel-Prize winners, and Facebook creators—the Bill Gateses and Steve Jobses—made sure to *create* the calculator in the first place. Now, think about how powerful America would be if it could turn its students into both human calculators and calculator creators.

CHAPTER 2
EDUCATION CAN CHANGE GOD'S WILL

In China's stratified society, education has historically been the chief and (at times) exclusive means of changing one's social class or economic status. Through education, a beggar could awaken as an official. Through education, men could change what God had set in place.

TO WIN OR TO HAVE FUN?

1

I've loved soccer ever since I was a child. It was my favorite hobby, yes, but it was also more than that. In a sense, it was the basis for my self-esteem.

I don't remember exactly how old I was when I started playing soccer. My earliest relevant memory comes from when I was around eight, about two years younger than my son Yan when he began to play. At that time, the Anti-Rightist Movement, a movement against freedom and openness in China, had been in full swing.

In China, the "right" wing is more liberal, closer to what we'd think of as the American Left, the progressives. The Chinese Right's central tenets are freedom and openness. The left wing in China, however, was quite conservative and ossified. As an intellectual, being labeled a "Rightist" was worse than slander. Rightists were guilty of the worst of treacheries and were considered counter-revolutionaries. They opposed China itself.

During World War II, Japan invaded China. Peking University in Beijing, where my father had majored in English, withdrew to Kunming City in Yunnan province. At that time, the US Air Force swooped in to aid China. Because of his background in English, my father often worked as an interpreter for the Americans. He used his language skills for various purposes, but primarily to help the American forces build airports.

Many years later, as a consequence of this contact with Americans, he was considered an intellectual who had been influenced by the "free and liberal" ideology of American Imperialism. My father was no longer a good comrade of the Revolution, but a liberal Rightist. Though my father was once a well-respected English teacher, in just one night, he lost his position and became the school's janitor instead.

This course of events had a profound effect on our family. Not only did my father have to carry this label, as his children, we did as well. I remember feeling great pressure even as a young child to be outstanding in everything I did. Whether it was my studies, playing sports, or any other activity, in order to stand my ground and be able to look my peers in the eye, I had to outperform all the other children. And as a boy, excelling in every area included, of course, soccer. I played soccer from elementary school through college with my own unique set of pressures. I rarely played to have fun. I played to prove a point. I played to win.

2

I saw my first American youth soccer game in 1990. At the time, I was living in a small college town in Ohio and working on my doctorate. My wife, my son, and I lived in a one-room efficiency dorm for international students. We had no car, few possessions, and very little money. As recent immigrants to this country, the world had revealed itself to be a strange and unsure place for us. We encountered small mysteries of American life on an almost-daily basis. Among these mysteries was recreational youth soccer.

To get to the classes from our dorm, I would often have to walk a mile or so. I didn't mind. In fact, I quite enjoyed it. At least part of the reason was the magnificent view. The main road was lined with massive green fields owned by the university but open to the public. Most striking of all was the color, a lush but stern green. Even with the sun shining upon it, this grass remained the color of cool, dark jade.

Though the fields were often used for a variety of events and leisurely activities, on the weekends in the spring and fall they were devoted to only one thing: soccer. Dozens and dozens of soccer games were played all at once by many different children of varying ages.

"What a find!" I thought to myself.

Growing up in China in the late 1950s and 1960s, soccer was one of the very few sports all young boys were able to play. Unlike other sports, you didn't need much at all to get a game of soccer going—just a ball, some feet, and some room to run. Games usually took place in the street, on concrete. To prevent our shoes from wearing down, we played barefoot. We created our own goals with our schoolbags and cast-aside shoes. The games themselves were brutal. With no equipment, skinned knees, sprains, bruises, and crushed bloody toenails were matters of course, as were thick, dry calluses on the balls of our feet and cracks in our heels. In place of organized teams, makeshift bands of kids or child warlords with a posse in tow ruled the day. Teams were decided by allegiances to the right people. Skill and sacrifice determined who got to play and in which positions. With no referees, toughness often mattered as much as skill (and sometimes more). Ragged, violent, and highly competitive—this was the soccer of my youth.

But the soccer games I witnessed in Ohio were something else entirely. Every child was dressed from head to toe in uniforms that resembled those worn by international-level players. The fields had been carefully measured and painted, and real regulation-sized goals had been dragged in and tied down with stakes. Each game even had its own dedicated scorekeepers and referees. While the games of my youth were contests of pride attended by no adults, parents and spectators dutifully lined the Ohio soccer fields. Accompanied by bright plastic coolers filled with drinks and food, the adults cheered, whooped, and laughed amongst themselves, casually training all manner of camcorders and cameras on the field as their kids played.

In over thirty years, I'd never had the opportunity to play soccer with such equipment or under such conditions. Indeed, not until my college team did I get to play soccer with shoes regularly, and even then I never dared to dream of *leather cleats* and *shin guards*.

When I saw American children playing this way, I thought about my son. He was already older than many of the kids on those fields, but, like me, he had no idea such games even existed. It occurred to me that I'd failed to provide him what all these kids were enjoying.

I became determined to sign my son up to play soccer. After saving some money, and with the generous help of our American family friends (who bought Yan his first uniform, cleats, and shin guards), we signed our son up for soccer in the fall of 1994. He was almost ten.

3

From the beginning of my son's soccer "career," my wife and son encouraged me to sign up as a coach for his team. I'd refused repeatedly. I told them that I was busy trying to provide for my family and study for my doctorate, delivering thousands of other reasons why I couldn't sign up, but the *real* reason I kept to myself.

My refusal did not last long. After receiving notice from the soccer league's organizers that there was a dangerous shortage of coaches, I was forced to reconsider. In the summer of 1995, rather than risk Yan losing out on the chance to play soccer, I decided to suck up my personal reasons and give it a go. I signed up as an assistant coach for my son's team.

The coaching position was interesting, to say the least. I worked alongside a modest, easygoing man named Bob. After learning of my background in the sport, Bob confided in me, admitting he knew very little about basic soccer tactics or fundamental skills. I was surprised when he told me this was relatively common for recreational-league coaches. He even stooped to repeatedly checking a coach's handbook while instructing players in the field. When he discovered I knew much more about soccer than he did, Bob delegated most of the substantive instruction to me, offering instead to handle the logistical aspects of running the team. With such responsibility thrust upon me (and with my own son watching), I felt tremendous pressure to ensure that the team did well.

On that very first day as an assistant coach, I was surprised to see the kids joking around and chasing one another rather than paying attention to me. How was I going to convince them they needed to listen to me? Finding my answer, I slyly asked Bob to throw a ball into the sky. All the children stopped what they were doing to watch the ball. They didn't quite know what was going on! I silently waited for the falling ball . . . and then, all of a sudden, I ran toward it and made a (likely not very elegant) bicycle kick. Everybody was dumbstruck, including Bob. Through this kick, I impressed the kids (and Bob!), building authority in everyone's minds. Later I implemented a very simple and direct strategy for our team: *win at all costs*. Before every single game, I made sure to tell Bob who should play which position. I placed our best players in the positions best suited for them. I relegated our weaker players to positions where they couldn't hurt our chances of winning. I only allowed our two weakest players to participate in games when we were already far ahead on points—and even then, only as forwards, where they were far away from our own goal so they could do whatever they wanted. During the games, I would stand beside our goal, running up and down the field to direct the game.

My short career as a coach proved very successful. Our team went undefeated for five straight games. Everyone was quite sure we would win first place in the league that season. Unfortunately, before the season ended, I had to go on a month-long business trip to Germany.

When I returned, I discovered that, not only had our team *not* captured first place, but they had actually lost very badly.

My son was puzzled by this: why had the team won the all games while I was there but lost almost every game as soon as I left?

The reason? Very simple: I was coaching the team to win, so when I coached, the kids played to win. When I left, and Bob took over, the purpose of his coaching (and the team's playing) shifted to something else—*to have fun*. That meant when Bob ran the games, he did so with little regard for what would be effective to win the game. He never discussed tactics (which he wasn't familiar with to begin with). Indeed, he ignored most of my careful allocations of players and recommendations, choosing instead to balance the team by allowing each child to take a turn playing each of the positions.

And that, right there, is the real reason I didn't want to be a soccer coach in the first place. My purpose was different than that of most Americans regarding playing soccer. I didn't care about the team having fun. I wanted them to win. I knew that most American parents would not agree with me. As you know, the position a kid would *like* to play is often very different from the position that child is able to play or ought to play. For example, every child wants to score goals, but usually only a forward has that chance. If the purpose of playing soccer is to have fun, rather than win, everybody would (and should) take turns playing as a forward. But to be good at scoring goals, a player needs to have solid ball handling and shooting skills. Beyond that, they need to be fast and have the right instincts. Not every player is suited to play forward. On top of this, in order to win, you have to put the players in positions such that there is a match between the responsibilities of the positions and the skill sets of the players. This, in turn, generates another issue, as certain players will invariably *never* get to fill the positions they *want* to play. On the one hand, certain players' desires (and perhaps rights) to play certain positions might be underemphasized, but on the other hand, the team's potential to win is maximized.

4

From the game of soccer, we can see that different ideas bring about very different attitudes, tactics, and results. Does the same hold true for education? Will varying educational ideas bring about different educational attitudes, tactics, and outcomes? Why are Asian-American kids synonymous with good students in so many elementary, junior high, and high schools here in the United States? Does the reason echo the story of my short career as a recreational soccer coach? Is it because Asian-American students want to win while other American students prefer to have fun?

The short answer is yes. Different ways of conceptualizing education create different approaches, which then create varied tactics to pursue differing outcomes. Here are some main differences between how American and Chinese-American students and families think about education.

Chinese American	American
Education is a life-or-death struggle; outside of studying, there is only more studying.	Education is a process that everyone faces, so you can certainly have fun while going through it.
Education is a passport toward achieving a goal, such as the American Dream.	Education is a social process to get to know people and enrich one's life.
Education is supreme and the highest goal.	Joy is supreme and education is a means and process.
Education is an intangible long-term investment.	Education is current, visible, and to be consumed.
Education is a battle of elimination won through selection and competition.	The purpose of education is to impart knowledge and cultivate people.

For Chinese and Chinese-American children, their introduction to education is the beginning of a lifelong battle that they must win at any and all costs. Little emphasis is placed on the experience or the process. Almost everything is focused on the end result.

There is an idea that is very popular in China with respect to education: "Don't lose the race, even at the starting line." Because most families in China have only one child, they see education as a war to be won rather than a process. Beginning as early as possible, Chinese parents push their children to be in the best position to win that educational battle. Indeed, whereas the starting line for this race was once infancy, now it has shifted to the prenatal stage of life. Future parents of Chinese children take all sorts of measures into account in order to ensure that their child is prepared to excel. One of the most popular topics among future parents is the exact time and date upon which to fertilize a child in order to maximize his or her chances of intelligence. This information can be found in various sources such as books, the Internet, and traditional Chinese secrets. Upon birth, early education programs await the baby, such as classical music lessons at six months of age, reading Chinese characters at one, learning English at two, and studying math and reciting Tang Dynasty poetry from memory at three. In order to get into certain kindergartens, the children have to pass a strict qualifying exam. If the Tiger Mother's methods scare Americans, shouldn't these early childhood education programs scare Americans even more? Such detailed itineraries would likely even scare the Tiger Mother herself.

This is not a hospital. It's a classroom in China. These Chinese high school students are preparing for the College Entrance Exam. The bottles that are hanging in the classroom are filled with amino acids, which parents, teachers, and students believe add energy and boost test scores. *Photo by CHImushroom.*

Beginning in elementary school, Chinese children start on what will soon become the focus of their lives: *studying*. Many Americans would be shocked to see how often and long Chinese kids study. They wake up very early, in many cases eating their breakfasts while they walk to school. In many parts of China, classes begin as early as 7:00 a.m. Students return home for lunch at noon and are back to school before 2:00 p.m. for a second session. They are then released for supper around 6:00 p.m. After dinner, high school and junior high students then turn right back around and head back to school at 8:00 in the evening, often not returning home until as late as 10:30 p.m. Any student who has not completed his or her homework by then will have to stay up until it's finished. Kids not only wake up much earlier than adults but also go to bed much later. Furthermore, adults only work five days per week, while many kids have to study six or seven days per week, only earning a brief time to rest on Sunday afternoon. In some big cities, children don't even go home at noon, spending the extra time at school. Indeed, though many kindergarten and elementary school students aren't required to attend school in the evenings, their parents send them to supplementary night classes for extra studies in math, music, dance, painting, and so on.

Obviously, the ones who are the most exhausted and endure the most suffering in China are students. It's not about going to school; instead, it's about waking up to a life-or-death educational battle every single day of the week.

This is the situation in China. And now, Chinese-American families have brought this educational battle to the United States.

5

While I was a student at Miami University, my wife and I conducted a comparative survey on how often Chinese and American children play after school.[1] One question we asked in particular was, "How long do you allow your kids to play after school?"

The feedback was very interesting.

Just about every American parent allowed their kids to play for some amount of time after school. About 30 percent said four hours; 30 percent said five hours; 10 percent said six hours; 10 percent said unlimited; and 20 percent did not know. A separate question asked about how much additional homework parents required their kids to do. None of the American parents required their kids to do any homework beyond what they were assigned at school.

In contrast, every single one of the Chinese parents surveyed added anywhere from one to three hours of extra homework to their children's workload and significantly limited their playing time. About 60 percent allowed their kids to play for only two hours after school; the rest said that their kids could play for three hours.

This is a part of the educational battle we know all too well. My son Yan once remarked, "I have changed so many schools, but the only thing that never changes is that I'm the *only* one who has homework on top of my homework!"

Perhaps none of this is surprising to you. After all, stories of the rigors that Chinese and Chinese-American families put their children through are quite common. The more interesting question is *why* this happens.

DIALOGUE

American parents: The idea of characterizing education in terms of a battle is very interesting. Can you describe some of the advantages that come through viewing a game, such as soccer, as something you have to win?

Huang: Let's look at this issue through the lens of soccer. Let's say your child is a soccer player; which of these lessons might he or she miss by viewing the sport as something that requires winning rather than as something that requires only that he or she have fun?

- Soccer is a fun experience and helps make life enjoyable.
- Soccer is good exercise.
- Soccer imparts good character.
- Soccer builds confidence.

Chinese parents: It's true that kids might or might not *completely* achieve the first and last points through the approach of having to win.

Huang: But having to win has its advantages as well! Now consider the following points and think about what children might not learn through the "having fun" approach.

- Soccer teaches the value of hard work and perseverance.
- Soccer builds a sense of responsibility.
- Soccer builds team spirit.
- Soccer makes kids tougher and more resilient.

American parents: Yes, kids could benefit from all of the above items using the approach of having to win while they likely wouldn't from the approach of just having fun.

Huang: Furthermore, please consider these even more intricate sociological and psychological results:

- Playing community soccer as a child provides children with a valuable opportunity to interact with others their age. They can learn at an early age how to negotiate social hierarchies in a safe and controlled environment that mimics adult work environments.
- Team sports (like soccer) teach kids the importance of assuming social roles and fulfilling one's responsibilities while also allowing them to simultaneously witness and experience the consequences of failure to perform one's responsibilities.
- Sports (like soccer) grant children an early chance to have a "mastery experience" through the orchestrated teaching, learning, and application of discrete skills in competition with peers.
- The idea of a "good sportsman" itself is a reflection of society's desire to promote certain characteristics and traits. Sports are simply one vehicle through which society can remind itself of the kinds of people it wants to produce.

American parents: We'll be honest, we are afraid the "have to win" approach might be too much pressure for our children. At the same time, it seems to educate kids better than the "have fun" approach.

WHY DO THE CHINESE HAVE TO "WIN" EDUCATION?

We've talked about the contrast between how average Americans and Chinese Americans conceptualize education—but why is education a life-or-death struggle for the Chinese and Chinese Americans? What explains this difference?

There are two primary reasons why Chinese Americans view education this way. First, the fathomless historical and cultural roots of China must be taken into account. Second, there are natural difficulties associated with the immigrant lifestyle that Chinese Americans have in common.

Let us address cultural and historical roots first.

Education Is a Game of Elimination through Selection and Competition

1

It's common knowledge that China was the source of four of the most important inventions in human history: paper, gunpowder, the compass, and the printing press. Despite the fact that the Chinese came up with these ideas, they didn't see their full potential or apply them effectively. For example, what do you think of when you hear the word *gunpowder*? Weapons, correct? Well, though the Chinese invented gunpowder, they didn't seek out the most effective way to use it. Instead of conquering their enemies with their explosive new discovery, they used gunpowder to make elaborate fireworks. This trend, sadly, continues with other Chinese inventions. Instead of sailing the seas and exploring the wider world with their early compasses, the Chinese used them chiefly to ward off bad luck by utilizing proper *feng shui*. Despite having paper for over one thousand nine hundred years and wooden printing presses for over a millennium, the ancient Chinese never thought to mechanize the process to mass-produce books. In fact, since the seventeenth century, European settlers have used China's own inventions (e.g., the compass and gunpowder) against it. As a result, European imperial powers were able to establish colonies up and down China's long eastern coast, which caused hundreds of years of strife. Though paper, gunpowder, the compass, and the printing press are widely known as China's great contributions to the world, they have had relatively little direct cultural impact on modern China.

However, what many people overlook is the fact that there is a fifth great Chinese invention. This was a creation so far ahead of its time that it has been lost in the shuffle of the passing years. Though less famous than its counterparts, this fifth invention, the standardized test, has had by far the most significant and long-lasting cultural impact in China and East Asia

China's history of administering national standardized tests stretches back well over a millennium, more than one thousand four hundred years to be precise.[2] And even today this tradition continues, as standardized testing remains the central and defining characteristic of modern Chinese education.

2

Modern Chinese education can be directly traced back to what is now known as the "Imperial Examination System," which developed during in the sixth century. Over a thousand years before Columbus landed in the West Indies, China's practice of administering standardized tests was already centuries old. Though its origins can be traced to an even earlier period of Chinese history (the Han dynasty, 200 BCE–200 CE), the first true version of the Imperial Examination System was introduced in 607 CE, during the Sui dynasty, which followed a lengthy period during which China was divided by war.[3]

The introduction of the examination system in China was a monumental change. It drastically altered the nature of the aristocracy in China and the nature and perception of education in China and much of East Asia. It helped shatter social boundaries that had been in place since what seemed to be the dawn of time. While the rest of the world was mired in the old ways of hereditary aristocracy, the Chinese took a massive gamble by creating a *meritocratic aristocracy*. This was revolutionary to the world, evidenced by the fact that the two basic tenets of the ancient Imperial Examination System, equal opportunity and meritocracy, remain pillars of education throughout the modern world. Even the college admissions process in the United States can be said to be built in part on the virtues of equal opportunity and meritocracy (among others).

More importantly, the Imperial Examination System opened up pathways to better lives for millions. Success on the exams came with many perks, including exemption from both corporal punishment and manual labor, an immediate change in social status and class, a state salary, prestige, and power. Under the Imperial Examination System, *anyone* who passed the relevant tests could serve as a learned civil official in the government. Even beggars and peasants could transcend the ghosts of their pasts and test their way toward becoming dignified and educated members of the Chinese gentry. Many of the constraints of existing social hierarchies—hierarchies that could previously have been upset only through war or rebellion—could now be cast off and circumvented simply by doing well on a test. The system prized talent and ability above blood and heredity, and, consequently, the Chinese people began to perceive education differently.

The nature of the exams themselves contributed to the change. The exams were not whimsical or administered in unpredictable ways. By most accounts, they were just the opposite. Much like many of the standardized exams given today, the Chinese imperial exams were administered at regular intervals (roughly once every three years), giving people ample time to prepare. More importantly, the tests generally covered material that, for the most part, remained the same (a set of texts derived from Confucian teachings known during the Tang dynasty as the "Four Books and Five Classics"). Unlike exams designed to prevent preparation (certain modern IQ tests, for example), the imperial exams offered by the Chinese government were predictable and, most importantly, *learnable*. That meant that anyone could do well on them simply through careful preparation and diligent study. The more you studied, the better you were likely to perform. Studying became a slow but sure route to success. Thus, a national attitude and affinity for intensive studying developed. An untold number of Chinese idioms sprang up singing of the rewards of studying and education.

The Chinese who created the Imperial Examination System not only changed the way the government was run, but they also transformed the nature of education itself in China. Before the Imperial Examination System was created, the purpose of Chinese education was to impart knowledge and cultivate people, similar to the goals of education in many other countries of the world.

Confucius, one of the world's great teachers and philosophers, had three thousand students. His free discussion style was somewhat similar the Socratic method made famous by the philosophers of ancient Greece. An A+ or a D− on an exam? It was unheard of! Later, the Imperial Examination System was created to identify intelligence and innate talent. While some were selected, uplifted through this meritocracy, others were eliminated. This was an unavoidable consequence of the Imperial Examination System's structure, and it has had a lasting effect on Chinese culture. Since then, Chinese education by its very nature has been about selecting a few and eliminating the rest. With the invention of the Imperial Examination System, quite suddenly, all Chinese people had a reliable and predictable route through which they could guarantee themselves a better life. Through the creation of the Imperial Examination System, the ancient Chinese forged a shield anyone could take up and utilize to shelter themselves against the misfortunes of birth and class. That shield was education.

With this historical context, it is easy to understand why the Chinese hold education in such high regard, why many Chinese would not hesitate to tell you even today that education is the single most important thing in life. The Chinese imperial exams were able to provide something to the common folk that no amount of hopeful thinking, ingenuity, hard work, resourcefulness, or prayer could have given in generations past.

3

I often tell my American students who don't understand the Chinese tenet of supremacy of education that Christians believe in a God who created all things in the universe and yet is not a part of the universe. This sense of a God who is above or outside the universe is quite foreign to Chinese tradition. We might say that while the Christians believe in God, the Chinese believe in 天. As this character doesn't have a proper English translation, I'll use the term *heaven* to try to describe one of its meanings. While this perhaps oversimplifies a very complex idea, heaven, for the ancient Chinese, referred to both a natural and a supernatural entity. It is said that the sky was so high, huge, and mysterious that people were unable to touch and understand it, and yet it related to people's everyday life. Even though human beings were unable to control heaven, they were able to create many things on earth. To further explain my point, let us examine two ancient Chinese characters: 大, which meant "big" and 天, which, as we have seen, meant "heaven." 大 ("big") is a pictographic character that symbolizes a spirited person with outstretched arms and legs. One might wonder why anyone would take the symbol of a person to represent the concept "big." After all, there is so much we can see on this earth—mountains, ocean, the ground—that is so much bigger than a person. Why not pick something larger to represent "big"? However, in Chinese culture humans were considered to be greater than all these things. Only human beings were able to create history, society, and civilization.

Now, looking at the character 天 for heaven, we can see that it contains two parts—a spirited person with outstretched arms and legs (大) and the sky above (一). The ancient Chinese did not feel that they understood the relationship between human beings and heaven. While they believed that humans were great, the sky above, or heaven, which they looked at each and every night, was greater. During the Spring and Autumn Period (770–221 BCE), Confucianism captured this idea in the saying: "Heaven and people combine into one." They emphasized that people must always be in harmony with heaven.[4]

Indeed, for nearly all of Chinese history before the adoption of the Imperial Examination System, one's station in life was determined at birth by 天 (heaven). If heaven made you an emperor, your life would be one of opulence, pleasure, and immeasurable importance. But if heaven saw fit to make you a peasant, your life would be spent in the fields, toiling and sweating, working alongside the beasts until the day you died. With few exceptions, the will of heaven was not malleable.

But the Imperial Examination System did something extraordinary. It gave each man no less than the power to change the will of heaven. It wasn't some miracle achieved through prayer, magic, or luck; it made miracles possible simply through *studying*, through learning. By putting forth simple human effort and educating oneself, a man could transcend the bounds of his own dismal ancestry. Through education, and education alone, man could exceed his own fate and rewrite his own part in the powerful play of life, perhaps achieving a destiny that even heaven itself could not envision.

This photo shows students reciting their lessons aloud. It is not unusual for Chinese students to read together from their textbooks for thirty to sixty minutes each morning before regular classes begin. *Photo by Bo Wang.*

4

However, by virtue of selecting a few, many had to be eliminated. As a system of selecting talents, the imperial examination had a tangential effect of gradually destroying the essentials of education. No longer were the goals of education in China to give rise to knowledge and encourage mental growth. Since education now served the needs of the government and was dictated by the requirements of the Imperial Examination System, the nature of education mutated. Education became a simple mechanism for elimination through selection and competition. The feeling that one *must* "win" at education is much more pervasive in Chinese education than anywhere else in the world.

Although China abolished the Imperial Examination System in 1905, its impact reached far outside China. Students in Japan, Korea, Vietnam, and other Asian countries, in particular,[5] know very well the feeling that one must win at education. The system? You can throw it to winds or leave it behind in history. The culture, however, has been melted into your blood. No matter how far you go, you will take it with you because it is a part of you. Therefore, Chinese people brought this emphasis on education across the vast ocean to the New World.

While the rhetoric of the West tells us that human beings are beholden to no fate in particular, and, indeed, can change their destiny through many different avenues, for over one thousand years, the Chinese have believed that education—*and only education*—can change the will of heaven. For this reason, they view education as a battle of elimination and selection that must be fought and won.

DIALOGUE

American parents: We find it difficult to believe that education can change God's will. Also, it's hard for us to see education as a battle of elimination through selection and competition. We'd like to know your suggestions and advice regarding this.

Huang: You don't have to believe in either of these tenets to apply the lessons that derive from Chinese-American parenting. My advice is this: Pay *much more* attention to your children's studies. Every morning when you wake up, make sure their schooling is one of your top priorities, something you're thinking about over the course of the day. American parents are regularly involved in their kids' extracurricular activities; after all, that's where the term "soccer mom" came from. But instead of just arranging their after-school sports, try handling and being involved in their studying in the same way. After all, in the long run a child's studies are at least as important as his or her extracurricular activities, and you'll make a big difference by being involved. I promise that you'll see a big improvement in your child's attitude toward studying and his or her grades, provided that you spend a *full semester* arranging their studying.

American parents: It's so much easier to handle their sports, which involve going to games and transporting them to their practices. Studying isn't quite as scintillating for us. In fact, it's downright boring!

Huang: It's because of those difficulties that your efforts will be appreciated! Even the smallest effort from you will go a long way. Indeed, start cultivating kids' study habits in early childhood; you'll see that it will make a big difference. Once they get used to studying and "get into the groove," you'll find yourself telling them to stop studying so much rather than constantly pushing them to study!

American parents: Wow! That sounds much better! Rather than pushing them to study, we'll encourage them to stop and take a break! But how do we make studying more interesting?

Huang: There are ways to make studying less boring and perhaps even fun for both your child and you. There are various math games you can play (see the example of 24 in chapter 6). Here's another example. In order to be able to read Chinese books, a Chinese-American child needs to memorize at least two thousand Chinese characters. The most difficult period for my son was after he'd learned about a thousand characters because it seemed as though for every one new character he learned, he would forget two others. I had tried various methods to help Yan, but these methods failed at every turn. Then I remembered that Yan had been crazy about a certain TV series based on Jin Yong's very famous Chinese kung fu novels. I decided to try to entice (or even trick) Yan into reading these books when he was in high school.

Chinese parents: Are you kidding? Jin's novels? They're semi-classical Chinese; how was he supposed to understand them in high school?

Huang: Yes, everyone (including my own wife) thought I was crazy to do this. I, however, endeavored to ask him to read just four pages per day with me—and it worked! After Yan finished one set of Jin's novels with great interest, it made many of my Chinese friends extremely envious because they had the same problem with their kids for years.

Chinese parents: Congratulations! You triumphed over that difficult period in which most of us fail.

Huang: It was funny because while Yan was able to read these novels, he had trouble with more modern writing. He couldn't even read the Chinese newspaper *People's Daily*! His wording and language use was semi-classical, which only scholars from a hundred years ago would use. However, if we had continued for just two more years, Yan would have reached the level where he would have been able to keep up with his Chinese by just reading the books he was interested in. After he went to college, though, he couldn't continue in this vein without my assistance translating and explaining key words in order to help him read smoothly and understand the story. It has become one of my lifelong regrets!

What I am trying to say is that being involved in your children's studying doesn't have to be mind-numbing. It can be entertaining for both of you.

The Actual Difficulties of the Immigrant Lifestyle

1

Any immigrant to America from China, whether a typical person or a student, struggles for survival. This hardship results in a single conviction: the importance and necessity of winning at all aspects of life. The children of these immigrants generally take the difficulties borne by their parents to heart; their parents' suffering becomes their life teacher and they adopt the have-to-win mentality.

In 1996, we finally were able to move out of the tiny student dorm and into our newly purchased house. Yan also achieved his own dream: he got a black Labrador puppy named Lucky. A new house, a dog—our friends teased us about finally achieving our own American Dream.

One day, while Yan was playing with Lucky and I was feeling content with our "lot," I asked him, "Let's say you divided your life into three stages, first, living in China, second, the small, cramped student dorm, and now our own house with a dog. Which one was the most meaningful for you?"

I was sure I knew his answer, but I asked the question anyway.

Yan pondered for some time and then finally said, "I was too young when I left to really remember the time we spent in China, but if I had to choose, it would be the student dorm."

I was completely surprised by his answer; for my wife and me, the time we spent in that small, cramped student dorm was almost too unbearable to recall. But it seems as though our son had eternal gratitude for the good memories we shared there—enough gratitude for all three of us.

2

I had a milkshake for the first time in 1989. I had been in America for just over one year at that point. While I was working on my doctorate at Miami University, my academic advisor and mentor, Dr. Charles Teckman, took me and another one of his students to do research at a local high school. I remember that that particular day was incredibly hot. It was late August, but the heat felt like the dead middle of summer. By the end of our research session at the local high school my shirt was soaked through with sweat.

As we were driving home, Dr. Teckman took a short detour. I looked at him, puzzled.

"Milkshakes," he said, smiling. This did not cure my confusion. At that time I had no idea that such a thing existed. I understood both of the component words ("milk" and "shake"), but I couldn't figure out for the life of me what it meant when you combined them. *What happens to milk when it is shaken?* I thought to myself in silence.

When Dr. Teckman handed me my strawberry milkshake from a place called "Dairy Queen," most of my most pressing questions were answered in the most satisfying way. I learned that milkshakes were not really milk. It was *ice cream*, but it was somehow also *liquid*. A deep plastic cup of swirling, light pink cream, dotted with flecks of red strawberry all the way through. It was intriguing to look at, and even more intriguing to learn how to eat it—not with a spoon but with a straw! The cream was so thick that it took some effort to work it out with a straw. I learned that two straws worked better than one. Most of all, however, I learned that milkshakes were *delicious*. Cold, sweet, thick, and unnervingly rich. I'd never in my life tasted anything quite like it.

But after a very small taste, I stopped and refused to have more. As Dr. Teckman drove us home, I covered my straw with my hand and held the cup close, hiding it from the sun. I pretended to have a taste here and there as we went. By the time we returned home, both Dr. Teckman and the other student had already finished their milkshakes and discarded their cups. I was still holding mine. I was sure that they could tell by glancing at it that it was still entirely full. If they could tell, though, they never mentioned it.

Dr. Teckman was like a father to me, and like a grandfather to my son Yan. In fact, to this day, Yan calls him "Grandpa Teckman." In the time that I've known him, Dr. Teckman has taken it upon himself to help introduce many aspects of American life and culture to our family. On numerous occasions he drove us to the grocery store instead of letting us walk. Once, rather than letting us spend money purchasing another plane ticket, Dr. Teckman willingly drove many hours in a single day to take my brother from Cincinnati to Kalamazoo, Michigan. On top of being my academic advisor, he was a mentor and guardian for my entire family.

When I saw that Dr. Teckman noticed I had barely touched my milkshake, I was afraid that I'd offended him. I began wondering whether he would think I didn't like the milkshake. I was worried he would ask why I hadn't had any, and I didn't feel comfortable explaining myself. By the time we reached my dormitory, however, I realized that there was no need to explain. Dr. Teckman bade me farewell and didn't mention the milkshake at all. He took care not to even look at it as we said our goodbyes. There is no doubt in my mind that he knew *exactly* what I was doing.

As his car pulled away, I turned and rushed home. Before I was halfway across the courtyard outside the dormitories, I broke into a light sprint. I held the milkshake out in front of me. I had felt it melting, getting softer and softer in the car. I was worried that it wouldn't taste like it had before.

Yan was sleeping when I opened the door.

I woke him up.

"Look, son," I said, "Look what Baba brought for you."

I held the cup up to my son, whose eyes were still heavy with sleep.

"This is *milkshake*," I said in English and out of breath. "*Dairy-Queen-milk-shake.*"

He took the cup and began to drink, still in a daze.

I asked, "Good? Do you know what it is?"

Yan didn't answer.

My wife and I looked at each other and then watched Yan silently.

When a slurp finally came from the bottom of the empty cup, my son raised his head and asked, "What is it?"

"Milkshake with strawberry!"

3

I don't know whether Yan could taste the ups and downs, the sweet and the bitter of life from that single milkshake. But what I am sure of is that he certainly did remember his first milkshake, something many children might not. To this day, whenever this milkshake is mentioned, he always silently smiles as if absorbed in thought. Indeed, this could be the beginning of many, many stories.

I like telling the milkshake story because it is a bit silly now that I think about it. Today, both my son and I can have milkshakes any time we want. But, oddly, we never do. Back then, however, it was truly something unique. Because we were living off the money I earned through my assistantship as a doctoral candidate, we had very little money to go around. For nearly a decade, we hardly ever spent a dime eating out. We simply couldn't afford it. That was the first time I'd ever had a milkshake, and it would be several years before I'd have one again. The second time was at an out-of-state conference, where I couldn't possibly preserve it for my son. I was forced to enjoy it all by myself. I did so quickly and without much complaint.

The difficulties of the immigrant lifestyle make parents and children realize that they have to work and study incredibly hard to change their life situation.

There is a Chinese saying: "Prosperity can never last for three generations." With hard work (and luck), the first wave of pioneers in a frontier are able to find great success. Their coming generations, however, can enjoy the success of their forebears without hardship. Eventually, the successors will forget the sacrifices of their forebears and will slowly lose any of that initial lingering spirit. After so many generations here, I wonder, how much of the original pioneering spirit of the American frontiersmen still remains? That is, of course, a massive question that we cannot possibly hope to answer in this text.

That said, in the 80s and early 90s, America was a new frontier for Chinese people like me. Many Chinese people who had very respectable jobs in China came to the United States to start new lives as dirt-poor students. In so doing, Asian Americans created a smaller version of the great American pioneer narrative.

DIALOGUE

American parents: Our forebears were immigrants, but we are not. We didn't live through your difficulties, nor do we have your backgrounds. How do we inspire our children to study hard?

Huang: My family owned two sets of rental houses for many years, so we have had the chance to get to know many tenants. Some of them were invested in making money and didn't make the time to spend directing their children's studying. But others realized that education is a means to change their children's lives. In the past, when we showed these families the houses, they would be very excited. "These bedrooms will belong to our kids so they can study without bothering one another. We'll set up our TV downstairs so we won't bother them either," they'd exclaim. The parents usually had a career goal, such as becoming a pharmacist, nurse, accountant, or lawyer, set up for their children. We were always deeply moved by their words, which recalled our old memories.

American parents: I think we understand what you're saying. The key is that education is a vehicle to change your life, but not necessarily your immediate economic situation.

Huang: Yes, exactly! In fact, families with a higher economic status should encourage their children to "experience" how education can change a life. When we were struggling through difficult times as foreign students, some professors consciously created the chance for their children to make friends with Yan by playing and studying with him.

American parents: Very interesting!

Huang: One day, one of the children said to his mom, "Yan's family's house only has one bedroom." His mother responded, "Yes, but where is he with his studying? At the top of your class, right? Studying can change his future. Believe it or not, one day Yan will have a house bigger than ours."

American parents: A very meaningful exchange.

Huang: More than twenty years have passed, but I found out about this conversation from the boy's mother (who is now one of my colleagues) only a few months ago. I thanked her for providing Yan with so many opportunities to understand and become a part of American culture when we were in a difficult situation.

American parents: She sounds like a very wise and nice mom.

Huang: Yes, she is, and her response to me was thoughtful as well: "We should thank you. I consciously created a chance for my son to associate with Yan and other foreign students' children. The immigrants' lives and their kids' study made a deep impression on my son. I'm convinced that, because of them, he always studied hard. That's to your credit."

HOW DO THE CHINESE "WIN" EDUCATION?

In Order to Win, One Has to Study Earlier and Study More

1

As an American, you've probably heard a fair amount of the ongoing discussion about why Chinese kids are good at math and science. Some people say it is because they use chopsticks; others say it's because they often play musical instruments. These people believe in a link between small, careful movements of the fingers and the exercise and growth of the brain.

I don't really know whether or not this is true, whether such a connection exists. I've forced my son to use chopsticks since he was very young, but he still hates math!

A more interesting and likely explanation came from Zou Jiayan, a professor at Hong Kong City University. He found that when students study the Chinese written language, it engages much more of their brains than typical Western languages. How and why does this happen? According to his research, the left part of the human brain is in charge of pictures and the right part is responsible for sound. Many Chinese characters have both visual and auditory meaning. In other words, Chinese characters force their readers to utilize both halves of their brains—your whole brain is awakened to process sounds, images, and meanings.[6] Does this make sense? Perhaps we'll just let scientists enjoy this headache while we move on to other explanations for Chinese students' proficiency in math.

2

Let's turn to the well-written, yet somewhat peculiar, explanation for Chinese mathematic success offered by bestselling author Malcolm Gladwell. In Gladwell's extremely popular *Outliers*, a text exploring the topic of success in general, he devotes an entire chapter to the question of why Chinese people (and other East Asians) are good at math. To begin with, Mr. Gladwell states that while some research indicates Asians may have an innate biological "proclivity for math," he believes the explanation may be *cultural*. In his words, "cultural legacies *matter*," and the Chinese mathematics phenomenon cannot be due entirely to innate Chinese biological characteristics.[7]

And I wholeheartedly agree; I am certain that this distinction is very important. Like Mr. Gladwell, I believe that the reason for the high performance of
Chinese students in early academics is primarily cultural, not biological. But
when Gladwell moves beyond this basic assertion, his logic escapes me and I can
no longer agree with him. In a chapter titled "Rice Paddies and Math Tests," he
advances very interesting but ultimately inadequate theories.

In regard to math, Gladwell says that the Chinese are simply willing to work
harder and longer than Westerners. This accounts for the difference in performance. Note that this is the same answer I gave above. But, as I stated previously,
the more interesting question is not what, but why? *Why* are Chinese students
willing to work so much harder than their Western peers?

Asian children and their parents prize education, even in the
poorest and most remote places. Unlike Americans schools, whose
classroom walls are often posted with inspirational messages for
the purpose of boosting students' self-esteem, the walls of this
Chinese schoolhouse are bare and crumbling. The shafts of sunlight
filtering through the porous wooden roof are light enough to read
by, and therefore all the inspiration they need. *Photo by Yue Wang.*

Gladwell's answer? Rice.

Yes, according to Gladwell, it is China's history of growing rice that makes the Chinese people willing to work harder and longer. This willingness to work harder translates directly to being "better" at math. I'll let him explain.

"Throughout history," Mr. Gladwell argues, "the people who grow rice have always worked harder than almost any other kind of famer."[8] Rice farming, he informs us, is unlike any other type of farming. By its nature, it is not only meaningful and complex, but also incredibly "exacting" on the peasants, who are pressed to grow a large amount of crop in tiny paddies that are woven together in complex tapestries to maximize production. Rice farming demands focused, hard work, and China, with its rich tradition of wet-rice farming, has somehow passed on these traits to its culture of education.

This cultural legacy of wet-rice agriculture, in Gladwell's view, has imparted upon Asian peoples an ability and desire to work "really hard"—and this has translated directly to excellence in mathematics.

Unfortunately, Mr. Gladwell's argument is rife with holes. Rice farming by itself simply cannot account for the difference observable between Chinese students and others in mathematics. I won't go so far as to say it has nothing to do with the real answer, but I certainly don't believe it is the main underlying cause. Below I raise some simple questions that I don't think Mr. Gladwell's theory can answer.

3

First, Mr. Gladwell severely overstates the prevalence and prominence of rice farming in China. While several regions of China do have long histories of rice farming, Mr. Gladwell's argument completely fails to account for those areas of China where no rice can be grown. Today, rice is actually only grown on about 25 percent of the cultivated land in China, limited mainly to parts of southern and central China, and even then it's not always the dominant crop. For many reasons, Chinese farms frequently rotate rice with other crops such as winter wheat, sweet potatoes, corn, and vegetables of various types, the same as they've done for thousands of years. Though Mr. Gladwell's argument extends to *all* Chinese people (and to other East Asian peoples as well), the subject of his argument is relegated to what ends up being only an isolated portion of China's vast agriculture.

Of course, Mr. Gladwell never argued that rice is grown in all parts of China by all Chinese people. But this highlights a second problem with Mr. Gladwell's argument. How exactly does rice farming by one section of the population foster or impart a culture of hard work upon the remainder of China's people? Not only are significant portions of China not historically reserved or used for rice farming, but even in areas of heavy rice farming, it is difficult to see how a "cultural legacy" was formed. That is, not only are China's farmlands stratified, but for hundreds of years, the Chinese people themselves have been heavily divided by class and social status.

Today, a Chinese peasant can't simply leave the farm and move into the city of his or her own accord; and this has been the case throughout Chinese history. Physical relocations require significant amounts of money and, in most cases, permission from the government. Consequently, those who grew up in a city—even one that is surrounded by rice farms as far as the eye can see—would likely know little more about rice farming than Westerners. At what point would these city dwellers inherit the culture of hard work from the rice peasants? By what vehicle would the rice-farming population bring the ethic of hard work to the city dwellers? The answer is unclear.

Additionally, if rice farming is capable of imparting such virtue upon an entire national population, why have rice-farming cultures from other parts of the world not seen similar results? In parts of Africa, particularly near the Nile River Delta, there is a nearly five-thousand-year history of growing rice. Rice was introduced in South America many centuries ago, and, for many Latin American countries, it remains a central staple food. Indeed, some of the largest rice crops in the world today are grown in countries such as Indonesia, Bangladesh, Vietnam, Thailand, Myanmar, Pakistan, and the Philippines—countries that also have rice-farming traditions that are hundreds of years old. *None* of these areas, however, have shown a similar propensity for the early academic successes seen in China. Why? Are they farming rice incorrectly? Are they not farming enough of it?

The problem is that Mr. Gladwell has found correlation where he believes he has found causation. In the chapter of his book devoted to the subject, Gladwell never truly explains *how* this cultural legacy of rice farming has translated into mathematical competence; he merely points out that they exist alongside one another. Which is more likely? That the Chinese people learned how to work hard in all other areas of life because a portion of its agricultural population has historically grown rice? Or that the success and prevalence of rice farming in China is one area (along with education) in which the Chinese people exhibit a pre-existing cultural readiness to work hard?

4

Finally, and most troubling, is the fact that Mr. Gladwell's entire argument rests on a flimsy and superficial definition of being "good" at mathematics. He starts with the assumption that the Chinese (and other Asians) are good at mathematics. Indeed, they are not only good, they are "better" than Westerners. As support, he cites international standardized tests such as the Trends in International Mathematics and Science Study (TIMSS)—a test taken by elementary school students.[9] But is the early success enjoyed by Chinese (and other East Asians) on such math tests enough to mean they are "good" at math? What about later, more noteworthy mathematical achievements? Why contain the question to only one type of success at mathematics? Why not include more remarkable accomplishments such as the Fields Medal or Nobel Prize?

Every four years, the International Mathematics Union awards the "International Medal for Outstanding Discoveries in Mathematics," also known as the Fields Medal. It is generally regarded as the highest honor that can be given to a mathematician, and it's considered the unofficial Nobel Prize in mathematics.[10]

Let's take a look at Fields Medal recipients. According to Gladwell's statements about Chinese people being "good" at math, you'd expect Chinese research institutions to have a large number of winners. However, with the aid of their specialized rice-farming culture, how many Chinese mathematicians have won the Fields Medal since its inception? *Zero.* Out of fifty medalists, not a single adult at a Chinese university has won. Despite being the country with the largest rice production in the world and supposedly the country that is "good" at math (and certainly "better" than Westerners), China hasn't managed to win the highest honor in mathematics a single time. Ironically, Terence Tao and Shing-Tung Yau, the only medalists of Chinese background, are products of Western academic institutions. Finally, France and the United States, Western countries with no strong traditions of rice farming or eating, are decidedly over-represented with ten and thirteen medalists respectively.

The prevalence of rice farming in certain parts of China is not enough to explain how Chinese children are able to find consistent success at the early stages of education. Nor can it explain how Chinese immigrants to the West and their children can realize similar results while other cultures with heavy rice-farming traditions cannot. Finally, there is no explanation for why success only appears on tests at the elementary and secondary level (such as the TIMSS and

PISA) and not at the highest levels of academia (such as the Nobel Prize or the Fields Medal).

No. As an explanation, China's history of rice farming is not enough.

5

So, then, why are Chinese-American children better at mathematics than American children? I return to my original conclusion: Chinese-American children are good at math, not because they are smarter than others, but because they start studying earlier and they study more. Thus, they are in a better position to answer seemingly difficult math questions that might put American children to shame. Have you ever watched the television show *Are You Smarter than a 5th Grader*? Provided that you have, you've probably discovered that there are actually quite a few adults who have difficulty with even first- or second-grade level math. Those who aren't confident in their answers would often complain, "I'm not good at math," "I'm scared of math," or "I was horrible at math when I was in school!"

I've heard many explanations for why Chinese kids are good at school subjects such as math and science. We've already discussed Malcolm Gladwell's theory on rice farming as it pertains to mathematics, but he also has a second theory that takes a different approach. In *Outliers*, Gladwell suggests that the Chinese language itself is better suited than the English language to help people learn and deal with numbers. Supposedly, it's easier and faster to memorize more numbers in Chinese than in English. Moreover, the way the Chinese language deals with numbers is also said to be more logical and easier to understand for children. These small advantages, Gladwell tells us, build up to wide gulfs in performance over time.[11]

My issue with explanations like the ones above is that they often make things more complicated than they otherwise need to be. They all tend to take the following form: because Chinese people do X, this stimulates the Y part of their brain, and this results in Z bonuses in math and science. These theories give the Chinese tendency for excellence in math an air of mystery and exoticism that is not only unnecessary, but also inappropriate. At times, these theories begin to sound dangerously close to biologically essentialist arguments along the lines of "Chinese brains are more logical and less creative" and "Western brains are less mathematical but more artistic." I believe that humans are humans and that biology matters less than our cultures and histories. Therefore, I find these biologically essentialist arguments, and those that trend that way, to be both uninteresting and insulting. Most importantly, these explanations ignore what I think is the simplest and best explanation for why Chinese kids are better at math and science (and school in general) at an early age: Chinese kids are simply willing to work earlier and harder.

I once heard an American quote that I think we can commandeer in order to examine education: "Winners have simply formed the habit of doing things losers don't like to do." If we think of education like the Chinese do (as a game or battle to be won and lost), this quote is equally applicable to children, parents, and educators.

Parents are waiting for their children who are taking the College Entrance Exam (similar to the SAT or the CAT). Parents are holding a banner that reads, "Kids, we will be liberated!" One's score on the College Entrance Exam, which is held once a year, is the sole yardstick to decide if one will be admitted to a college. Just one point more or less than others may determine one's entire life. Most high school students study six and a half or even seven days per week. Once the exam has been completed, kids and parents feel as if they've been liberated. *Photo by Bo Gong.*

Because the Chinese feel an immense pressure to win in the game of education, they have naturally adopted the strategy suggested by the quote above. They know exactly which things "losers" are not willing to do. Chinese students don't just turn these skills into habits; they make them second nature. This particularly applies to younger children. In traditional Chinese education, the early adoption of a full set of positive study skills is of the utmost importance. This has become so common that failure to push your child to develop these skills at the earliest possible opportunity inevitably means your child will fall behind. In America, however, few parents push their children to adopt these positive study skills, especially not at a young age. There is an underlying belief that to do so may stifle the child or hurt or hinder some other necessary developmental stage. To the Chinese, this is simply the behavior of "losers."

6

As a child, Yan was always good at math. Beginning in elementary school, he was generally the top math student in his class. This lasted through middle school, where he took high school math classes, and high school, where he finished all his math requirements by his sophomore year. From the outside, Yan's abilities seemed innate. Over the years, many of his teachers have commented on his "natural talent" at math. But truthfully, Yan was (and is) by no means a math genius. Not even close. I'd hesitate to even say that math came naturally to him. In fact, one could say that his math abilities are highly unnatural. They were, for the most part, created. Engineered. And I was the engineer.

When Yan first began attending American elementary school, I noticed a disturbing trend. As a first grader, he came home every day around 2:00 p.m. with a big smile on his face but hardly anything else.

Every day, I would ask him, "Do you have any homework?"

Like clockwork, he would respond, "No!"

At first, I was suspicious. Was he forgetting it at school? Judging from the way he proudly told me he had no work, that didn't seem to be the case. Was he hiding it? Was he leaving it behind on purpose? Could my young son already be that devious? But after a week or two, I realized that my son was telling the truth. This led to an even stranger realization: his teachers simply weren't giving him anything to do after school.

This was incredible. I didn't understand. I was already shocked at how short my son's school days were. In China, kindergarteners were expected to stay in school just as long as the rest of the students, and here my son was getting out in the early afternoons—at 1:30 or 2:00 p.m. But now on top of that, I realized he wasn't required to do any homework! How could a child come home from school with no homework? In China, kids his age would routinely come home with enough work that they'd sometimes have to skip dinner when they didn't start on it diligently. Even when Yan did bring back some "homework," I was shocked yet again at what they were asking him to do: write a few letters from the alphabet, do some cutting and pasting, or draw whatever he felt like.

What kind of school is this? I thought to myself. They weren't pushing him hard enough. He could do more than this. Much more. He should be doing more. In a few months' time, kids his age in China would be far ahead of him. *He's falling behind*, I thought, panicked. In fact, he probably was already behind, especially in math. His American class had been doing basic addition for weeks! If we ever moved back to China, I realized, my son would never be able to catch up.

I resolved to not let that happen. As a father, I saw it as my solemn duty to not let it happen. I couldn't let my son waste away like this. So, during that first-grade year, I began to intervene in his studying.

I said, "Son, shouldn't you study a little more math every day in order get a better grade in class?"

By asking Yan this, I was actually stepping away from traditional Chinese parenting. Chinese parents usually explain to their children why they have to study more math and then require them to do so. Others even force their kids to study more without even giving any sort of explanation. My style was different; I wanted to instill the concept of "have to win" into his mind with a discussion question. It would be so much better to bring his enthusiasm and initiative into play rather than forcing him to study. In addition, if I was going to add to his study burden, I thought I should at least "discuss" it with him. My parenting was much more democratic than many Chinese parents. Of course, though I began the discussion with a question, I knew there wouldn't be a question at the end! Yan might not be able to understand my question now, but provided that he tried and studied as I'd asked him to, he would understand it eventually.

After that point, I started giving Yan a regimen of daily after-school math lessons. We began with the basics, addition and subtraction. Under my careful tutelage, he picked these concepts up quickly. I wasted no time, then, and moved on to multiplication and division. By the time he was in first grade, he not only knew all of his multiplication tables, he also knew more complicated multiplication and long division. By American standards, this would likely have been deemed too much for a child his age. In China, however, this wouldn't raise a single eyebrow.

To my surprise, I found that the more I taught Yan, the easier it became. I could see his confidence growing lesson by lesson. My overarching goal was to instill in him the desire to be good at math, to be better than his classmates, to win. Things seemed to pan out by themselves. The more Yan learned, the more it seemed he enjoyed math. This was reinforced whenever his teachers would ask math questions in class. In no time at all, Yan was so far ahead of the other kids in his class that he was frequently able to show off his math skills in front of everyone. His teachers, amazed by his knowledge, praised him constantly. And this, in turn, kept him interested in our lessons. Yan didn't realize it, but what was actually happening was that he was slowly absorbing the need to win at mathematics. All according to my plan!

Unfortunately, after visiting a few bookstores I discovered that the textbooks Yan needed in order to study were incredibly expensive, costing far more than we could afford at the time. I was afraid that the Chinese textbooks we had at home would be too advanced. I also preferred textbooks written in English— Yan would be able to learn from the books on his own, studying math and English at the same time—it killed two birds with one stone!

The answer came one day when I walked past the local public library. From across the street, I saw tables full of books. It was a sale! The library was getting rid of its older books, including many used textbooks. I excitedly looked through them and found several sets of American math textbooks beginning from fourth grade up through high school. They were full of examples, key points, explanations, and exercises, and they were edited in a very logical fashion. At the beginning, I hurried through the stacks because I was worried I'd have too many competitors fighting me for these textbooks. But no! There was not a single American who was interested in them. So, after carefully checking and comparing them, I chose one of the sets. Most important of all: they were only a dollar per copy!

My god! I thought. *From now on, my boy has something to do!*

7

In 1966 the Cultural Revolution broke out in China. Though I had not yet finished junior high school, I was no longer allowed to study. Instead, I was forced to muddle along with the revolution. In 1969 I was sent hundreds of miles away to the countryside. I stayed there, away from my family and everything else I had ever known, for over three years. After working as a peasant, I was able to get a "better" job as a worker in a city factory. I stayed there for seven years.

For ten years I'd been uprooted and sent to work at difficult menial labor, my education interrupted.

During the Cultural Revolution only those whose parents were workers, peasants, or soldiers were eligible to go to high school and college. Because of my family's status, I was absolutely not allowed to study at any schools during those years. What's more, I never had a chance to go back to junior high school. Instead, I had to teach myself the subjects I thought I would have learned had the government allowed me to stay in school. Among those subjects was math. After securing old math textbooks from a friend of mine, I began secretly (and later openly) teaching myself algebra and geometry, which I needed to use for operating machines in the factory. This went on for nearly ten years. The possibility (and hope) that I would one day get to go back to a real school always lingered in my mind. I didn't know it at the time, but I was also learning a valuable skill that would come in handy later in life: I was learning how to study. I was also building self-esteem. If I could teach myself math, what else couldn't I do? I could teach myself other languages—English, for example. I could learn anything. This gave me the confidence and optimism that kept me going for all those years in the countryside and in the factory.

What did a kid who had just come from a foreign country need most in order to succeed in a completely strange education system? Confidence, of course! Self-teaching is an estimable ability. Knowing what I went through, and now armed with a new set of American math textbooks, I decided to cultivate my son's self-teaching ability.

8

The day after the library book sale, Yan was excited to return home from school and see those math textbooks. I picked up one sixth-grade math textbook and one eighth-grade math textbook to show Yan, saying, "These are all middle-school level textbooks. In terms of your ability, I could teach it to you and you wouldn't have any problems with eighth-grade math. But I want you to teach it to yourself instead. You just came to America and still have some problems understanding English; reading these textbooks will help with that. You should start with the sixth-grade math first, and assuming that goes well, you can move on to seventh-grade math next semester."

I handed him the first textbook from the set, a bright yellow sixth-grade math book.

"I want you to follow this book," I told him, "Start at the beginning and teach yourself four pages per day. You already know a lot of it. In cases where you don't, look at the examples and explanations first. I want you to do all of the exercises. Write them all out on these." I handed him a few semi-used notebooks I'd found at the university.

"When you don't understand something, keep working at it. Don't give up. You're too smart to give up anyway, right? Remember, understanding is a repeated process that comes from exercising and rereasoning. So don't hesitate to reread the explanations and rethink the examples. At the end of the book, there is an answer key. If you get some of the answers wrong, you should redo the exercises. They still might not be correct, in which case you should go back to the examples again until you figure out where you went wrong. Don't just come and ask me. I want you to figure it out yourself. Of course, it's possible that the answers given in the book are wrong. If you can find one, you'll get a big reward." (Note: he actually did find one error.)

"When you're done, then you can go play, but I want you to bring your answers to me first. I'll check your work every day, is that clear?"

Yan went along with this with little protest. Imagine, a first grader teaching himself sixth-grade math! Still, Yan was a bit disappointed because he thought the eighth-grade-level math would be more interesting and stimulating. Today I recognize that he was excited to challenge himself. The work he was asked to do in school was boring to him, and there was a part of him that was yearning for more mental stimulation. Even at that young age, I could tell he had it. Here he was, a first grader being handed a sixth-grade math book. It was a challenge and encouragement all at once. I was sure that he could see that I believed in him, that I expected this of him (and more), and, in turn, he started to believe in himself. I saw the pride behind his eyes when he began handing me his sheet of answers every day.

To be honest, after the first few weeks I stopped actually checking his answers. I'd hold the sheet up in front of me with his textbook open on my lap and I'd nod knowingly. I could tell from the eraser marks that Yan was doing his *own* checking before he handed the answers to me, that he truly made sure he'd gotten everything right before showing his notebook to me. I'd sometimes walk in on him while he was doing his problems and peek at his answers, at which point he would hide them, telling me that he "wasn't ready." That's when I knew. It was working. My son was teaching himself.

The effect snowballed. Yan reveled in knowing things his classmates didn't know, and this drove him to continue teaching himself more and more. By the time he finished the first semester of first grade, he was doing seventh-grade math. By the time he started second grade, he was working on eighth-grade math. In middle school we arranged to have him sent to the local high school for math. On all of the statewide standardized tests he scored in the 99th percentile for math. He excelled at math all the way through high school, where he achieved similar results on the PSAT, the SAT, his AP tests, and even the SAT II math tests.

Our American friends were puzzled. Not only was our son good at math, but we had also somehow tricked him into teaching it to himself! He never even bothered us for help. Since buying him the books, I'd barely had to lift a finger except to "check" his work intermittently. In fact, many years later I finally admitted to my son that I'd stopped checking his work when he handed it to me. To be honest, toward the end I stopped understanding the math he was doing altogether. Of course, I never told him that, but those were interesting days. By the time he was in middle school, every time Yan would give me his answers my heart would beat faster and I'd start sweating. I remember when Yan brought me his first set of trigonometry answers; I squinted at the page he handed me. I remember taking note of all the odd alien shapes he'd drawn and almost immediately getting a headache.

"Good job," I'd said, handing it back to him and trying to look solemn, knowing, and wise, "But son, I have to say, it's a little messy. Work on that."

9

From the perspective of millions of Chinese families, what I did with Yan is nothing special. In fact, compared to some Tiger Mothers, I suspect it's on the more lenient, easy-going side. Typical Chinese parents are almost always heavily involved in their children's school work and academic development.

This is a reflection of the "play to win" mentality of the Chinese in regard to education. Even though my son was only five years old when he came to this country, I felt a sense of fear that is familiar to all Chinese families with young children (and many more American families today): *I thought that my child was falling behind.* I felt that he was losing the game of education. Every second that passed was a second that other kids were taking advantage of to become smarter and more capable than my son. We were in a race, and we had to run, taking advantage of every step!

While at one time the anecdote of the Chinese and American delegates intrigued me academically, now it bothered me in reality. I couldn't trust the school he was attending to protect him against the possibility of losing, so I took matters into my own hands. I orchestrated a grand operation in which my son would learn math beyond his grade level so that he would never fall behind. It wouldn't matter whether he was here in America or back in China. More than that, I made sure that he learned to teach himself. This increased the likelihood that it would develop into a lifelong habit and that he would begin to assimilate and absorb the desire to win. In terms of my son's education, I wasn't taking any risks.

I was playing to win and I'd taught my son to do the same.

The state of mind of playing to win can drive children to study math on their own. As parents know, math is abstract and can be very boring for children. Harboring this unique way of thinking, though, means that children will start to learn a little early and learn a little more than normal. Little by little, they advance beyond their peers. With this state of mind, studying becomes a reward for the child's inner drive to succeed. Studying could perhaps even become a relatively relaxing or even enjoyable activity.

In Chinese tradition, studying wasn't just an unhappy experience. It was painful. As such, here are two ancient stories all Chinese children know: A man, whose name was Sun Jing, tied his hair on the beam that ran through his house when he studied so that he would wake painfully if he began to fall asleep while studying. Another man, whose name was Su Qin, jabbed his hip with a needle to keep himself awake while he studied. Therefore, the basic Chinese attitude toward studying is characterized by toughness, diligence, and perseverance. Chinese children are cultivated and trained to have this attitude toward studying. American parents tend to emphasize the fun in everything for their children, so American children are often spoiled, always asking for fun. No fun, no way. So many American children are scared of math not because they lack the ability to think logically in abstract terms, but because of their attitude toward studying.

10

But there is a second half to the story of Yan's amazing achievements with math, a half that I've been reluctant to tell. If you track my son down today and you ask him how he feels about math, I'm sure he'll waste no time in telling you that he hates it. He can't stand math.

"I haven't done any math for five years, and I don't plan on starting up again anytime soon," he once proudly said. Indeed, after he finished his AP math classes in high school, fulfilling his college mathematics requirements, he never touched the stuff again. Yan went on to college and majored in creative writing, intentionally and admittedly staying as far away from math as he could.

"Toward the end of high school," he once told me, "I figured out that I could take AP math classes and that they counted for college credit. Once I discovered that, I took as many of them as I could just so I wouldn't have to deal with it again in college."

When I heard this, I couldn't help but feel sad and confused. As a father, I took it particularly hard because I was the one who introduced him to the subject. I was the one who taught him his first lessons. I was the one who bought that set of textbooks. How could my son just abandon math? How could he turn his back on all our work?

What I didn't realize at the time was that the pride I'd taken for so many years in my son's math abilities had blinded me to something else. Something I'd never thought to consider: his *appreciation* of the subject. While I taught my son to be good at math, to constantly strive to be better than his peers, I never really gave any thought to whether he was developing an appreciation for it. More importantly, I never bothered to think about whether what I was doing would create animosity or resentment.

11

Looking back, this was foreshadowed long ago by Yan's first-grade teacher. In the middle of his first-grade year, my wife and I decided to approach the school and propose that the administration allow Yan to skip to the third grade for math. We'd heard that other children had been allowed to do this in other schools, and we believed that this would be a suitable solution to our worries about whether he was being challenged. In all honesty, we'd thought we were being modest. After all, Yan was already doing sixth-grade math at home, and we were only suggesting a jump to the third-grade level.

After meeting with Yan's teacher, we eventually received the following letter. The names and locations have been shortened to preserve anonymity.

January 14, 1992

Dear Mr. and Mrs. Huang:

I have spoken with Dr. R, our principal, about your concerns regarding mathematics for Yan. She in turn spoke with Dr. M, the assistant superintendent for curriculum and instruction. I would like to clarify some information for you about our first grade mathematics program before I share with you their opinions.

I am enclosing a list of the fifteen units that we cover in mathematics in first grade in the T District. I am also enclosing the instructional objectives so that you can see in more detail the mathematics curriculum. These units and objectives are based on recent recommendations of the National Council of Teachers of Mathematics and the Ohio Model Curriculum for Mathematics. As you will see, there is much emphasis on having children understand the concepts behind the mathematics, to be able to communicate both orally and in writing about what they are learning, and not rote memorization of arithmetic fact. Our goals are for children to become problem solvers, to learn to reason, to become confident in their own abilities, and to value mathematics. Our program actively involves the children in learning through the use of concrete manipulatives while learning from developmentally appropriate activities. Some of the arithmetic skills that Yan would be working on in Chinese schools, such as multiplication and division facts, would not be considered developmentally appropriate activities here for most first graders. We do activities with grouping objects that certainly lay a foundation for multiplication and division so that children will hopefully understand what multiplication and division means before they memorize the facts.

Yan is certainly an exceptional student in arithmetic skills. However, arithmetic is only one part of the total mathematics curriculum. There are many activities that we do during the mathematics lessons which will challenge Yan to think and will challenge him.

Dr. M and Dr. R both feel that having a college tutor work with Yan one-on-one is preferable to having Yan go to a third grade class once each week. If you would like to borrow a third grade math book to use at home, I will be happy to make the arrangements.

Please let me know if you have further questions after reading the mathematics curriculum and this letter.

Sincerely,
Mrs. P. T.

12

Rejected! When my wife and I first read this letter, we were in shock. We were also completely unconvinced. *What does she mean?* I remember thinking. She readily admits Yan is an "exceptional student in arithmetic skills," but then she says that is only "one part of the total mathematics curriculum"? What is math if not arithmetic? At the time, it sounded like a lot of hogwash to me.

I reread the letter in 2005 when I was writing a book for Chinese audiences titled *Gifted Education in America*. After thirteen years, I was surprised that I felt the same pang of negative emotion I had felt the first time. I was *still* not convinced that Yan's teacher had made the right decision. But by this time, I was much older. By this time, Yan was already in college. He'd already declared to me that he hated math and that he would never have anything to do with it again. With this in mind, I took a closer look at the letter.

I noticed one sentence in particular, a section that I'd merely skimmed over the first time I read the letter all those years ago: "Our goals are for children to become problem solvers, to learn to reason, to become confident in their own abilities, and to *value* mathematics."

I compared this with my own goals for Yan at the time. While I wanted him to be confident in his abilities (and he did indeed develop that confidence), I was surprised to realize that the school's three other major goals, the last one in particular, did not match mine. My goal was simply to make sure Yan kept up with Chinese kids his age and was ahead of all his peers in his class. I hadn't thought much about teaching him to "value mathematics," and looking back now, I certainly hadn't been able to do that.

It was as though Yan's teacher knew something thirteen years earlier that I'd only just discovered: though my son was good at certain mathematic skills and would continue to excel in those areas, he never learned to appreciate math. He never valued it. In China, there is a saying that someone who can predict the future with divine accuracy would know that certain calamities were going to happen three years before they occurred. Yan's teacher, however, beat that by a full decade. She seemed to know something about my son that I would only discover when he entered college. She knew thirteen years before I did.

For many years I puzzled over exactly what had happened with Yan. How could someone who grew up doing math problems every day, who excelled at the subject—how could he end up *hating* math? It was one of his top skills, after all, and aren't we supposed to enjoy the things we're good at? Over time, the answer came to me.

Studying too much will produce negative side effects. No matter what, taking anything too far doesn't lead to good results.

DIALOGUE

American parents: The Tiger Mom definitely scares us, but the early childhood education programs in China scare us even more. Even President Obama said that America should take notes from the Chinese and start to educate its children "earlier and longer." What are your thoughts on this issue?

Huang: I wish President Obama would read *The Besieged City*! I have been strongly and firmly against the early childhood education programs in China for years because the programs have simply gone too far. A vicious cycle has formed in China: as parents push their children harder and harder to study, the children hate studying more and more. But then again, American schooling is a little too slow, and pupils don't study long or hard enough. Therefore, it wouldn't be a bad idea for children in the United States to study a little earlier and a little more.

American parents: What is the best way for kids to accomplish that?

Huang: Fostering kids' ability to self-teach is definitely the best way. When I was in junior high in China, I made a bit of effort to preview material that had not yet been taught. Instead of reviewing what we'd done in class, I briefly *previewed* what we were going to be doing each day. I taught myself daily a little bit, and thus finished homework before it was even assigned. Not only was I able to relax when I played with other kids while they were constantly worrying about finishing their homework, I also cultivated a sense of superiority and confidence in my own abilities.

American parents: We can see that you're right; self-teaching is absolutely the way to go. But do our kids have the ability to teach themselves through studying?

Huang: Of course. It's normal to doubt whether your children have the capacity to self-teach, but in actuality, self-teaching is an innate ability that almost everyone (including kids and adults) should have. The key is to create an opportunity and environment for self-teaching. I cultivated Yan's, my brother's twins', and many others' self-teaching ability. When you doubt children's ability to self-teach, look at the technology wave that this generation has grown up with. Cell phones, tablets, video games, computers—did your children need you to teach them to use these things? Most likely they taught themselves how to use them, and thus they can teach themselves about math and other school subjects as well.

In Order to Win, One Must Hold High Hopes Starting in Childhood

1

It's standard for American college students to wait until their sophomore or even junior year to decide their major. Even when senior year comes around, many of my students aren't certain of what they want to do.

I asked, "What do you want to do after you graduate from college?"

My student responded, "I don't know. The only thing I know is that I love thinking."

I then asked, "Do you want to be a philosopher?"

The student thought for a while and then answered, "Well, I'm not sure. . . ."

I said, "I like your ambition, but you must be sure. You need to be able to feed and support yourself after you graduate, and philosophy is not food."

2

Chinese-American families always ask their children to set ambitious goals starting from childhood. No matter what they will be in the future, great ambition must be cherished as early as possible; which is to say, cultivation of ambition and goals must happen early. Chinese-American parents instill great ambitions, such as attending Harvard or becoming a scientist or astronaut, into their children when they're very young. There are two reasons that parents do this.

First, if children set ambitious goals, they will have a strong inner drive to succeed. Therefore, the higher the goal and the earlier it's set, the better. Greater ambition will bring about greater motivation; those who start earlier will get into gear earlier.

Second, ambitious goals are better than readily achievable ones. If you imagine bargaining in a flea market, when vendors set their prices high, it creates room for a counter bid. A child may not end up being able to reach a very ambitious goal, and that's okay. But having greater ambition will at least produce strong motivation to work hard toward something.

When Yan was two years old, he declared that when he grew up he wanted to be Company Commander Huang, a Chinese military officer who commands tens of soldiers. We considered it a joke, but his grandmother was uneasy, as she had other career ideas in mind for him. After that, she started to cultivate more ambitious goals for Yan, such as becoming a scientist, professor, or doctor.

Sometimes the ambitions Chinese parents set up for their children are an extension of the parents' own ideals. For example, let's say a parent wanted to be a pianist when he or she was a child but could not achieve that goal for some reason; the burden of the parents' hopes and dreams could subsequently be placed on his or her child's shoulders.

Many American parents may also have their own thoughts regarding their child's future career, but their methods are very different from Chinese parents'. An American friend of ours once told us (in front of her ten-year-old daughter) something to the effect of, "Her fingers are very nimble; she'd make a great hairdresser!" Another friend of ours said her young son wanted to be a construction worker when he grew up; she and her husband had nothing but praise for his choice. We were surprised by how pedestrian their goals were for their children.

Chinese education wants students to pursue a higher ambition. American education, however, wants students to cherish their ideals, which could be very common. The speakers Chinese schools invite to lecture are always great scientists, well-known professors, or at least, like me, a bestselling author who earned a doctorate from an American university. Those who are qualified to lecture in Chinese schools are models for students, the people students should strive to emulate when setting their goals. Those who are invited to address students in American schools are from of all walks of life, such as firefighters, doctors, policemen and women, dentists, auctioneers, etc. In Americans' eyes, all trades and professions have their own strengths. In Chinese peoples' eyes, the goals must be set high; otherwise, they are not considered ambitious enough. Above all, the Chinese pay great attention to the hope that one's son or daughter will be extremely successful; this is called being a "dragon." To do that, a child must have great ambition from an early age. In contrast, Americans emphasize the hope that one's child will grow to be a happy adult who has good health and a strong moral character.

3

What is a dream? Some may say that a dream is something that is so far out of reach that you have to chase it forever. Some believe that dreams are the prime power and dynamics of evolution for human beings. With a dream, people have something to pursue. With a dream, people have a motivation to pursue it. Without a dream, a somebody could become a nobody. Without dreams, human beings would still live in caves.

As I have previously mentioned, the supremacy of education in Chinese culture stemmed from the Imperial Examination System. Therefore, Chinese people believe that education is the sole method they can use to reach their goals, to make their dreams come true. For many Americans, on the other hand, the dream of education is less focused. Americans more often view education as a means to develop one's own interests, find happiness, and live a healthy life.

Hoping your child develops into a healthy person (both physically and mentally), rather than a dragon (a phenomenally successful person), has become more and more accepted among Chinese parents in recent years. In 2010, *Educational Selections from Quanyu Huang*, a series of eight books I authored, was published in China. Unexpectedly, it was the book titled *Helping Your Child to be a "Person"* (in contrast to a "dragon"), which talks about American parenting, that became one of the most popular titles in the series. Of course its popularity might not mean that Chinese readers were ready to accept the concept, but at least they seemed to be willing to learn about different ideas. Current Chinese parents are gradually paying more attention to children's self-esteem, self-confidence, and individual development while continuing to instill great ambitions in their children. Obviously, these changes in Chinese parenting are influenced by Western education. But regardless of what alterations Chinese parents make to the way they raise their children, setting high goals and encouraging great ambition will continue to produce powerful effects on modern Chinese education.

Believe it or not, if you go to a preschool and ask Chinese-American children what their goals are, the word *Harvard* will likely exist within their very limited vocabularies. All Chinese-American families I know have aimed their children's sights at Ivy League schools starting at an extremely young age. A Chinese-American father I know set the goal of attending Harvard for his daughter when she was five years old. Because her ambition was created very early, she approached that goal one step at a time from elementary school through high school. Eventually she was accepted at Harvard after more than a decade of hard work. Creating big goals for children has its advantages, but at the same time, it's important not to burden children at so young an age that they're completely unable to understand that ambition. It might actually end up being counterproductive for parents.

When children truly understand the goals and ambitions that their parents direct them toward—and that they set for themselves—it will fuel their inner drive to succeed. As a result, their ambitions, and all of their actions, will work toward their end goal. This is what I call "self-education."

4

Asian-American children are different from their American peers in terms of culture, family backgrounds, language, appearance, and physique. This sometimes creates a sense of inferiority for Asian-American children. This sense of inferiority clashes with the lesson of self-education—of aiming high and having great ambition—that they receive at home. While most Asian-American children are able to overcome this contradiction in their daily lives, it helps immensely when they find a *teacher* in their American schools who will help to start their inner drive, which is to say that self-education should be supported by all three legs of the tripod. For example, Yan attended five different schools before proceeding on to college. He had the privilege of meeting and learning from many outstanding teachers. One of them, Ms. Schultz, was his gifted program teacher when he transferred to a new school in the sixth grade.

I heard Yan mention Ms. Schultz quite often, but I didn't really know her until seven years or so after Yan graduated from that school.

In 2003, when Yan was about to leave for college, he was informed by his elementary school friends that Ms. Schultz's students were going to hold a retirement party for her. Because he was preparing for college, I didn't think he'd bother to attend. Unexpectedly, he readily agreed to go to Ms. Schultz's party, to which I accompanied him. I have to admit that I was astonished when I arrived in the school's dining hall where the party was held. Several hundred people had come from near and far to pay tribute to their teacher. I thought a woman who sat next to me was, like me, the parent of a child Ms. Schultz had taught, but when she gave her speech, I realized I was wrong. Twenty years earlier she'd been one of Ms. Schultz's students. Now? She was a newspaper editor. One by one, the students excitedly recalled the details of their favorite experiences with

Ms. Schultz. When her students put a crown on her head, I was deeply touched. I had seen how much my mother's students in China respected her, but this was the first time I saw so many students showing their great reverence to a teacher in America.

5

In 2006, Ms. Schultz passed away of ALS.

Yan knew his beloved teacher was ill and had already bought a plane ticket to return home to see her. Unfortunately, there was a very heavy snowstorm on the day Yan was supposed to leave. Yan wasn't able to make it home before Ms. Schultz passed on. In his grief, he wrote an essay to commemorate her.

When Yan moved to a new school as a sixth grader he felt very lonely and did not know how to adapt to the new campus life. The very first day he went to Ms. Schultz's class, she asked the prettiest girl in the class to give Yan a campus tour. Yan wrote:

> I remember Ms. Schultz moving the two of us to the doorway, opening it, pushing us out, saying, "I hope you guys get to know each other," and winking at me and smiling. With that smile, she closed the door.
>
> But in that one short moment, pushing the two of us out of the door, Ms. Schultz, in her own way, showed a faith in me that even I did not have. She made me feel like I *deserved* to be out there with Sara (a rather dastardly attitude that has come into its own in my time at college). Ms. Schultz had a quality about her that made her believe each student was her very personal favorite. She taught me the complete power a good teacher can have over a student.[12]

6

On several occasions Yan and I have discussed why he felt such a connection to Ms. Schultz. Yan believed that Ms. Schultz showed immense trust and faith in her students. And the way she expressed that trust was contagious; her faith in Yan turned into faith in himself. That trust, that faith, became Yan's inner driver. There's nothing more precious than that lesson, and this, by far, was the most valuable thing that Ms. Schultz could ever have done for Yan.

After Ms. Schultz found out that Yan had published two books in China, she invited us to her house for dinner. She gave a crystal sea star to Yan and said, "Yan, I hope you will be a star!" She then played a tape Yan's class had made about eight years earlier in which they discussed what they wanted to be in the future (a teacher, a lawyer, a doctor, a screen writer, and, of course, President of the United States). The child who wanted to be the president said that if he were elected, he'd designate Ms. Schultz's birthday as Teacher's Day in the United States.

The name of the tape was *Be a Star!* This was very meaningful to me, as Ms. Schultz was the *first* American teacher I knew who tried to instill great ambitions into her students' minds.

The classroom of Yan's favorite American teacher, Ms. Schultz.
Photo by Lois Schultz.

Of course, influenced by American education, many of Yan's career goals were very American. At different times throughout his childhood he wanted to be a zookeeper, a rainforest explorer, a high school teacher, and a comedy actor, among others. A child's ideals are important, but more important is the child's confidence to achieve his or her goal. Nevertheless, it's even more important to have a positive life attitude and continue to improve on one's own abilities.

Dialogue

American parents: Our kids *do* have ambition and goals, but they're not nearly as motivated to achieve them as Chinese children are. What can we do to motivate them more?

Huang: There are four points of which you should be aware. First, a kid's goals need to be specific, as we've discussed previously. When they aren't clearly defined, children will have trouble finding the motivation to struggle toward them. Second, if kids don't set their goals high enough, the motivation to achieve them won't be as strong because they know they won't have to work as hard. Third, the goals your sons or daughters set must be realistic or they won't motivate your children to succeed. My student who "loved thinking" is a perfect example for these three points. As we can see, there is a great distance between loving to think and becoming a philosopher or philosophy professor. Furthermore, because his goals weren't specific, ambitious, or realistic, the only thing he could conceive of was that he "loved thinking." Finally, children must learn to withstand pressure; otherwise, they won't be motivated and they also won't be conscious of their responsibilities. When children don't understand their responsibilities toward themselves and toward others they will have trouble becoming fully mature. This is why I prefer the idea of having to win, rather than always having fun, because when you feel that you have to win, you have to set goals and cultivate ambition.

American parents: But we do worry about our children's happiness. They may become depressed when their goals are set too high and they don't achieve them. We want our children to be happy.

Huang: Happiness is relative. Temporary happiness (in high school or college) may not bring lifelong happiness. Because competition is independent from human will, competition is everywhere and forever. No one (including individuals, families, organizations, and countries) can avoid competition. In 1957, a human-made satellite from the Soviet Union crossed the skies of the United States every single day. How could Americans be happy? That one small satellite inspired the Americans to set a seemingly unreachable goal, to go to the moon, which they accomplished in a matter of years.

Happiness is always connected to competition. Therefore, setting goals and cultivating ambition early is best.

In Order to Win, One Must Be Able to Withstand Suffering

1

In general, the American tripod—family, school, and social education—fails to pay adequate attention to the importance of helping children to set goals and cultivate ambition, as Ms. Schultz did so well. Why? I believe there are three primary reasons.

First, many people think ambition comes from want and need. If you desire what you don't possess, you'll find within yourself a motivation to pursue it. Most kids today have everything they want: food, clothing, toys, games, you name it. If they don't have it, their parents will likely provide it for them, as they do with everything else. The one thing they do lack? Time. Time to play, time for fun, time to do what they enjoy. That's why it seems as though kids have little ambition these days. They don't need to have ambitious goals.

Second, some parents believe that the primary goal they should pursue for their children is happiness. Anything that could possibly make a child less happy will hurt their health and development. And let's face it: no child really wants to study without some guidance, encouragement, and perhaps pressure. Because parents don't want to make their children unhappy, they don't pressure their children to study in school. They don't encourage their children to set high goals or have great ambition. As long as their children are happy, many parents seem to think, does it really matter how they go on to earn their living?

And finally, some people believe in foreordination or predestination. A person can't determine the outcome of his or her own life because it's already been determined. Not everyone can achieve something great; some of us are destined to remain on the lower rungs of the ladder. Cultivating ambition will be a low priority for those who believe that one should just be content with one's lot in life. This is the sad philosophy of fatalism.

When I discussed these three reasons with my American friends, they agreed with what I was saying. Surprisingly, they all acknowledged that Americans forget to encourage—or willfully resist encouraging—their descendants to set lofty goals that they must work hard to achieve.

A friend of mine named Lisa taught English in China for a year. She was extremely impressed by how hard Chinese students study. She said, "Our American children have too much, and everything comes too easily for them, so they're short on motivators. I always tell my children, 'If you don't study hard, you'll lose everything, and don't even think about a vacation to the beach!'"

Lisa let out a sigh and said, "You know what? My children responded: 'Mommy, don't worry about it, we can go to King's Island's Beach!'" (King's Island is an amusement park in Cincinnati.)

I wanted to laugh, but I couldn't. I understood her distress at her children's resistance to the values she was trying to teach them.

Lisa continued, "I really want to help my children understand that life isn't always as wonderful as they think it is. I want to plant the roots of ambition in my children's hearts, but it's just so difficult."

2

Of course, you could be happy without having ambition, but the type of happiness that comes from achieving a goal that you feared was out of your reach—one that you had to work hard and strive for—is distinguished and special. To reach your goals, you must face many difficulties; this adversity will make that particular happiness special and meaningful. Think about a soccer game. Isn't the goal you score during a difficult and closely contested game worth much more than the many goals you can kick when the field is empty and you're practicing alone? Americans often say, "No pain, no gain." But, if I may be allowed to modify the phrase a bit, I think "No pain, no game" makes sense as well. Can a child who always gets poor grades without effort in school be satisfied and confident? Without confidence, can he or she truly be happy? Competition is an objective reality independent from human will. Can avoiding competition at all costs really make a person be happy? If instead we give children opportunities from a young age to acquire the type of happiness that comes from overcoming adversity in order to achieve, they will gradually form earnest and confident spirits.

3

One way to make sure your children have ambition is to allow them to experience some suffering and adversity and then enjoy the delight that comes with achieving something after they've worked hard to reach it.

Mencius, an ancient Chinese sage who was as famous as Confucius, said, "If Heaven is going to place a great mission on a man, it always first frustrates his spirit and will, exhausts his body, makes him go hungry, harasses him with troubles and setbacks so as to stimulate his spirit, toughen his nature and enhance his abilities."[13] These words are critical to understanding Chinese education, as well as the self-education aspect of my tripod theory.

In China, my generation endured many hardships. When I was sixteen most of my classmates and I were sent to the countryside to be peasants, to learn "real Chinese values," as the authorities put it. The intention of Chinese authorities was to punish us, but we actually benefitted from the suffering and hardship. Every day I had to labor in the fields from sunrise until sunset for only thirty-two Chinese cents (approximately $0.08 at that time). Malcolm Gladwell has pointed out that "the people who grow rice have always worked harder than almost any other kind of famer."[14] I know firsthand what it was like to be a sixteen-year-old Chinese rice peasant. Even worse than the extremely hard work Gladwell described was the fact that we didn't have enough food to eat. The so-called three meals per day were actually two meals of diluted rice congee, which was so thin that we could see our reflections in its watery surface. The rice soup was lackluster and often left us hungrier than we were when we started eating. For dinner, we had rice, but it wasn't nearly enough to fill our bellies. There were very few vegetables to be had; grinding salt over a few peppers was enough to be called "a dish." And meat? We dreamed about meat at night; having meat at our meals was incredibly rare. The pain in our stomachs from hunger was almost too much to bear. In our desperation, we'd make a "spiritual banquet." We'd blow out our oil lamp then lay on the beds, taking turns describing our favorite dishes to one another. We'd skip no detail, discussing how they were cooked and then how to eat them—smell, shape, color, taste—until we were all moaning from the thought of food and crying in pain. We would become crazy from hunger and from imagining delicious food; luckily there was no light, so we didn't need to worry about seeing how crazy everyone else was acting!

While this experience was one of the most difficult times in my life, I wouldn't trade it for anything. My time in the poor countryside taught me about true hardship and adversity. After that, I was able to understand things about myself and the world that others might be unable to figure out. I was able to continually rouse myself and cultivate my ambitions toward something greater.

4

The wisest way to protect children from hardship is to give them the experience of suffering hardship.

In the summer of 2005, after Yan left for college, he went to China to raise money for Chinese orphans. We also sent him to my father's hometown. He directly saw and experienced how difficult it was for his grandfather, who had been born into a poor peasant family. He also saw how hard his grandfather must have studied more than sixty years earlier in order to achieve admission at Peking University.

My father's hometown is located near the border between China and Vietnam. It's a drive of several hours from any major city. The small village he lives in is surrounded by mountains; his house is old and run down. In the days before roads were built in the more remote parts of China, it took several days and nights to get to a city.

We had an agreement with Yan: for seven days, he would stay in the small room where his grandfather once lived. It was a different kind of life, poor and rough, so if Yan really couldn't handle it, he could call my sister and she would bring him back to the city.

Upon arriving in my father's village, Yan said, "This is a corner of the world that has been completely forgotten by human civilization."

I told Yan that Chinese people think of their families and hometowns when they see the moon. He didn't understand, and asked, "What? When Americans see the moon, it's just a moon. How can the moon have anything to do with families and hometowns?"

Yan never loved taking pictures, but he took a camera with him on his Chinese journey. One night he went onto the roof by himself and took a picture of the big, bright, yellow moon. We haven't discussed the photo since then, but I like to think that maybe the moon is for him no longer in the sky, but in his heart, following him wherever he goes.

Though when Yan lived in the United States he often failed to pick up our phone calls, delivering a litany of excuses—low battery, he didn't hear the phone ring, his phone wasn't with him—when he was in my father's village, he punctually went to the roof (where the reception was better) every night to wait for our phone call.

The village had no power and no fresh water. There wasn't even a toilet. Yan always said the worst part of his experience in the village was using the cowshed as a toilet. He said, "Even only ten yards away from the cowshed, you can hear the buzzing from mosquitoes and flies." My wife bought the best and strongest calcifuges for Yan, but unfortunately the mosquitoes "made in China" didn't seem to care anything about "made in America" mosquito repellent.

All the young people had left the village to pursue education and jobs in the cities, so only old men and women were left in the village. Yan worked with them in the sugarcane fields, and not only was it boring, it was incredibly hot and no one talked to break up the monotony of being in the fields. Yan struggled each day with the decision of whether or not to stay.

Every night, Yan slept shirtless with no sheets because it was so hot and uncomfortable. But one night the weather turned a bit cooler, so he asked for a blanket. That night, he also decided to sleep in a different position; rather than lying down with his head directly under the window, he turned and put his head on the opposite side, away from the window. To this day, Yan can't explain why he changed his usual sleeping position.

Later that night, around midnight, a heavy storm moved in. There was thunder and lightning along with a heavy gust of wind, and BANG! The window shattered into pieces, and all the glass fell on Yan. Without his thick blanket and altered sleeping position, he could have been seriously injured. What's more, Yan refused to tell us about the incident until after he returned, knowing that had we been told about what had happened, we would have insisted he return to the city immediately.

We all shook when we saw the photos Yan took, as he described what had happened to him. And it's still a puzzle for us, all these years later. Why did Yan ask for a blanket that night? Countryside blankets in China are very thick; he probably didn't need it, even with the slightly cooler weather. And why did he turn the other way to sleep? These little things caused him to escape serious harm.

I have to think that my father reached out from the afterlife to protect his grandson.

Yan really tried hard, and to this day we admire his resolve. Despite the window-shattering incident and the fact that he contracted painful shingles because of the stress he was under, he kept his word and stayed at his grandfather's house for the full seven days. His relatives tried to make things easier for him, and in some cases, trick him. One relative tried to coax him to leave the village for a night on the town, promising that he would keep the excursion secret. Yan refused. Another relative lived in a nearby town and had a normal bathroom in his house. He told Yan to use that instead of the cowshed, and though Yan admitted he was very tempted by this offer, he refused.

When we asked Yan why he didn't take advantage of the bathroom, he smiled and said, "If I needed a regular toilet, I wouldn't have had to go to the countryside in China. I could have just stayed home." He labored in the field with peasants. He chatted with them under the shadows of the trees. Even though they didn't really comprehend one another's lives, he tried to understand the life of the local people and tried to open himself up to new experiences and live a life he'd never previously imagined.

More than sixty years ago, Yan's grandfather, a poor peasant who was not even twenty years old, was curious about the world beyond the mountains that surrounded his village. He used the money that Yan's great-grandfather had raised by selling their farm cattle to journey, step by step, along the rugged countryside paths that ended, for him, at the best university in China. It was my hope that Yan, by spending time in the village and walking along those same rugged paths, might gain some insight into his grandfather's state of mind and perhaps come to understand how his grandfather had been able to rise up from that difficult situation.

5

Yan later wrote a few essays about his experiences in China. I'm quoting from one here.

> I wake at four in the morning after one caustic shout of *"Hey, American boy!"* I remember where I am, what I'd left in my e-mail auto reply a week ago: *In China, farming, do not disturb*. Through the thin walls, I hear my older cousin Chong rouse. The shout that woke me had done the same for him. I hear a frustrated sigh and the slow, methodical shuffling of clothes. Chong has come back to the farm from his life in the city to, as he put it, look after me. He has decided to leave today. It has only been two days.
>
> I put on a shirt and coarse plastic slippers. I look out over the dark silhouette of the mountains. They look like great folded backs, weary, leaning against one another. The village sits below them. This is where the *Zhuang* people have lived for millennia, where a few waning members of my family *still* live. I walk out into the dimness, feeling my way down the crumbling stairs made of overwatered cement.

"Where is he?" a voice says in the dark. It is my second uncle. "No time. Go get him."

"Don't bother," Chong says from atop the stairs. His voice is flat, and tired. "I'm right here."

"Please, the corn is waiting for you," my second uncle scoffs. "Walk." We walk. Repellant-immune mosquitoes amass, form lines, and wait, hissing, before descending on us in invisible volleys.

"*Aiiiya!*" Chong says, slapping at his neck. "Another one. A big one. Malaria, for sure."

I left China when I was five and my last memory of my cousin Chong was a beautiful one. During one of my mean streaks at that age, I'd latched onto Chong's hair and pulled until he cried. Instead of fighting back, Chong kept his hands behind his back and, through tears, said to my furious father, "He doesn't know any better. Don't punish Yan, he doesn't know." Due to China's one-child policy, I had no true older brother, so Chong was the closest thing. He was five full years older than me, wise, and tall. He was like an adult in most ways that mattered, yet he was also a well of wisdom on things that other adults did not know (such as Manga comics, fighting, and guns). I looked up to him, and I loved him.

A few years ago, he failed his college exams and left the farm for a city named Shenzhen to find work. Now, more than a decade later, we meet again. I am taller than him. The Chong of my memory has been replaced with a hunched, gaunt man; a man full of complaints of the farm (the food, and heat, and the insects), of condescending lectures, and of brags. Chinese city life, unforgiving of farmers' sons, seems to have hurt him, misused him, but we do not talk about this. We do not talk about America. Or anything.

This day, we are to spend the entire morning uprooting corn. This is, apparently, a necessary part of the growing process. My second uncle hands us gloves and shovels. He demonstrates what he wants me to do. Walking backward, he straddles one of the long rows of infant corn. Wherever there are two or more plants growing next each other, he stabs his shovel deep into the earth and uproots all but one.

"Do you understand yet?" he says after four or five plants. I nod; he grunts. He does not say anything more for hours. I hand a pair of burlap gloves to Chong and we go to work. The sun slowly rises.

I think back to when I'd first left for America. Upon finding out that my father had received a scholarship at an American university and my mother and I would be moving there, Chong, only ten, fell into a deep silence, not speaking for several days. Years later, he would admit it was because he, the eldest of my generation in our family, had always secretly thought *he* would be the first one in America.

I claw an elusive, bulbous root from the dirt with my fingers. Why does the corn always grow in groups of two or three? I wonder. When I finish my first row of over two hundred plants and I look back, it dawns on me. Many seeds are planted in each hole to ensure that at the very least one will grow. To maximize the likelihood of success, at a young age, the other plants must be sacrificed and left for decomposition, devoting all available resources to one single plant. When I get to the next pair, I find myself suspended. The shovel is heavy. I linger foolishly and feel absurd. *I am deciding between corn!*

I stop. I look over to my cousin Chong. Sweat drags down his sharp, set jaw; he breathes through his nostrils and stares numbly at the ground as he works. I am not tired, but I find it hard to go on.

Chong would go back to Shenzhen later that day, leaving me on the farm. Soon after, he would pack his things and ride the train to Guangzhou. He had a friend, he said, who had a good position lined up for him, a teaching position—quite promising. My mother would see him a year later on a separate trip. He would be living alone, working random jobs, eating powdered milk and ten-cent steamed buns every day. My mother would take him out to Korean barbeque and he would eat like he had not been full in months.

Nearly noon, when it is too hot to continue, my second uncle stops us. Chong walks over, panting. Our shirts are soaked through. Dried mud cakes our feet, and our hands are pink and raw. Chong puts his arm on my shoulder. We look out over the work we've done: a pleasant field of tall-standing, lonely corn.

There aren't many days that people will remember for their whole lives, but I'm hopeful (and truly believe) that the seven days Yan experienced in that small Chinese village will benefit him for the rest of his life.

I've also wondered about my own experiences. If I didn't labor in the countryside as a peasant forty years ago, if I'd had a million-dollar check in my hand when I left China for the United States, if Yan hadn't experienced adversity early and late in life, would we still think of studying and education as a life and death struggle?

Dialogue

Chinese parents: On this topic of encouraging your children to experience a different kind of life, Americans have done a much better job than us, haven't they? We coddle our children with life experience.

Huang: Yes, it's true. The United States was established over two hundred years ago. Because of that, people really understand the threat of "prosperity never lasting for three generations," though it is a Chinese saying. Many wealthy families send their children to work minimum-wage jobs. American kids travel to impoverished areas and countries, volunteering their time to help those less fortunate. The Peace Corps, Teach for America, and other programs are designed to extend this American spiritual wealth.

Chinese parents: You sent Yan to China, to his grandfather's hometown, which isn't a typically Chinese thing to do. Did you learn this from Americans? Does this make you a "Tiger Father"?

Huang: Yes, I learned this from American education, but I am in no way a "Tiger Father." Many Chinese people, including our own relatives, did not understand why we did this to Yan. When they heard about Yan's experiences and the danger he faced in the countryside, they asked us, "Are you crazy?" We took our Chinese heritage and culture and combined it with our American experiences. In this case, we learned from American education, applying my Co-Core Synergy theory of education to Yan.

CHAPTER 3

DEVELOPING KIDS' AMBITIONS BEFORE DISCOVERING THEIR INTERESTS

Confucianism placed emphasis on social status, on the obedience of subjects to their monarchs, of sons to their fathers.[1] As a result, Chinese parenting usually forces children to obey their parents' will. Taoism, however, recommended "to govern by doing nothing that goes against nature."[2] When it comes to children's interests, college majors, and careers, American parents prefer Taoist over Confucian ideas.

SHOULD KIDS BE ABLE TO CHOOSE THEIR CAREERS?

1

Many times I have asked my students, "What will you do after you graduate from college?" And every time I'm shocked by the answers, "I don't know what I should do," and "I haven't really thought about what I'm going to do."

This phenomenon among my American students is worth noting: many of them don't even know what majors they want to pursue until they've already graduated. Every year I inevitably end up rushing to find jobs or graduate programs for my students at the last minute, just before they graduate. That is to say, because the school forces them to choose a major at a certain point, they make their selection, but it's clear they haven't thoroughly considered what majors are really appropriate to them. Not only are they not certain of what they'd like to

105

do, many don't even know what they're able to do. Put another way, they don't seem to realize the differences among these questions:

- What do I love to do?
- What am I able to do?
- What can I realistically do?

2

I had a student, Cheney, who was among my best. He was incredibly bright. Another professor first discovered his language talents and then strongly recommended him to me and asked me to look after him. Cheney decided to sign up for an independent-study course with me for a year.

People always believe it is difficult to find a good teacher, but because I have perspective from the other side, I would say it is more difficult to find a truly good student. I couldn't help Cheney develop and reach his potential without first understanding where he was heading and what he wanted academically and professionally.

I asked Cheney during his senior year, "What are you going to do after you graduate?"

He pondered this for a few minutes and then said, "I want to go back to H University in China." Cheney had studied for a semester at H University, one of the top universities in China. His desire to return was understandable.

I then asked him what he meant to study.

"I don't know," Cheney said, shrugging.

This surprised me. How could he know he wanted to go back to H University but not know what he wanted to study there?

Upon further inquiry, I was even more surprised at Cheney's reasons for wanting to go back to China. "Well, my girlfriend is there right now. She's from Russia," he said. "That's probably the main reason I can think of right now."

"But what you'll be studying at H University doesn't really have anything to do with your girlfriend, does it?" I asked. "Don't you have any ideas?"

Cheney shrugged once more.

"You *really* need to think about what you want to do with your life first," I told him. "Only then can you decide what you want to study!"

Over the following months, we often discussed the course of study Cheney would choose to pursue at H University. But it soon turned out that it didn't matter what he wanted to pursue academically. We hadn't considered the problem of the HSK.

The HSK is a Chinese-language proficiency exam that any American student wishing to study at a top university in China must pass. However, there were no HSK centers around our area for Cheney to take the test. More importantly, even if there had been a testing center in close proximity, Cheney had already missed his first opportunity to take the HSK. The remaining tests would occur too late for Cheney to apply for school in China. Even with my help and guidance, without a good score on the HSK (or indeed, a score at all), Cheney would have a very difficult time getting into H University.

As I was trying to find a way out of the quandary Cheney had gotten himself into, the Confucius Institute Headquarters in Beijing sent out a notice that it was organizing a regional qualification trial for the Chinese Bridge Competition. The Chinese Bridge Competition is a famous contest allowing students of Chinese to perform and demonstrate their mastery of the Chinese language. It struck me immediately that this might be a great opportunity, as Cheney spoke excellent Chinese. Not only that, he also had learned Chinese kung fu and had fantastic performance talents. Since the Chinese Bridge Competition itself is a strong credential in the eyes of many Chinese admissions committees, I suggested that Cheney participate in the competition on behalf of Miami University.

I found myself shocked when he refused. Without giving it much thought at all, Cheney told me that he wasn't interested. I was, once again, surprised and confused, as I'd worked hard to find a way to help Cheney attend H University.

Students who won the Chinese Bridge Competition would have a strong advantage over their peers and would even have a good chance at winning scholarships to pursue their studies in China. Because it was clear that Cheney would not be able to take the HSK before his application deadline, this was his best chance! He could win a prize from the competition and that would provide powerful evidence of his Chinese-language comprehension. With that, I could help him argue to H University that he should receive a waiver from the HSK score requirement. Moreover, it would likely result in him winning a scholarship and saving on tuition (which Cheney had admitted was an issue).

Wasn't that a perfect situation in which to kill two birds with one stone? I thought it was an especially good idea because I was confident that Cheney was proficient enough to win the regional competition.

But try as I might, Cheney simply refused to take part in the competition. "*Why?*" I asked him. "At least tell me why!"

Cheney looked at me and simply offered, "I don't really have any reasons; I just don't want to do it!"

I pleaded with him, "But for your own future, you should! You're going to miss a very good opportunity here." After I repeatedly explained the advantages of participating in the competition, he didn't say anything further. His face, however, told me he still wasn't willing to consider participating.

This is clearly good for his future, I thought to myself. *Why doesn't he understand that?* Soon I became frustrated enough that I took a different route altogether.

"It doesn't matter what you say," I said to Cheney. "You must take part in the competition."

For a moment, I realized that I'd blurred the lines of our relationship. This isn't something American professors do, I thought. But I didn't care.

"You don't have a choice!" I told him.

And that was it. I'd presented Cheney with a clear ultimatum: if he wanted to continue in my independent study course, he had to take part in the competition.

Cheney could tell that I was angry. Not knowing how to react, he almost wept. Even my own colleagues were surprised to see me so upset with a student.

A week or so later, after speaking with his uncles (who agreed with me), Cheney reluctantly agreed to participate in the Chinese Bridge Competition. To his surprise (but not mine), he won a prize. Based on that prize, I helped him obtain a concession: our university would prepare Chinese-language proficiency exams for Cheney in place of his having to take the HSK. As a result, he received a full scholarship to pursue his doctorate at H University.

3

More than a year later, on a trip back to the United States, Cheney met up with me and we had the chance to have a profound conversation about what had happened.

Cheney confided in me that even as a senior in college he had never given any focused thought to what he would do with his future or career. He had never sat down to plan out what his next steps would be, and he'd certainly never considered what kind of career he wanted to pursue. The Chinese Bridge Competition was just one small example. He couldn't see the potential consequences that his decision would have at the time; all he knew was that he didn't want to do it. Cheney had come to realize how aimlessly he'd been wandering in college, but he still didn't have a clear picture of what he wanted to do with his life.

"Have you given any more thought as to what you'll do in the future?" I asked him once more.

"Yes, but . . . I'm not sure. A teacher, maybe. Or something else?"

"Have you thought about how you might use your Chinese talents and skills?"

"Not really. . . . Maybe I'll teach in schools? Maybe I'll work for some sort of company? Maybe as an interpreter?"

This was a step in the right direction, I thought, but I was still deeply worried about him. His graduation was coming up soon, but he was still confused about his future.

"I think lots of kids are in my position," he told me. "Many of my friends are graduating without jobs. And a lot of them are going back home to live with their parents . . . in their basements!"

As a professor and a father, this was a startling revelation to me. Moving back home with your *parents*? Why was this pattern developing among so many American students? How could this happen? In many parts of the world, a twenty-four year old is no less than a seasoned adult. Indeed, twenty-four year olds in other parts of the world are heads of households. From the perspective of a Chinese father, nothing could be a greater cause for concern than an adult child without clear career goals. And here we see another great difference between the values of Chinese and American education: the early, ambitious (but achievable) career plan.

While American students who have these kinds of early goals aren't rare, there are too many who haven't given the subject enough thought, and thus, are moving home to live with their parents after they graduate from college.

4

Whether or not a child has cultivated that early ambition absolutely relates to how they select their career.

According to a study conducted at Yale University in 1953, the 3 percent of graduates who had written out goals they wanted to accomplish in life had more wealth later on than the other 97 percent of their graduating class *combined*. A study at Harvard Business School cited by Tom Bay in his *Look Within or Do Without* assessed how its graduates were doing financially ten years after graduation. Surprisingly, just 10 percent of them were comfortable financially, and only 3 percent of them were financially independent. The percentage that needed some sort of financial assistance was a shocking 27 percent, while 60 percent had no savings, living paycheck to paycheck.

Viewing this through the lens of goal setting, the study had some interesting things to say about that 27 percent receiving financial assistance. Specifically, they had absolutely no experience when it came to setting goals. The paycheck-to-paycheck percentage had *very* basic goals, mostly based on survival until the next payday. The more comfortable 10 percent knew where they wanted to be in five years and had general goals to pursue while the 3 percent had specifically outlined their long-term goals as well as the steps they would need to take in order to achieve them.[3]

5

Through my firsthand experience as a professor, I am able to divide my students into one of two basic categories.

The first group consists of those who don't have clear aspirations. These students believe that being happy and enjoying life is more important than setting goals. They don't study hard; as long as they don't fail their classes they feel as though everything is fine. When there are difficulties in front of them, they avoid facing them and search for some other source of happiness. When Monday hits, they're still thinking back to the parties over the weekend and looking forward to Thursday, when they'll start partying again.

The second group consists of those who outline their goals and set up their ambitions very early. Their study attitudes and motivations are very different from the first group.

Even with the second group, I've only seen one pupil among my American students who had a definitive career goal in the first semester of his freshman year. He wanted to attend law school. Because he had this goal in mind early, he was able to work on it over the course of his entire college career. He asked me questions about law schools during the second semester, wondering about the practical experience emphasized by the "Big 14," the top law schools, as well as what GPA and LSAT scores would be required to attend one of these schools. Because his goal was clear early, he not only had a strong inner motivation but also a clear plan for his course selections starting his sophomore year. I had no doubt that there would be one more aggressive lawyer in this country soon.

6

Chinese and Chinese-American children usually set up their goals earlier than American children. This means that their careers are also quite clear, such as doctor, lawyer, engineer, accountant, actuary, or computer programmer. Many Chinese-American children have made up their minds regarding their careers during their high school years or possibly even earlier. After they get into college, some may change their majors once or twice. In general, they'll have established a basic idea about their future careers by the end of their sophomore years. Of course, this comes from the kids' inner motivations, but it also results from their parents sharing their concerns, consulting with them, being involved, and having thorough discussions with them about the future.

We often discussed Yan's future career at our dinner table when he was in high school. At that time, what he disliked most was that we tried to help him decide what his career would be. As many Chinese-American parents do, we once suggested that he should become a doctor. But Yan was having none of it. He responded, "This is my career, let me decide what it will be on my own. I will tell you, though, that I do not want to be a doctor."

After he went on to college, he told us over the phone that he had decided his major would be in writing. Yan played a bit of a trick on us here. His actual major was *creative writing*, but he knew we wouldn't find that acceptable. He chose to tell us it was simply *writing* because he believed he could convince us that writing could be a tool for any professional and academic career. He also knew that I enjoyed writing; here, he was using the Chinese strategy of catering to another's pleasure. I said, "A writing major is alright because writing could be a tool for any professional or academic career. However, creative writing is different because it must be its own career. As a business, my first concern is whether such a career would enable you to feed you and your family." To make my point, I shared a joke with him: I loved creative writing when I was his age. At that time, the royalty for a poem was fifty cents per line in China, which was enough for a meal. A friend of mine, who was concerned with buying more meals, thought for hours about where he could add a line with a single word into his poem—"Oh!" Since then, his nickname has been, "Oh, fifty cents!"

Yan laughed but ignored my suggestion. I wanted him to choose a major that could help him get a real job so that he'd be able to feed himself after graduation. But he loved creative writing and even imagined living and writing in a log cabin in the woods.

We did not know about the true nature of his *creative* writing major until his sophomore year. However, we knew that American universities allow students to change their majors. We decided to step back and see whether Yan would eventually choose a different course of study. Therefore we didn't try too hard to change his mind immediately.

Theoretically, Chinese universities also allow students to change their majors, but in reality it is almost impossible to do so. Chinese students are divided into two categories: liberal arts and science (including engineering). The nationwide college entrance exams are also separated into two different exams. This means that students must decide what schools they want to attend and what they want to major in before they even start high school, much less choose which college entrance exam they want to take. After they are admitted, their career has been decided. This system is unreasonable, to be sure, but because of it, many Chinese students have quite a clear understanding of their careers at an early age.

In contrast to this rigid system, many American children choose their majors using their emotions. Too many think that as long as your major makes you happy, it will all be okay. They, of course, are happy during their four years in college, but when they graduate they discover the problems with that approach: it's often difficult to secure a job after college with certain majors.

When we visited universities with Yan before he graduated from high school, a junior at one university guided us on a tour. He said that he had changed his major five times, "Maybe one more next month. But for sure, this will be the last time." He smiled.

I said, "Why is this one the last time? Because there will be no more chances?"

He sighed and responded, "You're right. If they give me more chances, I'll probably keep changing it."

Allowing students to change their majors is a good thing. It helps students discover their interests and determine what major will suit them best. But the approach of choosing a major based on emotions or happiness is problematic; while a child might be happy in college, they will face difficulty when they graduate. What job can they get? What will their career be?

7

When Yan went to college, he did not have very clear goals laid out. He joked, "The campus tour girl was cute, so that's why I chose that university." Even though he chose creative writing as a major, he did not have clear goals about his job or career. As most American students do, he was more concerned with being happy about his major and enjoying college than with planning his future. Yan was a devout student of Jujitsu, so as soon as he had time at the beginning of his freshman year, he went to a Jujitsu club in a nearby city, where he took a Brazilian world champion as his master. At his Jujitsu club, someone told him that a GPA of 3.5 would be good enough to be admitted to a prestigious law school. He was thrilled because he'd already achieved a GPA higher than that, which meant he was able to enjoy himself even more. But after that, his GPA fell; he received straight B's during his third quarter. Later that year, he and his friend established their own Jujitsu club. Only then did my wife and I realize that Yan might have chosen his university based on the quality of the nearby Jujitsu club.

Starting in his sophomore year, Yan really started to think about his goals. He gradually set up a clear path: he wanted to attend one of the "Big 14" law schools.

When we went to pick up Yan for winter break that year, my wife noticed something new hanging up on his dorm room walls. She quietly pointed it out to me without Yan noticing. On the wall, among the posters, there was a sheet of paper with two big numbers on it. I immediately realized Yan had put his target GPA and LSAT scores up on the wall, where he could see them every day and they would inspire him to work harder to achieve his goals.

Yan always said that going to law school and becoming a lawyer was his own decision. Of course he made this decision by himself, though our parental guidance was vital as well. One day Yan disclosed some news over the phone: a member of his Jujitsu club was a lawyer, and they had discussed law school. I responded, "Yes, a lawyer can be a writer, but a writer may not be a lawyer. When you have rich experiences, particularly in law, you can write whatever you want. You don't have to think about where your next meal will come from and whether you should add an 'Oh' into the poem for fifty cents."

Yan waited until his sophomore year to seriously think about the future and set his goal, but fortunately it wasn't too late. After that, his behavior and attitude changed greatly, and his grades improved drastically. When Yan started applying for law school, his GPA and LSAT score were higher than the target numbers he had put on his wall, and they were high enough to ensure him entry into the top tier of American law schools. Finally, Yan decide to accept admission to a law school that offered him a sizeable scholarship and allowed him to defer for one year. I admit, I wondered whether his decision was based in part on the size of the city the law school was located in and the proximity of a good Jujitsu club. Only God knows! I will say that even though his law school orientation lasted for less than two days, he still brought his Jujitsu coat with him.

8

Most children will change when they leave home for college; this is particularly true of Asian-American kids. Children not only physically break away from their parents; they do so psychologically as well. One step after another, they become independent. During this time, most Asian-American children have not yet become economically self-sufficient, but, through their new experiences on a college campus, they gradually begin to think independently. Their parents' influence begins to decline, and the influence of their peers begins to rise. At this time, they're also facing a critical decision: choosing their long-term career. Though this process of change can be painful, many children successfully muddle through it and go on to great careers. Others, though, end up struggling for the rest of their lives.

Yan had a junior high classmate who was a capable tennis player. He decided to attend college far away from home in order to take advantage of a tennis scholarship he'd been offered. During his sophomore year, he began to wonder whether he should continue with tennis. After all, though he'd won acclaim and been successful at the sport for so many years, he knew that he wasn't good enough to play professionally. It made his friend even more uneasy when Yan decided to attend law school because he was so unsure of what his next step should be. What career should he choose? He had no idea. This friend often talked on the phone with Yan and was often quite upset by his self-doubt and insecurity. When he turned to his parents for guidance, they'd say, "You can choose whatever you want! As long as it makes you happy, we'll be happy!" The problem was that he didn't know what would make him happy, and the uncertainty that comes with not knowing was making him even more unhappy. He tried many different areas of study—psychology, history, Chinese, religion— and still was unsure of what to do. Finally, he decided to go to medical school to be an ophthalmologist. Since setting that clear and ambitious yet achievable goal, he's completely changed. He's now a happy, confident young man. What amazed me was that his parents weren't appreciative of his choice, as they feared it would be too hard and thus make him unhappy.

9

Everyone thinks that Chinese parents spoil their kids too much. And it's true, Chinese parents really do spoil their children, but American parents, in a way, spoil their kids even more.

In China, parents take care of their kids too much. They are too involved in their kids' lives and select their careers and majors, not allowing them any independence.

On the other hand, American parenting is often too lenient. American parents allow their children too much independence, sometimes even completely letting go after their children leave for college. As long as their kids are happy, the parents are fine. They don't want to even attempt to discuss serious, difficult topics with their children. As a result, children lose the opportunity to talk through career choices and goals with their parents. Parents lose their chance to guide their children and advise them.

Chinese-American parenting is different from both the Chinese and American methods. Many Chinese-American parents respect their children's independence and allow them to make their own final decisions. While they do take this step back, even it's just one step, they are still involved in their children's vital decisions, unlike many American parents. They give their thoughts, suggestions, advice, and guidance through various methods, and sometimes even use pressure to influence their children's decisions.

DIALOGUE

American parents: As American parents, it's very difficult to decide whether we should offer strong guidance regarding our kids' career selection. Can you tell us why we should do so?

Huang: I am happy to share two with you! First is the metaphor of broccoli, which I will discuss later. If your kids don't like broccoli, wouldn't you still make them eat it? And second, when a kid eats too much ice cream or chocolate, won't you stop him or her? Parents have more experience than their children and thus they're able to view things maturely and apply reason to situations. This is the reason that Chinese parents involve themselves in their children's career selection.

American parents: Don't parents sometimes try to choose their kids' careers based on their own interests, replacing what the child might want to do or be good at?

Huang: Yes! This is actually a problem with Chinese parenting. But on the contrary, American parents don't involve themselves enough in their children's career selection. Many let their children do whatever they want to do or even completely neglect the questions as an outsider would.

American parents: What is your advice?

Huang: Here are my two cents. Involve yourself early and provide skillful guidance. Involving yourself early means cultivating ambition and the habit of setting goals while they're young, which we've discussed; otherwise, kids won't even know what they want to do when they graduate from college. Skillful guidance emphasizes that parents ought to keep the communication channel completely open with their kids and always analyze both sides—advantages and disadvantages—with their kids.

American parents: What do you consider your parenting style, Chinese or American?

Huang: The two are opposed to one another, as you've seen here. My style is in between—a "retractable dog leash," as I'll discuss later. A puppy has the freedom to run anywhere within the expanding leash's area, but it's not completely uncontrolled. When necessary, the puppy can be brought back under control.

American parents: You've combined the Chinese and American ways together.

Huang: Yes, Co-Core Synergy Education!

TALENTS OR INTERESTS?

1

When parents try to help their children decide their paths in life, parents often have a difficult time distinguishing between what their children like to do and what their children are good at. Some parents may put an emphasis on their own interests rather than their children's; others might overvalue or underrate their children's talents.

Sometimes, a person's talents and interests are the same. But they often conflict with one another, and sometimes one's interests become one's weaknesses. A good example is some of the contestants who try out on national television programs such as *American Idol*; many are passionate about singing but at the same time are so bad that the audience is barely able to bear listening to them.

Have you ever attended your community's kids' soccer games on the weekends? Whether you know a lot about soccer or not, you can observe that many children not only have the talent to play soccer but they are very interested in it as well. You will also likely find children who enjoy playing soccer, but they aren't necessarily good at it. Of course, there are also some kids who have the talent but lack the interest in playing soccer.

Obviously, what you're "able to do" and what you "love to do" are two very different concepts.

The relationship between talents of children and interests of children has always been complicated. It becomes even more difficult when you add parents' talents and interests into the mix.

2

The relationship between the talents and interests of children and parents can be described as follows.

Kids' interests versus parents' interests: Sometimes these two can be in conflict, but at other times they're harmonious. If they are at odds with one another, Asian-American parents will probably pay more attention to their own interests, especially when their children are young. Believe it or not, this phenomenon has happened in American parenting as well. Family businesses are a prime example, such as roofing, air conditioning, and furnace businesses. I once met a furnace and air conditioning company's owner. He told me that the business had been in his family for several generations. He fell in love with painting, but because he was the sole son in the family, he was expected to continue his father's business; otherwise he would be the one responsible for ending it. His father had forced him to sacrifice his own interests in favor of the family's greater interest. He had to quit high school and start working at his father's business. While he was telling me his story, he was drawing on a sheet of steel. I said, "See, you're using your painting talents!" He didn't raise his head to look at me, but he gave himself a small smile.

Kids' talents versus parents' talents: Many parents believe that because they are good at something, their children should be good at it as well. Or, on the other side of the spectrum, kids see their parents' talents and believe they should have the same strengths. The parents of some of my American students had successful businesses in China and were hoping their children would continue their legacy. These students saw their parents being successful, and naturally they hoped to continue their parents' hard work in China someday. In the end, there are three possibilities. First, what their kids are able to do, the parents may be good at as well. It's also possible that the children didn't inherit the same abilities as the parents. And finally, there's the situation in which children are able to do something that parents don't have the talent to accomplish. It can be complicated and confusing, but this is the reality of the situation.

Kids' interests versus their own talents: It's quite possible that children's talents may conflict with their interests. This is fine, as long as their interests don't become their weaknesses, as is the case with the *American Idol* hopefuls we previously discussed. Chinese and Chinese-American parents would seize kids' talents and neglect their interests. In other words, as long as the kid has the talent, Chinese or Chinese-American parents would ask them to give up their interests in order to pay full attention to their talents and natural gifts.

"Face saving" is an integral part of Chinese culture. As a result, Chinese and Chinese-American parents sometimes have a lot of trouble acknowledging their children's weaknesses, particularly when their weakness happens to be something they are interested in.

3

Like anyone else, there are things Yan is unable to do well no matter how hard he tries. One of these was singing. Yan loved to sing, but he was tone deaf, so he was unable to sing well. I, on the other hand, can sing reasonably well. My wife always complains that while she taught Yan to draw I never bothered to teach him to sing. When she says this, I inevitably respond, "How can you possibly complain about this? As soon as I turn on our karaoke machine, you and Yan flee upstairs and I'm left with the dogs for company!"

I love to sing Chinese songs, but Yan loves to sing American songs. Because of these divergent interests, I wasn't able to teach Yan to sing. Besides, everyone has their weaknesses. There always will be something that you are unable to learn or be taught.

One year, on a sudden impulse, Yan decided to try out for the school play. The song that everyone was required to sing was *Amazing Grace*. The afternoon before he went to try out, he practiced the song again and again. It was honestly quite painful to hear him sing, and I had difficulty facing the fact that there was something my son loved to do yet obviously could not do well. I really wanted to tell Yan that he should stop singing and that the school play would likely reject him. I asked him to come to my office so I could have a talk with him. Yan, who was a supercilious child, never stooping to ask me for help and always grinning cheekily and fooling around, was suddenly very serious. He piously asked me, "Daddy, can you please coach me in singing this song, particularly this line?" I unconsciously swallowed the words that were already in my mouth.

Though I did accede to his request, this was a very big dilemma for me.

I was very uneasy waiting for Yan to come home that afternoon. But I was surprised to find out that he had been asked to play a small role! Looking at my son's excited and happy face, so many thoughts and emotions filled my mind.

I carefully and indirectly inquired about the singing test.

Yan said, "There were not enough people, we are all OK, and nobody was rejected."

So, that is how it went.

All this anguish was for nothing. Because he had to miss some rehearsals in order to attend a students' conference in Washington, DC, he ultimately did not end up playing that small role.

There were two different tragedies that could have occurred here. I knew Yan couldn't sing well, but I could have forced him to sing anyway. On the flip side, if I had been unaware (or didn't care) that Yan was unable to sing well, and only knew that he loved to sing, I might have encouraged him (or forced him) to sing. Either way, I would have dreaded sitting in the audience and suffering through this tragedy.

However, these tragedies occur in both America and China *every single day*!

I'm a father who is engaged in education as my profession, yet I still found it difficult to handle one of my son's hobbies. How would I handle his major in college and career selection? I was having so much difficulty with this issue; how would parents whose jobs don't relate to education at all handle it? It's a huge problem!

4

Regardless of the daily hobby, college major, or career selection, many Chinese-American parents only pay attention to their children's gifts or talents and neglect their interests (look at those many Chinese-American children who struggle in premed programs). Quite a few American parents, however, pay too much attention to their children's interests but ignore their gifts or talents (look at those parents who accompanied their children while they made fools of themselves on *American Idol*).

Therefore, the best combination of Chinese and American family education is to consider both your child's talents and his or her interests during the process of setting his or her goals and ambitions.

We were really happy for Yan when he decided to go to law school. He had already shown his eloquence and debating skills in junior high. Upon graduating from high school, he won a scholarship from my wife's company. During the celebration ceremony, the CEO asked Yan to say a few words. That was the first time I saw my son officially speak in public. He made the adults in the hall laugh so hard that they bent over in their chairs. No wonder he wanted to be a comedian telling jokes in a bar! The CEO simply said to the room, "Well, you all like him better than me. When he graduates he can be the CEO, and I can simply retire."

We thought that with clear and logical thinking, eloquence, and writing skills, he would be a good lawyer.

We knew that he was able to do law, but we still were worried about whether he would enjoy law because he hadn't yet had any real experiences in law school or at a law firm. We were concerned until he attended his law school orientation and sat in on a few classes. When he finally got to the airport, he was so excited to call and let us know that he had found these seemingly dry classes very interesting! He believed that the study of law fit both his talents and his interests and was excited to learn and explore.

After this conversation, we dropped our worries like a stone and were able to breathe evenly again!

DIALOGUE

American parents: Americans overvalue kids' interests.
Chinese parents: Chinese only emphasize kids' talents.

Huang: You both are right. But Co-Core Synergy Education brings balance to both sides. It seeks to maximize both talents and interests.

Chinese/American parents: When something our child loves to do conflicts with what he or she is able to do, what should we do? What advice would you give us?

Huang: In this case, I would follow the Chinese path. What a child is able to do stems from his or her innate capacity. However, people can be capricious, and what they love to do may change.

Chinese/American parents: Can you please give us an example?

Huang: Of course! Let's take singing as an example. A isn't able to sing, but he loves to sing. On the other hand, B is an amazing singer but doesn't enjoy singing. Obviously, since A simply cannot sing well, and no one enjoys his singing, A will never achieve his goal. However, when people appreciate and enjoy B's singing and he sees what an effect his voice has on people, it may gradually change his interests toward singing.

An innate ability can be lost but can't be taught; an interest can be changed but can't be passed on.

SHOULD WE MAKE CHILDREN EAT BROCCOLI?

1

If you ask American kids whether they like broccoli, many, many will say, "No way!"

If you ask American parents whether they like broccoli, many of them may answer, "Not really."

However, whether American parents like or dislike broccoli, when you ask them, "If your children refuse to eat broccoli but you know that broccoli is good for them, will you make them eat it regardless?" the answers will likely vary.

President George H. W. Bush once said, "I do not like broccoli. And I haven't liked it since I was a little kid and my mother made me eat it. And I'm President of the United States, and I'm not going to eat any more broccoli."[4]

We know that despite the fact that the elder President Bush hated broccoli, his mother made him eat it. It's a pity I can't ask Barbara Bush, as a mother, whether she made their children eat broccoli.

When you ask typical Chinese parents whether they would make their children eat broccoli, all of their answers would be the same: "Of course we'll make our child eat broccoli!"

2

Many Chinese and Chinese-American children play various music instruments, but how many of them are really interested in them? Most likely many of them were forced to learn by their parents because of Chinese tradition: lute playing, chess, calligraphy, and painting were considered scholarly accomplishments in ancient China. Chinese parents usually ask (or force) their children to learn at least one of these skills. The best is to learn all four whenever possible.

Yan was sent to learn Chinese traditional painting at an evening school when he was three. He was so young that he drew on his face and clothes more than on paper. His teacher was a well-known professor from a college of fine arts. His reputation attracted a lot of "students." During every class, the back of the classroom was crammed with parents. While the children were learning, parents were also busy writing down notes in order to supervise their child's painting later on.

A three-year-old child certainly did not select this painting class. Obeying was his only "option."

There are no grounds for blaming parents for choosing activities for their children when they are very young. However, as the children grow up, they may discover that the interests their parents chose for them are different from their own interests. It is said that there are more than fifty million children who learn music in China. How many of them really love music? Nobody knows.

3

There's no doubt that the very famous young Chinese pianist Lang Lang is excellent at music. Every Chinese child who learns to play the piano knows the story of how Lang Lang's father forced his son to play against his will, and how Lang Lang almost committed suicide.[5] Horribly, rather than this story steering parents away from forcing their children to play the piano, they've seen Lang Lang's professional success, and thus it has encouraged Chinese parents to push their kids even harder toward playing the piano. Because of Lang Lang's story, countless Chinese children bear physical and mental suffering.

While Lang Lang is adored by thousands of children, people (including myself) also question how good his cultural education was under his father's cruel methods. A recent event involving Lang Lang surprised me and made me certain that the cruel training he was forced to undergo has left serious blemishes on Lang Lang's moral, cultural, and educational character. On January 19, 2011, Lang Lang played the piano at a White House state dinner hosted by President Obama in order to honor President Hu Jintao of China. The music he played was from a Chinese movie about the Korean War. Unsurprisingly, this caused much consternation and provoked discussion in both Chinese and American circles. Some thought that Lang Lang was trying to shame and dishonor the United States by playing this music. Others thought that the music was just that—music; that it didn't have political significance, and that people shouldn't confuse art and politics. I, however, think that Lang Lang was either ignorant or senseless. If a pianist does not know the background of the music he's playing, he is ignorant. If he knew the background but played it anyways at a friendly diplomatic occasion with two presidents and countless important people in attendance, he is senseless. I would rather believe it was the former. After the event, Lang Lang defended himself to the mass media by saying he did not know the background of the music because when the movie was produced and released in 1956, his mother was only two years old; therefore, there was no reason he should know its history.[6] When I read this news, Lang Lang's childish defense made me sad. According to his statements, it's apparently not important to study and understand history. His defense was obviously nonsense, and his refusal to apologize made it even worse. This happened to a world-renowned pianist; shouldn't it have made Chinese parents who were recklessly forcing their children to play music ponder more deeply the potential consequences of doing so? Of course, many may not care, as long as their child can be a pianist at the level of Lang Lang.

Confucianism emphasized obedience and holding to your place in society, which is especially clear with his statement, "Monarchs should have a monarch's manner; subjects should have the behavior of a subject; a father should have a father's air; a son should be a son."[7] This idea of Confucianism has profoundly influenced Chinese people for thousands of years. Therefore, Chinese parenting always forces children to obey their parents' will and decisions. Lang Lang is a successful model of this educational style in so many parents' eyes.

Interestingly enough there was another doctrine, Taoism, whose teachings conflicted with Confucianism in ancient China. Taoism emphasized governing "by doing nothing that goes against nature."[8] To follow nature, and what was natural, was the key to Taoism.

When it comes to choosing children's interests, selecting their college majors, and planning their careers, Chinese parents hold the ideas of Confucianism dear. American parents, on the other hand, follow the ideas of Taoism, whether they realize it or not. Quite a few American parents choose to step aside from guiding their children's self-education, instead deciding to "govern by doing nothing that goes against nature." However, as a consequence of this, children's neglected interests, gifts, and talents may gradually decline.

4

When I was writing my book *Gifted Education in America*, I sent an e-mail to a teacher of the Gifted Education Program at Yan's junior high school in order to get information on where the students of Yan's class currently were. He responded in a brief letter in which he told me that many of the students had gone on to study at Ohio State University, Miami University, the University of Cincinnati, Indiana University, Northwestern University, and other respected schools. However, he noted that one young man was touring the western part of the United States, one was making plans to move to Alaska, one was looking to start a rock band, and another was working at a lake, restocking the fish supply, among other assorted duties. He added that some kids had to experience some of life's hard realities before focusing in on a sound career path.

According to the teacher, the four boys who had not yet identified their career paths were extremely smart. Among twenty high-IQ students, there were about 20 percent who did not go to college, which is unbelievable and unacceptable according to Chinese expectations.

These children were extraordinarily smart and showed special promise as middle schoolers, but they seem to have floundered on their journeys to adulthood. The fact that they were allowed to choose their own paths (such as touring the western part of the United States and looking to move to Alaska) with no input from their parents is unimaginable and would almost never happen in a Chinese family.

5

Regarding our child's extracurricular activities and interests, our parenting style was much more reflective of that of an American family, with a Taoist "govern by doing nothing that goes against nature" approach. For instance, around Yan's tenth birthday, he started joining in community soccer games. At that time, Yan had not shown obvious interest in soccer. Our friend Helaine bought soccer shoes and other gear for Yan. After she purchased these items for him, Yan was driven to play soccer. Of course, Helaine knew I loved soccer, and we made a decision to steer Yan toward playing soccer as well. We succeeded; he played soccer through his freshman year in high school and was one of the top goal scorers on his team. However, Yan decided not to play soccer after that year, so I decided to encourage him to play volleyball. I could have coached him because I was a very good setter, and I believed he would make a good setter as well. Yan, however, refused my suggestion and chose tennis. Several years later, Yan confessed to me a small secret: "I didn't choose volleyball because you knew how to play volleyball, but as for tennis, you don't know how to play it at all, so you would be unable to make any indiscreet remarks or criticism." During high school, the wrestling coach at Yan's school wanted him to join the wrestling team. I thought it was too dangerous, so I did not agree to it. Instead, Yan began to pursue Brazilian Jujitsu, which he still practices today. I did not stop him, but I could never watch him do it. As a Chinese parent, this was the best I could do, even taking into account all the education we received from American parenting.

As for Yan's career choice, we kept our strategy closer to traditional Chinese family education. The only difference was that instead of forcing Yan to do what we thought was best, we tried to guide him toward a good career choice. Strictly speaking, this is neither a Chinese nor an American way, since we were involved in his decision but did not try to force him to follow one path or another.

Yan once compared my Co-Core Synergy Education to a retractable dog leash, which is a dynamic and vivid metaphor. A cute little puppy can have a certain amount of freedom to run out anywhere within the leash's expanding area. However, it is not uncontrolled. When necessary, the puppy can be drawn back under control. So, in a sense, Co-Core Synergy Education allows your child to wander and explore freely but only to a certain extent. When you feel your child has gone too far, you can guide him or her back toward the correct path, something even Yan accepts and appreciates. When Yan presented his comparison to me, I said, "Does that mean you're a little dog?"

He laughed and said, "Why not? Human beings are social animals anyway."

6

The following is a story in Yan's book *My Seven American Teachers*. The events in the story occurred during Yan's freshman year in high school.

This Is Your Future

Around the end of the year, I was facing a very difficult dilemma. Should I or shouldn't I continue on in art class?

With all the conflicts in my schedule, if I took art, I couldn't take a computer class that I thought I might need for my maybe future career in computers. So it was one or the other.

This art class is hard to get into. Most students who enter art have decided their future even before the entrance test. Most of them know that art is an important part of whatever career they will have in the future.

Also, the reputation of this art program is very good. Every one of the graduates should be able to earn scholarships from numerous schools and organizations. The expectations for the class are much higher than normal. So those who enter art have been expected to finish the four years and get a lot of scholarships.

With difficulty, I made my decision. The hardest part was probably telling the Brother, my art teacher, that I had to quit art next year.

How should I tell him?

One day, the Brother was extremely happy. I couldn't wait any longer and took the opportunity to tell him my decision. Starting next year, I wouldn't be taking art class anymore.

What killed me was, the Brother thought I was joking. He stood up and walked away while giggling at me. I followed him and grabbed his arm and said it again.

He listened to me and once again started to laugh, interrupting me in a humorous tone, "Yan, get to work or no fortune cookie for you."

The Brother really didn't believe me. He genuinely thought that I was still kidding around with him.

I took about a full fifteen minutes convincing him over and over that I wasn't playing around. And even then he still didn't believe me.

Then he showed a side of himself I rarely saw, he said very seriously with a blanketed expression of shock, "Yan, you're serious?"

It seems that I had unintentionally hurt the Brother's feelings.

The Brother looked me in the eyes and said very plainly to me, "Yan, you have the potential to be very good. Do you know that? I mean your work ethic in here is sort of funny and you mess around a little, but you have the raw talent."

The Brother was trying to persuade me to stay, but my decision had already been made.

At that moment, I felt that the Brother had suddenly become much older. That type of humor and cleverness had instantly vanished.

The Brother slowly mumbled, "I don't know what to say. . . . This is your future."

In fact, I felt quite bad at that moment.

I had never seen this type of sad emotion from the Brother, something that will stay with me for decades to come.

I pretended to smile and tried to kid with him. I swore to him that I would come here every day for the next three years to play and make fun of him.

At the time I wrote this, sophomore year had already started. My friends in art this year told me that the Brother always mentioned me.

He threatens those kids who don't work, "Be careful, if you don't work, I'm going to kick you out and keep this spot open for Yan!"

Good Old the Brother, I can never make this up to you. In this life, I'm afraid I'll never get another opportunity to take your class again. But the things I learned from you will accompany me to the ends of the earth.[9]

Yan's struggle between his interests and the classes he thought would be most relevant for his future career was difficult. We only provided him our advice and guidance: he could draw very well, but was he good enough at it to make it his career? We were not sure. In the end, we gave our thoughts to Yan on the subject but stepped back and allowed him to make the final decision. And his computer skills turned out to be a powerful tool in his present legal career.

Children's career choices will vary as they grow and change. For example, Yan expressed interest in many different careers, such as zookeeper, explorer, high school teacher, comedian, and writer (living in the mountains), before settling on his final choice as a lawyer. The key is that we, as parents, had to guide Yan's career choices when he was too young to understand the goals he was setting. However, we also had to know when to take a step back as Yan grew and allow him to explore his own choices and make his own decisions. The intensity of parents' involvement in a child's career selection must change over the years. We encouraged Yan to become a doctor at a young age, which was completely our will. In the middle, when he was a teenager, Yan's will was very strong. In the end, his choice to be a lawyer combined both wills: he wanted to be a lawyer, and we guided him toward that career choice.

We can't simply view parents' willingness to be involved in their children's career choices as a negative thing. Development occurs over a long period of time, with varying maturity levels. When children are not mature, parents can point out a direction for their children's development. As we can see, when parents are involved, the child's thinking changes; his or her desires rise and fall, varying wildly. For example, when Yan was in high school his interests ranged from "writing in the mountains" to "studying in a big city," which were poles apart. When we saw Yan's goals swinging between high and low, we got involved in his goal setting. We could have chosen not to be concerned and to let things drift, but the results would have likely been similar to those aimlessly wandering students in Yan's gifted class. It's so important for parents to guide their children and involve themselves in their career selections.

Chinese parents' ideas about what their children should do will likely be an extension of the hopes they had for themselves but weren't able to achieve. For instance, if a Chinese-American parent could not go to an Ivy League school, he or she might want his or her children to try for admission. Many people see this type of behavior as a negative thing, but it's not completely bad, particularly when parents' ideas are not wrong. These hopes and expectations might affect a child's willingness to work hard and set goals. High hope and ambition from parents can be a motivation to push children to continue to move forward, just as human selfishness and greed are also motivations for making progress. Without the ambition that comes from selfishness and greed, humans would never have advanced as far as we have today.

But parents should not simply bend a child's will; rather, they should seek to combine their will with their child's. If an egg is broken from the outside, you're making breakfast. But if an egg is broken from the *inside*, a life has been created. Therefore, no matter how wise, intelligent, and brilliant the parents' ideas are, it's only when they combine with the child's that good things will happen. This is the most subtle and delicate aspect of parenting, and it's incredibly important. It's at the center of my Co-Core Synergy Education theory.

DIALOGUE

American parents: We follow our kids' lead rather than forcing them to do things they don't want to do.

Chinese parents: We, on the other hand, usually compel our children to do what we believe is best.

Huang: Neither of these approaches is best. Allowing kids to set their own paths with no guidance isn't good for kids, but forcing them to do things against their will isn't good either. There should be a balance, a healthy mix, of the two approaches.

American/Chinese parents: Could you please be more specific?

Huang: Here are my ideas.

When there's a conflict, parents ask themselves

(a)   whether it's an issue of right or wrong (Is there a morality problem? Might it involve breaking the law [this could involve alcohol or drugs]? If the answer to either of these questions is yes, parents will have to force their children to change.),

(b)   whether it's clear who is correct and who's not (For example, your child may absolutely love singing but may not be good at it at all. It's a tough situation, but my advice would be to compel your child to change, but only if he or she wants to pursue singing as a career. If singing is an interest or a hobby but not a career aspiration, it's fine to leave your child be.),

(c)   whether it's a value judgment (For example, which is more beautiful, a traditional Chinese painting or a modern oil painting? In this case it's good to explain your point of view but leave it to your child to make his or her own decisions. You shouldn't try to compel your child's interests or replace their interest in oil paintings with your interest in traditional Chinese paintings.),

(d)   whether it's really an essential conflict (When it's not, parents should follow the kids' lead. Kids may have trouble finding their interests and hobbies; in this case, parents should guide them toward interests that the parents believe are suitable.).

To sort out the conflict, look at the categories first and then decide on a proper way to handle the situation, rather than recklessly involving yourself without thinking about it.

American/Chinese parents: Your advice is very interesting; it's neither completely American nor purely Chinese. Now what are your thoughts on kids' talents?

Huang: This will be a more Chinese approach.

- If a child chooses an interest for which he or she has no talent, particularly when it is career related, parents should compel the child to change course.

- If a child is talented at many things, try your best to make him or her select the best or most appropriate activity. For instance, let's say that Yan had decided to stay in the art program in high school. We would have tried our best to convince him to change.

Listing items kids can or can't do and being overly controlling was the approach of the Tiger Mother. Allowing children to do whatever they want without any control is the American way of doing things.

The key of Co-Core Synergy Education is to be involved and control properly, but only to a certain extent.

CHAPTER 4
WHAT DOES "PARENTING" MEAN IN A CHINESE-AMERICAN FAMILY?

Chinese parents make their child's education the highest priority and central goal for the entire family. As such, Chinese parents are willing to do things for their children that many Western parents simply would not conceive of doing.

CHINESE PARENTS AND "SACRIFICE"

1

One evening we went to the country club for a party. We happened upon our friends, who were drinking at the bar by themselves.

We asked, "Where are your kids?"

They answered, "They're at home with a babysitter."

We were shocked. We didn't understand how parents could hardheartedly go out and enjoy time alone without their children. They probably noticed the puzzled expressions on our faces, so they explained further: putting emphasis on the husband-wife relationship after the children came was supposed to be good for the marriage.

They could tell that we were still bewildered, so our friends asked, "How do Chinese parents do things?"

I shared a joke with them:

Gentleman A and Gentleman B encountered a tiger on a hill. Gentleman A wanted to work together with Gentleman B to fight the tiger. Gentleman B smiled and tied his shoes, ready to run.

Gentleman A said, "Are you able to run faster than a tiger? Absolutely not. We'd better fight the tiger together. We might have a chance to survive."

Gentleman B answered, "Of course I can't run faster than a tiger. But as long as I can run faster than you, I'll be okay."

After hearing this story, the couple embarked on a delicious bit of arguing.

The wife was a sales executive and went to China very often. She said, "Asian culture stresses the collective. So Gentleman A's idea for fighting the tiger together is the Asian way of thinking."

The husband was a high school teacher who was familiar with Western culture. He said, "Western culture likes to talk about individualism. So do you mean that B represents Western culture?"

I shook my head.

An old gentleman involved himself in our discussion. "Individualism does not mean running away. American cowboy culture relished the idea of fighting alone. Two people fighting together or escaping together? Neither are representative of Western culture."

The arguing went on.

I said, "It's wrong to oversimplify this story by classifying these two gentlemen into either Asian or Western culture."

People were in an uproar.

The wife said, "We understand ... well, at least we think we understand Western culture. Would you please use Asian thinking to explain and analyze this joke?"

I said, "You visit China relatively often. You've probably seen that people who are complete strangers grapple with one another to grab seats on the bus. Thus, from that incident you may conclude that this behavior would be similar to Gentleman B's approach."

She vied for the topic. "Yes, but if A and B are a father and a son, fighting together would be Chinese culture, right?"

Everybody laughed to show agreement with her.

Playing with my cup, I said softly, "Wrong! A Chinese father would sacrifice himself and let his son run away! Of course, at this crucial moment of life or death, an American father would fight the tiger as well."

I knew parental sacrifice was a very interesting topic, and I was curious to see what they had to say, so I hesitated to speak my next thought.

These parents are volunteering to block traffic in order to reduce any noise that might distract the students taking the college entrance exam. *Photo by Bo Yang.*

The husband jumped in, saying, "Then what would you use to maintain the relationship between husband and wife?"

"The kids!" My wife and I were quick to speak.

As soon as a Chinese family has their own child, the center and heart of the family moves to that child.

2

When Yan was about eight or nine, he came home and told us about "vitamins." At a family friend's house, Yan had gotten the chance to sample a Flintstones vitamin. He came home indoctrinated, telling us of the endless benefits of multivitamins. Eating multivitamins was good for you, he said. People who eat them live longer.

"I want us to live longer," he said. "They taste really good, too!"

Eventually, we acquiesced. The next time we were at the grocery store, my wife agreed to buy some vitamins. When she entered the pharmaceutical aisles, she was shocked to discover just how expensive vitamins were. More than $10 for a little bottle! After some internal debate, she bought the cheapest one, a small orange bottle of fifty vitamins. After all, as we both agreed later, the vitamins would be good for him.

When we got home, Yan forced us to eat one with him after dinner (as he'd also learned). My wife and I convinced him that we only needed half because we weren't still growing like him. Our bodies didn't need it, we told him. Though slightly suspicious of our reasoning, Yan agreed. After a few days, we eventually stopped eating them altogether, leaving them all for our son.

I like telling this vitamin story because it highlights a point about Chinese parenting and family education that I have rarely seen properly emphasized. Chinese parents *always* put their children ahead of themselves. When it comes to the good things in life, the average Chinese parent will do exactly what I did with the vitamins and with the milkshake I saved for Yan: they will find some way to preserve it for their child. Chinese children wear the best clothes in the family. They eat the best foods. When there isn't enough of a good thing to go around, you can rest assured that Chinese parents would relinquish their own claim to it in order to give it to their child.

In China, it is normal for parents to willingly give up their own desires, wishes, and dreams for their children. There is no controversy. The father doesn't get the big piece of chicken. The child does. The father and mother eat the leftovers. The parents don't get to have a day off or a "day to themselves." Every day is an opportunity to provide more for the child. The father doesn't get to go on a fishing trip. The mother doesn't get a day of indulgence at the spa. Indeed, few Chinese fathers and mothers ever celebrate their birthdays. Apart from basic filial respect and obedience, children are *never* expected to affirmatively do nice things for their parents.

Perhaps the best word in English to describe how most Chinese children live is *spoiled*. The Chinese are not ashamed of this. They openly call their children "little princes" and "little emperors." Like serfs in China, parents are expected to pay fealty and work hard for the betterment of the emperor's kingdom. No true emperor would ever think to go out of his way to do something nice for his subjects. Unfortunately, for many Chinese children, this much is true. They are *beyond* spoiled. They grow up as the center of their entire family and may receive a rude awakening once they enter the outside world.

3

There is a very popular saying in China: "The sad plight of all parents." This saying means that parents would give up anything or do anything for their children.

Americans will probably be surprised to discover that *so many* Chinese parents come to America not for themselves, but for their children's futures.

Anna was Wei Chen's English name. She was a former professor at Peking University. In the early 1990s Anna came to America as a visiting professor. In order to give her children better opportunities, she decided to stay in the United States so they could study here. To do this, Anna, a former professor, has been working as a nanny for over ten years.

When she was interviewed by a reporter from the *Global Times*, she acknowledged that she had a sense of inferiority for a very long time after working as a nanny. She did not tell anybody that she had once been a professor because she worried that what she was doing would hurt the reputation of Peking University. Anna, however, finally moved past her psychological obstruction and just tried to survive and help her son and daughter come to study in the United States. There's no reason she should have felt ashamed of herself; she did what she had to do in order to help her son and daughter.

This boy was two minutes late for the College Entrance Exam. Because of the high stakes, his mother knelt down to beg the gatekeeper to let him in. *Photo by Tielin Liu.*

The money she made from being a nanny was the main source of income for her family, which helped her children finish their undergraduate studies in China. Her children didn't realize she'd taken a position far beneath her previous job in order to support them. When they came over to the United States to pursue their graduate studies, they discovered her secret. Anna said, "They held me and cried bitterly and swore that they would study extremely hard, graduate as early as possible, and repay me with a very good life."[1]

Anna's story is not unique. There are quite a few Chinese senior intellectuals, such as professors, scholars, doctors, and musicians, who are engaging in menial jobs to make a better life for their families. Creating an opportunity for their children to study in the United States is the apex of their hard struggles.

In fact, I could serve as an example as well. If I had returned to China with a doctorate in Higher Education Administration in the early 1990s, I would almost certainly have been hired as a president of a Chinese university. However, by the time my wife and I graduated with our degrees, Yan would have not been able to return to China, not only because of problems with Chinese reading and writing comprehension, but also because of his adoption of American culture, study habits, and modes of thinking. We had seen our friends bring their children back to China, but due to the differences in ways of teaching and schooling between American and Chinese primary and secondary education, their children were held back one or two years in school. Some children would never be able to catch up with their Chinese peers because they were unable to adapt to their ways of study, behavior, and modes of thought. Many Chinese students choose to stay in the United States after they graduate with doctoral degrees; most often they do so not for their careers but for their children's future. I, too, gave up my career and decided to stay in America for my only son.

The first several years after I graduated, I found various ways of supporting my family. I worked as an interpreter and translator. At one point, I had my own import/export business. Sometimes, when I had to deal with rough salesmen, I would withhold information about my academic work, as one salesman had denigrated the honor of having received a doctoral degree. One day my son, who had just started the sixth grade, said, "Daddy has no one to talk to at home, so he has to talk to the dog all day!" I took this as a joke and smiled, but in my heart I was crying. . . .

4

The "one family one child" policy was implemented in China in the 1970s. After these only children began to go to college, something new appeared in society, the concept of *Peidu*. There's no direct American parallel for this Chinese concept (*pei* means "to accompany" and *du* is "to go to school"), but a rough translation is "to accompany one's child in studying." To put it simply, parents gave up their careers to follow and support their children in their educational endeavors. Even though the tradition of education being supreme in Chinese culture had endured over centuries, in the past there were usually several children per family and parents' incomes were much lower. Even if parents wanted to follow children along on their studies, there were too many of them and not enough money to do so. Furthermore, the government prevented people from choosing their jobs freely; the system of registered permanent residents wouldn't allow people to move from city to city or from the country to the city. Therefore, accompanying children during their studies was absolutely impossible at that time.

Because the College Entrance Exam is highly competitive, parents often feel duty-bound to sacrifice their personal careers or other life pursuits in order to provide their child with any possible advantage.
Photo by Fang Wu.

Today most families in China have only one child. Two parents take care of one kid, so a family with a high income would be able to have one parent give up his or her job to accompany their child in the child's studies. Even parents from lower income families can find jobs around schools. In many parts of China, in order to attend good middle schools and/or high schools, many children must move away from their parents and hometowns, often hundreds or even thousands of miles away. In order to ensure that their child is doing well, one parent will often pick up and follow their middle-school- or high-school-aged child. As a result, a marvelous and strange phenomenon has appeared around some prestigious Chinese schools: adjoining streets or neighborhoods have apartments occupied solely by parents who are accompanying their children on their educational journeys. What are they doing there? They are doing anything and everything necessary to aid their children in their studies. The parents attend to their children like squires to knights, preparing their meals, washing their clothes, and doing whatever else it takes to maximize their child's chance of educational success.

A middle-school classmate of mine resigned from her job in Liuzhou to accompany her son in his studies in Beijing. She's been separated from her husband for three years.

This forty-five-year-old father sold his company and sat in the classroom with his son to study with him for the College Entrance Exam. *Photo by Weibo Li.*

"It is worth it, if he can get into the College of Fine Arts in Beijing," she stated very stubbornly. "My child likes drawing. We have done our best for him. Whether or not he can get into the college, we only can pray for him."

One year of tuition in Beijing is around 25,000 Yuan. Total expenses are approximately 45,000 Yuan per year. If he had studied in his hometown of Liuzhou instead, his tuition would have been less than 2,000 Yuan per year.

She said, "He's been studying for twelve years just for this one exam. Do you know how much pressure he's under? Why shouldn't I have accompanied him here?"

Very cautiously, I asked, "If by any chance, his exam—"

She interrupted me, saying, "He will take the exam again next year!"

I didn't have the courage to ask what would happen if he failed a second time.

5

I have a Chinese friend in the United States who goes by the English name of George. His wife is good friends with my wife, and, on occasion, we'll get together.

Once, on our way to a banquet, we decided to carpool. We'd all be there anyway and it'd save some gas and maybe even a tree or two, I'd decided. When it came time, George picked us up in his Toyota and we were off.

I sat in the front while he drove, and our wives sat in the back. On the way, I happened to glance back and noticed that his wife (who goes by the English name Leslie) was reading a rather large book.

"Is that a textbook?" I asked her.

"Yes," Leslie said, looking up. "It's my son's."

"Oh?" This piqued my interest. Why was Leslie so fervently poring over it in the back of the car on the way to a banquet?

"I'm reading his assignment," she explained, perhaps sensing my curiosity. "I'll go over it with him later tonight after the banquet."

I nodded. I'd met her son before. A good, albeit shy, boy. If I remembered correctly, he was preparing to go to middle school.

"Do you mean the homework that he's done?" I asked, confused. "You're reading something he wrote?"

"No, no, no," she said. "I'm reading what he was supposed to read. His homework. We do it together. He reads it, and then I read it, too, so that I can understand and help him with his work if he needs it."

"Ah," I said. "I see. But he's not struggling at school, is he?"

"No, he's getting all A's."

I said, "Well, then, I know which university he wants to attend!"

Each of us laughed simultaneously, since Chinese-American kids and parents are all in agreement that Harvard is the dream college.

A few months later, I heard that Leslie had quit her job in order to stay at home and study with her son. She learns all the material from the courses that her son takes at school. When he comes home at the end of the day, she talks to him about what he learned, discussing specific issues with him and making sure to highlight the more difficult aspects of his lessons. Because Leslie's son has a companion in studying, he feels a strong motivation and a special challenge to understand the material; as a result, he studies vigorously. He not only makes excellent grades but also does very well at his many extracurricular activities, including sports and art. Though he hasn't yet graduated from high school, he has attracted the attention of several Ivy League schools, including his dream school. Many of my American friends are very impressed by what this Chinese-American mom has been doing. They say that they often forget to even remind their kids to do their homework, much less teach themselves the material that their children learn at school every day.

I wasn't surprised by George and Leslie's story. Leslie is actually one of several Chinese parents we personally know who have taken similar measures with their children. Substantial and direct involvement in a child's education is the norm in China. It is one of the central characteristics of Chinese parenting. Within a Chinese family, a child's studies are rarely left up to him or her alone.

Chinese parents feel a deep and personal responsibility for their child's success in school. For many parents, the centerpiece of their parental responsibility is ensuring that their child succeeds in education. Few Chinese parents would hesitate to sacrifice any amount of time, money, or effort to ensure that their child stays ahead of the curve. While parental involvement can take all shapes and sizes— from harsh and strict to warm and accommodating—the result is that Chinese parents become inextricably bound up in their children's education.

Since many Chinese families have only one child, a child's performance in school often becomes the sole focus of the entire family. This is why it is not uncommon for one parent to completely give up his or her career to stay home to instruct, tutor, and guide the child in his or her studies.

One incredibly important concept of Chinese parenting culture that has been lost in the shadow of the iconic Tiger Mother image is *guan*. There is no direct translation for the concept of guan, but it involves an amalgam of other verbs. To *guan* means to manage and, when necessary, to control or restrain your child—but it also means to care for and about them, to be involved and invested in their lives, and to offer protection and guidance for them. A Chinese professor once joked, "My university *guan* [controls] my thinking, but also *guan* [takes care of] my food [tenure position]." Though the joke has lost much of its humor in translation, it still expresses the subtle differences in the meanings of guan. While guan can have an authoritarian feel to it when the child is seen as being dangerously out of line, its main component—its heart—is the aligning of parental interests with those of the child's. In China, good parents guan their kids. Bad parents do not.

In business circles, important businessmen often toss around the term "agency costs." When two (or more) entities are working together for some common goal, it is important that every participant has the same interests at heart. If, for example, a family hires a broker to sell its house, the family would try and seek out a broker whose chief goal would be to obtain the highest price possible from a potential buyer. A broker who, instead, had other interests in mind (such as giving a good deal to a friend or intentionally selling it at a low price to hurt the family) or simply did not share the family's interests (a broker who is paid a set fee regardless of the sale price) would *not* be the ideal partner for the transaction. If the family were to proceed with such a broker, the family would likely lose out, incurring agency costs.

When it comes to a child's education, the traditional Chinese family is set up in such a way as to reduce agency costs. The family does this by making the child's education one of the *highest* priorities (if not the single highest priority) of the entire family. The child's education is the central goal *for the family*. As such, Chinese parents are eager to do things for their children that many Western parents simply would not be willing to do.

6

More and more Chinese students are studying abroad at younger and younger ages. Along with them, large numbers of Chinese parents are accompanying their children in their education. They are beginning to appear in countries such as the United States, Canada, and Australia.

Recently a reader of mine sent me a story from the *China Daily* (October 8, 2012). Kevin Brown, vice president of Sotheby's International Realty, was helping a Chinese woman find an apartment near Central Park in Manhattan. The Chinese lady said that the exorbitant prices in the area, roughly $5 million for an apartment, weren't an issue. What was important was that she wanted to send her daughter to Columbia University. After several hours of looking for an apartment, Brown finally asked the woman, "How old is your daughter?" She answered, "*Two* years old." Only *two*? Brown was shocked. He thought to himself that he didn't even know what food he should serve his daughters that evening, much less what their education plan should be for the next two decades. A few weeks later, the woman bought a $6.5 million apartment at One57.[2]

It's clear from this story, and from the other examples I've given, that Chinese parents are willing to give up everything and do anything for their children's education. There is a story that every Chinese parent knows about Mencius, the second most important sage of Confucianism. The story describes how Mencius' mother moved three times in order to find a good place for Mencius' education. The third time they moved near a school. After that third move, Mencius became more polite and disciplined and exhibited a love of reading. His mother said, satisfied, "Eventually, I found the right place for my son." This story has influenced Chinese parents for more than two thousand years.

Parents are scrambling to buy tickets to receive consultation regarding the College Entrance Exam. Students and parents hope to receive vital information that will give them an advantage over other exam takers. *Photo by Junsheng Jia and Yong Zha.*

Chinese-American parents are all "modern mothers of Mencius." No matter how expensive the houses are, as long as it is within the realm of possibility, they will move to an area with a good education system. If they are not wealthy enough to buy a house, they will rent a tiny apartment near a good school.

While American education is calling on parents to spend more time with their children in order to understand their children better, Chinese parents have been contributing their entire lives to their children.

7

It's true that money can't do everything, but without money it's hard to do anything at all. Let us turn the discussion toward the expenses for children's education.

How much would it cost a Chinese student to earn a bachelor's degree in the United States? Let's take as an example Miami University in Ohio, where I am a professor. Right now, the total cost for one year's tuition is about $40,000. For four years, it's over $160,000. Some Americans may think Chinese people are rich because they spend so much money on and in pursuit of their children's education, but that's often not the case. In fact, many Chinese families scrimp and save on every expense, including food, and use all their savings, sometimes even selling their houses and cars, in order to send their children to study in the United States. An ordinary professor at a regular Chinese university makes around $10,000 to $20,000 per year. Therefore, it's a lot of pressure for a Chinese professor to send his or her child to pursue a degree here in the United States.

A reader once sent me a letter explaining how she was saving money in order to send her one-year-old child to study in America. Her yearly income was about $15,000. Right now, she's paying very expensive educational fees for her daughter to attend a good nursery, but despite this, every year she deposits $4,500 into a fund, which yields 8 percent. In twenty years, she'll have $200,000 for her child's education, more than enough for four years of college—assuming, of course, that tuition doesn't rise at the same current exorbitant rates!

I was deeply moved by her magnificent goals.

Chinese families usually save 40 percent to 50 percent of their income for their children's education. In terms of a survey (based on 749 families in Shanghai), people spent 46 percent of their incomes on junior high education, 51 percent on high school, and 52 percent on college.[3]

Many Chinese-American families are also willing to contribute everything, at any cost, to ensure the success of their children's education.

When Yan was in the process of applying for law school, he received many scholarship offers because of his high LSAT scores. With the level of generosity of many of these offers, it meant he could go to law school basically for free. However the law school Yan wanted to go to was the most expensive in the country. Even though Yan received scholarships for $20,000 per year, it was a *small* sum compared to what we would have to pay on a per-year basis toward his education. My wife and I carefully calculated our financial status again and again. We decided to contribute all our savings and also take out loans to support Yan so he could attend the law school he really wanted to without worrying about the cost. The thought of Yan taking out his own loans to go to law school never crossed our minds; it was our job as parents to support him and provide for his education. There is a Chinese saying, "Even needing to sell the last pair of pants is still worth it to send children to school." This is very common within Asian-American families of every socioeconomic status. In particular, new immigrant parents who have fewer working years will often have few financial resources to use for their own retirement. When they contribute all their savings and borrow as much as possible in loans for their children, it indicates that they have already allocated their retirement savings.

I discussed this topic in my classes. Most students said that although their parents were wealthy, they would give their children two options: (1) accept the full scholarship to the less-preferred law school, after which the parents would buy a new car for the child to drive to said law school or (2) allow the child to take loans in the tuition amount, whether from the bank or from the parents, and then drive the parents' used car to said law school.

An American friend once told us that one day his minister had asked the same question to more than six hundred people in his church. Only four people raised their hands to indicate that they would share the Chinese-American parents' choice.

DIALOGUE

American parents: As parents, it's difficult for us to describe our feelings after reading this section.

Huang: When your children are young, you do sacrifice and spend a lot of time and energy on your kids, particularly with regard to sports. A friend of mine who was interested in football actually switched to soccer because it was what his kids were interested in. Not only did he learn all about soccer, he even took exams to be a referee and became a coach for his kids' soccer teams. But with regard to spending time, energy, resources, and money on your children's studying and education, American parents are extremely far from Chinese parents.

American parents: Yes, this is one of the reasons we don't know how to describe our feelings. We feel guilty, but it's almost impossible for us to emulate Chinese parents in this regard.

Huang: Yes, it is virtually impossible for American parents to sacrifice themselves as Chinese parents do for their children's education. However, it is possible to make small sacrifices toward your kids' studies. For example, you can give up something when your kids' interests conflict with yours. Spending time tutoring your children isn't fun, but if they need it, try sitting down with them in order to help them. In other words, sacrifice yourself a little more in order to involve yourself in your children's studying. While it's boring, it will get easier with time. You never know, after a while, you might gradually, without even noticing, begin to sacrifice yourself more than Chinese parents do!

TURNING POWER INTO AUTHORITY?

1

The first time I experienced authority was many years ago.

I don't remember which year it was; all I know is that I was a small child. One day someone knocked heavily at our door. I opened the door, and a large man threw himself on his knees in front of my mother and said, "Teacher He, do you remember me? I am —, and I am a criminal. While I was in prison I always thought that if I had listened to you I would not be the person I am today. Every single day in prison, I told myself that you, Teacher He, would be the first person I would come to see the first day I was released. . . ."

I was shivering with fear.

My mother calmly said, "Stand up, please! You do not need to kneel."

The large man started to kowtow, touching his head to the ground in an ancient Chinese symbol of respect. "Teacher He, if you do not forgive me, if you do not recognize me as your student, I cannot stand up!"

My mother sighed and said, "As long as you mend your faults, you will be fine. You will still be my student!"

I curled up in the corner, not understanding why my very thin, weak, and frail mother had such strong and frightening power over this big self-professed lawbreaker.

In front of that strong criminal, my physically small mother showed intangible awesome power. It turned out that an ordinary middle school teacher could have spiritual strength even more impactful than the power in the police's hands. What was that?

Authority!

It's true that a teacher has power, just as the police do, but that doesn't automatically mean that he or she has authority.

2

Yan published a book in China, and in it he classified his teachers into four different categories. I was surprised at his daring in doing so and considered suggesting that he delete this passage from his book, but the publisher said, "If you delete it, it won't be a fifteen-year-old kid's opinions, but instead a fifty-year-old father's argument."

In his *New Heights in America*, Yan identified four different types of teacher motivation. He pointed out that some teachers are motivated by their paychecks. These teachers simply want to collect their salary to feed their families. They tend to do the bare minimum. Other teachers are motivated by pride. They can be very effective teachers because they want to be able to have pride in their students, which motivates them to go beyond the bare minimum. However, they can feel shamed and become very frustrated when students do not cooperate, as is often the case in American schools, where unruly students sometimes pick on teachers. In such cases, this type of teacher will have limited success in the classroom. The third type of teacher is motivated by a sense of duty to society. He or she believes that teaching is a way to serve society, and beyond conveying information, he or she will also behave as a role model for his or her students, showing them how to become moral and righteous. Such teachers are capable of changing students for the better. Finally, there are those teachers who consider their job to be a labor of love. These teachers do not require any type of external motivation or reward. Rather, they are successful simply because they love what they do and enjoy thinking of ways they can become even better at it.[4]

While Yan did not use the concepts of power and authority to make his arguments, they're relevant to his observations. The first and second types of teachers have power, but no authority. The third and fourth types of teachers, the types Yan says have something that make the difference between "a teacher everyone hates" and "a teacher everyone looks up to," have not only power but authority as well.

Just like teachers, every parent has power, but not every parent has authority. One of the vital characteristics of Chinese-American parenting is to turn parents' power into their authority.

3

What are *power* and *authority*? What are the differences between them?

Power is granted by culture, society, and/or legislation, but you must build authority on your own. Power is held by certain people in certain positions; authority is influence that you build in others' minds.

The key here is the subtle difference between power and authority.

Legislation and culture grant certain positions the ability to exercise specific rights and/or use certain forces. This is power. That is to say, as long as a person is appointed to one of these positions, regardless of whether he or she is moral or intelligent, he or she may exercise these rights and/or use these forces. This power is not just legal power; it could be cultural power as well. Legal power is more readily understood, whereas cultural power may not be so easy to understand in American society. For example, laws don't grant any rights to parents to beat their children in China, but almost every Chinese parent has spanked his or her child. Police don't have the right to interfere with parents physically disciplining their children unless a child's life is in danger. Who gives parents the right to spank or even beat their children? Society and culture. It is difficult for Chinese parents to believe that American children have legal rights to call the police if they are beaten by their parents.

Authority implies a force that can make people obey you willingly. Authority includes not only power, but also prestige, might, and dignity, among other terms. In fact, the Chinese concept of authority is close to German sociologist Max Weber's concept of charismatic authority, but the Chinese put the emphasis more strongly on internal influence.

Authority could imply power, but power does not necessarily include authority. Authority can sincerely convince people, though it may not change their minds. It can exert mental and spiritual pressure and influence people internally. Power, on the other hand, is physical and external; you can force someone to do something differently with power but rarely will you convince them that you are correct.[5]

People who have power may not have authority, and people who have authority may not have power. The President of the United States undoubtedly has tremendous power. Some presidents, however, do not have any authority in the minds of the common people; these presidents become targets to be ridiculed. Teachers who have power may not have authority in their students' minds. They can yell so loud that their throats become sore but none of their students will listen to them. In contrast, some students who have no power in the classroom speak one word that ends up being more powerful than a thousand sentences spoken by the teacher. It sometimes is hard to describe where authority comes from. One glance from someone may be enough to build his or her authority in another's mind.

My father was forced to endure all kinds of hardships; in terms of academics, I have learned much from him. However, though I understand my father's power, he never built his authority in my mind.

My mother didn't teach me much in terms of schoolwork, but I have an intangible reverence for her that I simply cannot describe. She loved to visit her students' homes (which was the Chinese educational tradition). It didn't matter whether they were good, bad, or weak students; as a teacher, she would visit their homes at least once during the school year. My mother not only visited good students' homes, but she also paid particular attention to the bad and/or weak students. She had very serious myopia, so my mother always brought me, her eldest son, as her "little cane" when she visited her students' homes in the evenings. The visits often lasted so long that I was asleep by the time they were over. My mother had to carry me home, staggering under my weight, at the end of the night. My mother called me her cane, but in reality, she was my cane, guiding me through life. Though I lost my mother in 2003, she built authority in my mind that will last forever.

Power implies a material social relationship. For instance, a teacher has power over his or her students. As soon as this relationship is finished, the power won't exist any longer. In other words, without the subordinating relationship of student to teacher, a teacher's power will disappear. However, authority is a transcendent influence. Even after the binding of power has been released, the influence still exists. For example, my mother's former students, who had left school over thirty years earlier, collected money to rebuild the gate at the school where my mother once taught. The only caveat the students gave was that they wanted to carve my mother's name, the name of an ordinary middle school teacher, on to the gate. This gate now represents the eternal authority a teacher built in her students' minds.

This is the difference between power and authority.

4

American education and parenting generally rely on power as opposed to building authority. How many American children remain close to their parents and feel gratitude toward them after they have left home, particularly after marriage? How many American students contact or even remember their teachers years after they have graduated?

As a professor, I remember almost all my students and think about them very often, even miss them sometimes, but how many of them remember me? I have been trying to build my authority in my students' minds, and according to the teaching evaluations I receive, I believe I have succeeded to some extent. One thing we Chinese-American professors often sigh about is that some American students do not remember anything about you no matter how much you have done for them.

Chinese-American parenting does not rely on power but on authority.

Everyone says parents are the first teachers for children because, from the perspective of time, as soon as children come into this world and open their eyes, the first people they usually see are their parents. They also associate with parents for a large part of their lives. From the perspective of space, the distance between the child and the parents is the closest—from being held in the parents' arms to the parents patting the child's shoulders when seeing them off from home.

However, as time goes on, this first teacher also becomes the target that children rebel against. The child will hear advice from and listen to anyone except his or her parents. If the parents tell the child to go east, then the child will head west. In this phase, children manage to do only what their parents don't want them to and refuse to do what their parents ask them to do. Often, the problem isn't what the parents are saying, but rather, who is saying it. How many times have you heard the word *no* come out of a child's mouth before the parent has even finished speaking the first word of a sentence? The first teacher becomes the first target during a child's rebellion. Many parents can only shake their heads and let out a deep sigh at this stage.

5

Of course, this phenomenon happens in both American and Chinese-American families. This kind of conflict, however, may not be very strong and often does not last very long in new Chinese-American immigrant families, particularly the first generation of immigrant families. Why? Let us compare the differences between Chinese and American families in how parents convince children of what to do and what not to do.

Chinese	American
Parents convince children.	Parents, teachers, and religious figures convince children.
The actions of parents convince children.	The words of parents, teachers, and religious figures educate children.
Silence is the tool to convince children.	Yelling is the tool to convince children.
Convince children using facts from parents.	Convince children using reasons from parents and teachers.
Parents' sacrifices convince children.	Parents' offers convince children.
Convince children with authority.	Convince children with power.

In new immigrant families, parents are the sole source of guidance for children. Because of the cultural divide and the psychological distance that language barriers create, immigrant children often don't trust American schools and society right away. It's parents who hold sole authority and power over their children, not schools and churches.

6

An important character of Chinese-American parenting is to use the authority parents have built in their children's mind to educate them.

After Yan went to university, the three of us had a discussion about our parenting style and choices. We often have this kind of theoretical discussion; it's a way for us to keep the lines of communication with Yan open.

We compared American parenting with Chinese tradition. We found out that they represented two different ways of parenting: lenience versus compulsion.

"What is our . . . or your style?" Yan asked.

"Authority," I firmly said, "which lies between these two."

My wife and I have not involved ourselves with Yan's study habits and lifestyle too much. We asked him to teach himself the material in advance, and once he was in the habit of doing this, we took a step back. As long as his grades were good, we didn't care much when or how much he studied; we allowed him to manage his studying himself. We usually didn't even know about important exams until after the fact, when he showed us how he did. When Yan was in high school, he struggled through a painful and difficult period, prioritizing his social life and fun experiences over his schooling. We kept our eyes on him and tried to talk to him as much as possible. And when some improper behavior came into play, we seriously warned him against acting out. For the most part, we let him listen to his own conscience and learn his own lessons.

After Yan went to college he said to us, "If I hadn't gone through that period of struggling during high school, I'd probably still be naïve and immature today."

The authoritative parenting style uses authority, which is built into a child's mind, to keep communication open with him or her. It instills education and activates that inner drive in a child's mind while also respecting the child's rights and needs.

In the West, most people claim to belong to a church or believe in some kind of religion. Therefore, teachers are not holy. However, there is no religion for the vast majority of the Chinese population.[6] Therefore, parents are holy, and due to the Confucian tradition teachers are also sanctified. As such, parents have a chance to build their authority in children's minds.

7

How do Chinese-American parents build their authority?

Many immigrant families, particularly the first generation, started from poverty and built their achievements step by step. More importantly, the children experienced this firsthand; the parents' difficulties and struggles live on in the memories of the kids. When parents silently sacrifice themselves, contributing whatever they can toward their children's wants and needs, they simultaneously build authority in their kids' minds.

Parents who do not value hard work yet yell at their children to study will likely have no effect on their children. On the contrary, just one look from parents who work hard toward their goals and make sacrifices for the family can shock a child. The parents who started from nothing and reached their American Dream are models for the child reaching for his or her dreams. Obviously, this model has inexhaustible authority and special persuasive abilities.

I don't want to brag, but I can use myself as an example. With only $55 in my pocket, I came to America when I was thirty-six years old. I used my second language—English—to pursue a master's degree and then a doctorate. After I graduated in 1993, I published two books and one dictionary in America and eight bestsellers and another dictionary in China. One of them was the top best-selling nonfiction book in China in 2000. Because of how my educational theories strongly influenced Chinese educational reform, Miami University granted me the Profound Impact Award in 2007. On top of this, I once had my own import/export business.

I really love to research and write. Every day I set aside writing time after I come home from work. I even have a writing plan, with a goal of writing three pages per day, and I have adhered to this plan for years. Through this process, I've not only written quite a few books, but I've also built an intangible authority in my son's mind. Yan has loved writing ever since he was very young. Regardless of what the contents of his writing were, he always achieved good results. He published two bestsellers in China and Taiwan when he was only a teenager. After he went to college, he still pursued writing, publishing essays, short stories, and a dictionary, all while attending a prestigious law school.

In order to establish parental authority, it's important to build a harmonious relationship between parents and children. While children will take examples and inspiration from the parents' behavior, it's also important to respect the child's independence and interests. If you have authority in a child's mind, he or she will be willing to listen to your guidance.

It's difficult for parents to maintain authority during a child's teenage years. Not only will children begin to rely more on their social experiences and increasing personal knowledge, they will also naturally begin to reexamine their parents. This is a critical time in maintaining parental authority. If parents fail to negotiate this phase with care, they will lose the opportunity to educate, influence, and guide their children.

Of course, quite a few Chinese-American parents utilize the power parenting style as opposed to one of authority. They force children to obey their absolute power and develop solely according to their design and plan. The kids may be outstanding in school, but they will probably not be so outstanding in society. Their creativity and career achievements, as compared to others', may not be so excellent.

8

Many American children see signs of their parents' success—driving a Mercedes-Benz, living in an expensive house, boating during the summer, skiing in the mountains during the winter. In a child's mind, this success seems as easy as buying chicken from a grocery store. Without seeing how hard their parents worked and the difficulties they faced to achieve this success, they will never understand how valuable it is. If the parents' work on a daily basis looks simple and easy, what chance do the parents have of building authority in their children's minds? Not a very good one; therefore, they have only power.

Parents who believe in a lenient parenting style not only do not have authority, they also give up their power to others, such as school, churches, or their children's peers. They allow their children to do whatever they want, letting them run their own course and follow their own whims without interference. This amount of freedom isn't conducive to a child's healthy development.

DIALOGUE

American parents: It's very interesting to read this section because we're surprised to realize that we, as parents, have power, but we may not have built authority in our children's mind. Now, how do we turn our power into authority?

Huang: First of all is sacrifice. If you sacrifice yourself for your children in whatever way you think is best, you will be more persuasive. Second, involve yourself in your children's education and studying. If you don't, they won't think you have any right to speak on the matter, and indeed you won't know what you're talking about regarding their schooling. If that's the case, how can your children respect you, and how can you possibly build authority in their minds?

American parents: American kids are very independent, so it's very hard to turn power into authority.

Huang: Yes and no. They are independent, but you must build authority in their minds rather than use your power to coerce them. The way to build this authority is to model for them the virtues of setting goals and working hard to achieve those goals. If you wish to convince your children to work hard and achieve ambitious goals, you will not be persuasive unless you succeed in modeling that behavior for your kids.

American parents: What else can we do to make building authority easier?

Huang: In addition to the other suggestions I have outlined, you should avoid treating the relationship between parent and child as a purely material relationship. It should be treated as a spiritual relationship as well. Parents are not only materially responsible for their children (providing them food, clothing, shelter, and such); they are also spiritually responsible for them. Americans can follow the example of ministers and religious figures as well as that of American teachers like Ms. Schultz, my son's beloved teacher, to see how power can be turned into authority.

CHINESE PARENTS AND "GREED"

1

Last year, while I was in Beijing for a conference, a friend of mine invited me to dinner. He wanted to discuss children's education, but he looked blue and drank silently when I brought up the subject.

I asked, "How is your son?"

When he was reluctant to respond, I added, "If you don't want talk about this right now, you'll have to treat me to dinner again tomorrow night so we can discuss it then!"

He sighed and said, "Please don't even bring it up. His grades are low, in the bottom 5 percent of his class."

"The bottom five?" I asked incredulously. It was no wonder he was anxious and looked as though doomsday was coming.

With some delicacy, I asked, "How many students are in his class?"

He didn't even raise his head when he said, "More than sixty."

With even greater care I inquired, "What's your son's grade average?"

He didn't answer, instead drinking deeply from his glass of wine. Finally, he gathered up his courage and said, embarrassed, "He has a 95!"

I couldn't help but laugh at this, especially considering how low my friend's spirits were. "A 95? You never know, your son may be the most promising kid in his class!"

His eyes glistened. "Excuse me . . . are you joking? Why do you say that?"

I said, "You're the CEO of a large, successful company. What was *your* class rank when you were his age?"

"I don't know," he responded suspiciously as he refilled his wine glass. "We weren't ranked then, but it was probably above average. My average grade was about an 80."

I took his glass of wine from him triumphantly and said, "That's it! What are the people who were ranked at the top of your class doing right now? Not much, are they? It's like this cup. It's full right now, and just like it, students who do perfectly in school are full. But that means there's no room for individual development; their heads are stuffed only with what their teachers have told them. Your son has a 95; it's a good average, and it still leaves room for his own individual development." I couldn't help myself as I teased, "Actually, to be quite frank, 95 is a little high. There might not be enough extra room for him to develop. . . ."

My friend was screaming in frustration by this point. "This is my punishment for drinking a full glass of wine, isn't it?"

I smiled and said, "Why are you worrying about a 95? Don't you think that's a bit silly?"

He shook his head and smiled bitterly.

I said again, "You think your son should do better than a 95? You're being greedy."

By now, others at the dinner were listening in on our conversation. They interjected, "Punish him with one more drink!" In Chinese culture, drinking is sometimes considered a game. The person who drinks the least wins, and the crowd was intent on making sure my friend lost.

By this point, he was happier because he realized that I was correct. He yelled at the crowd, "Come on! Are you guys any different? Who doesn't want their kids to do better in school? Anyone?"

I couldn't tell how much of my friend's happiness that night was from our discussion and how much was because of the wine. But after I returned to my hotel, I lay in bed thinking over our conversation. Aren't I greedy as well with my son's grades?

2

What happens when an American child brings home a bad grade on a test? Is it any different from what would happen to Chinese children? Imagine that nine-year-old Johnny just came home clutching a math test with a big, bright red D+ in the corner.

Based on popular media, we suspect that, although Johnny's parents would be disappointed (and perhaps even concerned) if Johnny got a D+, they would take care not to hurt his feelings or self-esteem.

On the other hand, in the image of the Tiger Mother, there is a popular belief that Chinese parents are harsh, authoritative, uncompromising, and even cruel.

Having lived in both China and America, having raised my own Chinese-American son in America, and having been in contact with countless American and Chinese parents, I must emphasize again that the popular view of Chinese parenting on this point is, for the most part, wrong. If you go looking, you're sure to find a few fierce Tiger Mothers like Amy Chua out there, throwing tantrums and hurling abuses. Those Chinese parents do exist. I'm sure American parents like that exist as well. People often misinterpret what Chinese parenting is all about. But looking at only what some Chinese parents do instead of why they do it makes it too easy to mistake the forest for the trees.

3

In 2006, Dr. Florrie Ng, a researcher at the University of Illinois, and her colleagues conducted a fascinating study that looked into what I would describe as the main difference between Chinese and American parenting. To do this, Dr. Ng asked over one hundred fourth and fifth graders, half of them from Hong Kong and half of them from the American Midwest, to take a short logical reasoning test. Each child was accompanied by his or her mother.[7]

Dr. Ng's intent was quite different from what it appeared to be on the surface. The point of this exercise was not to study reasoning but to uncover the different approaches Chinese and American parents utilized with their children, which was what made it so interesting. How do Chinese and American parents react when they're told their child has done well, but not perfectly, on a test? How do Chinese and American parents react when they're told their child has failed to do well on a test?

Dr. Ng was able to design two versions of the tests:

(1) a SUCCESS condition test full of very easy questions and a few difficult ones, and

(2) a FAILURE condition test full of difficult questions and several *very* difficult ones.

None of the children taking the tests (nor their mothers) knew that there were two versions of the test. Children taking the SUCCESS version of the test would naturally do very well overall but not perfectly—missing only a few out of twelve total questions. Children taking the FAILURE test were doomed to do poorly, missing the majority of the questions.

Under these conditions, about half of the Hong Kong children and half of the American children were chosen at random to take the easy version of the test. As expected, these children all received relatively high but not necessarily perfect scores. The other half of the children were given the very difficult version of the test. This resulted in a relatively low score for most of them, and this is where things get interesting. The children's answer sheets were graded, and their scores were written on the top part of the answer sheet. Those in the SUCCESS condition were all told, "You have done well," whereas those in the FAILURE condition were told, "You didn't do too well."

After informing the mothers, the experimenter then left the room, giving the children and mothers a five minute break together in the testing room. The mothers were informed that, after the break, the children would be asked to tackle some more problems similar to those they had just completed.

What did Dr. Ng discover after reviewing the tapes?

- The Chinese mothers issued less overt praise and more negative comments.
- The Chinese mothers were far more focused and interested in immediately preparing their children for the second test.
- The Chinese mothers asked their children many more questions about the test.

Other interesting findings:

- Though Chinese parents made more negative statements, their general affects—their tones and the ways in which they behaved with their children—were not harsher or more negative than American parents.
- For most of the experiment, there was no noticeable cultural difference in the ways Chinese and American mothers behaved toward their children.

- In fact, the only difference was seen in the group of children who did "well," where the Chinese mothers' affects were generally far more *positive* than the American mothers.

Though they seemed to be more interested in general, Chinese mothers made noticeably fewer positive child-centered comments compared to American mothers. In general, the Chinese mothers—even the ones whose children had been in the SUCCESS group—made few positive comments.

The only cultural difference in affect Dr. Ng did observe was that Chinese mothers showed *more* positive affect than American mothers in the SUCCESS condition.

How can we explain this disparity? What does Dr. Ng's study tell us about Chinese parenting? Is it consistent or inconsistent with the stereotypical view of Asian parents? Based on her study, what would you say is the main difference between Chinese and American parenting with regard to children's education?

4

I first learned about Dr. Ng's study when a colleague of mine showed it to me. We often discussed educational concepts and ideas, particularly ones having to do with Chinese education.

"Can you explain that last part?" he asked me. "I always thought that Chinese parents were stricter with their kids. We always hear about how Chinese parents never praise their kids, how they're never happy with their child's performances, and how they always demand that they be better and better. Is this just an error? How come the researchers didn't find that the Chinese mothers were more negative overall? How is it possible that they seemed to be genuinely happier in some cases? Is it still true that Chinese parents praise their kids less and punish them more? Do we have to throw that out now?"

At the time, I looked at him and I shrugged.

"I don't know," I said. "Let me think about it."

The truth was that I was also initially confused by the study. I had the very same questions as my colleague. Upon consideration, there could have been many different reasons for the test results being different from what we expected. For instance, the test featured Raven's Progressive Matrices instead of standard academic (math, science, or reading) questions. Chinese mothers may not have known how to react to these problems, which could have been why Chinese mothers questioned their children more about the test. Additionally, because there were many different mothers and children in the same room, mothers may have acted differently for face-saving reasons. They could have also been apprehensive about the second test awaiting their children. I pondered these questions, but it was once again on the soccer field that the spark, the igniting breakthrough moment, came to me.

Yan continued to play soccer every season until his sophomore year in high school, when he picked up tennis instead. During this period, I'd attended just about every single game he played. Over the course of eight years and sixteen seasons (including both spring and fall), I estimated that I'd watched my son play about two hundred games.

Since I was my son's first coach and I'd taught him most of his basic soccer skills and tactics, we had a tradition where I'd give him a critique after every game. On the car ride home, I would replay portions of the game in my head and issue my analysis and assessment, such as, "When you are approaching the goal with the ball at that speed, son, don't just think about kicking it hard. Shot placement and timing are just as important, if not more!" I made many similar comments to Yan about his playing over the years.

Reading over Dr. Ng's study, it occurred to me that she would place my feedback to Yan in the "neutral" or "negative" task-related-statements categories. I realized that the balance of what I said to my son after his games consisted of direct assessments of where I thought he could improve. It was almost never "positive." Thinking back, it hit me that in the entire time I'd watched him play soccer, I'd only really praised him a few times. I could count on one hand the number of times I ever told him that he played "well": four times.

In Yan's very first game, when I was unofficially involved in coaching (our best friend Helaine was the coach), Yan scored three goals in a row on his own. One of those goals was what I call a "Pelé" goal, where he retrieved the ball deep in our own end of the field and then carried it singlehandedly down field and scored, dribbling past half of the other team's players. After the game, however, as I debriefed our team, I didn't mention Yan's Pelé goal. Instead, I pointed out that he had missed an easy penalty kick in the last quarter on which he should have scored. "You used the wrong type of kick," I told him. "You *chipped* the ball, that's why it went over the goal. You have to STRIKE it with your instep. Don't chip the ball. We worked on this."

Almost immediately after that, Helaine came over and pulled me aside. She asked me why I was being so hard on Yan.

"Why didn't you tell him he did a good job? Why didn't you mention that goal where he carried it all the way down the field?" she asked.

"There was really nothing to say about that," I said. "He didn't make any mistakes there."

5

The truth was that I rarely felt disappointed by Yan's performance at soccer. There were a few times that Yan did not play well at all, but, to be honest, I was not just pleased but genuinely happy with how he played the vast majority of the time. When Yan played well, I would often smile for the entire day and well into the next day. Anyone who has ever taught or coached someone else knows that wonderful feeling of elation and validation when the student is able to successfully implement the things you've shown them.

But I never openly told him I felt this way. Apart from those four games in which he played exceptionally, I rarely praised his performance on the field. Instead, I would constantly try to highlight areas where I thought he could improve. Even when he played very well, I would make it my policy to always point out a few things that I thought he could do better.

I did this to keep Yan from getting complacent. I didn't want him to stop *feeling* like he needed to improve. I watched other American parents around me openly throwing around lavish praise for what I would describe as mediocre performances. I often wondered what the child thought in that situation. Does the child actually know how well or poorly he played? If he doesn't, doesn't this further skew his ability to self-assess his performance? If he cannot properly assess how well he is doing, how can he ever improve? If the child does know how well or poorly he played, does hollow praise do anything at all? Does it raise his spirits? Could it, instead, dampen them if he suspects those who praise him are not being forthright?

I decided this route was far too complicated. I wanted my son to know where he stood, to have the ability to self-assess in an objective way, and, in the end, to constantly improve. I wanted my son to know that I said what I meant, not only when I criticized him but also when I praised him. I wanted him to know that when I did praise him, it was a heartfelt and genuine compliment.

When Chinese parents watch their children do something well, but not perfectly, they are put in this same odd position. Traditionally, even when the child does something well, the issuing of verbal praise is not a matter of course. No matter what the child is doing, whether it is school, sports, or playing an instrument, Chinese parents tend to keep the outward praise to a minimum.

6

Many Americans know the Chinese proverb: "Give a man a fish and you feed him for a day. Teach a man to fish and you feed him for a lifetime." But there's another Chinese story about fishing that most Americans probably are less familiar with.

An old man fished daily off reef of a beautiful beach. He would arrive at an appointed time each day and cast his line for only two hours regardless of how lucky or unlucky he was. A young man who observed this strange behavior asked his elder with amazement, "Why don't you continue to fish the entire day when you are lucky? If you do so, you can catch more fish and sell them to get more money."

"Get money for what?" the old man calmly replied.

"You can buy fishing nets to catch more fish to get more money."

"Get more money for what?"

"You can buy a fishing boat to put out to sea and catch more fish to earn even more money."

"Earn even more money for what?"

"To set up an ocean going company to catch fish or to ship goods and materials to major ports around the world. You can command great wealth!" exclaimed the young man.

With a hint of mockery in the old man's tone he retorted, "Command great wealth? Why?"

The young man flushed with rage, "Why don't you want to earn as much as you can?"

The old man smiled passively, "I fish two hours a day. I dress warmly and can eat my fill each day. As for the rest of my time, I can greet the golden sunshine of an awakening day or enjoy a crimson sunset at eventide. I can feel the moist warmth of the earth as I snuggle a seed into its bowels. I can enjoy the subtle scent of flowering plants. Why should I earn more money?"

The young man remained silent for several thousand years. He and his progeny have thought deeply about its essence for many generations.[8]

7

This is a very interesting but contradictory phenomenon: in regard to money, people's states of mind have changed drastically over the years. In China, after the Cultural Revolution, the government instituted a policy called "Reforming and Opening." Deng Xiaoping openly encouraged the acquisition of wealth and working to become rich. China has officially embraced a market economy since 1992; these days, you would have an extremely difficult time finding people in China who have the same views on wealth as the old man in the story. If the old man represents the old views about money, of being content with one's lot in life, then the young man can be thought to represent Chinese and Chinese-American parents, who are greedy about their kids' scores and achievements.

When it comes to Chinese parents, I've never found or heard of a single one among my countless friends, colleagues, readers, and acquaintances who isn't greedy about his or her child's grades. It doesn't matter whether they live in America or China; the fact is, all Chinese parents want their children to do better, even if, by American standards, the child is excelling in school. If a child's GPA is a 3.5, his or her parents would want a 3.8. After he or she has struggled to achieve a 3.8, the parents will respond, "Our neighbor's son has a GPA of 3.9. How come you only have a 3.8?" If by any chance the child reached a 3.9, the parents would say, "Our friend's daughter has a perfect 4.0 GPA. If she can do it, why can't you?" It's a continuous cycle that goes on and on, never stopping.

When Yan was in high school, he told his friend, Brian, "You know, my SAT score was almost 1500 but my parents said if I could actually get a 1500, they'll buy me a PlayStation 2."

Brian joked, "See, that's the difference. My mom said if I can pass Chemistry this semester, I'll get an Xbox." (Actually, poor Brian didn't receive an Xbox when he passed Chemistry.)

It sounds like a joke, but this really does happen in almost every Chinese-American family. The LSAT, the test that students take for law school admission, is an extremely difficult test. We were thrilled when Yan brought home a very high score on the test. At least, we were at first. One day, Yan admitted that he had made two very stupid mistakes in the reading comprehension section. If he hadn't made those errors, his score would have been even higher. We lamented to ourselves, "Oh, if he hadn't made those two mistakes he could have gotten an almost perfect score!" Though we didn't mention our thoughts to Yan, we often indicated our regret to others. We knew that if he had received that higher score, we still wouldn't have been satisfied, desirous instead of a perfect score. And if he had achieved a perfect score? We would have been greedy about something else—our greed never stops!

In addition to setting continually higher goals for their children, Chinese-American parents also like to compare their children's weaknesses with other children's strengths. "Oh, his son got into Harvard, but my son only got into Yale!" "Her daughter plays the piano very well, but our daughter doesn't play the violin nearly as well." For good reason, Chinese parents have been labeled greedy.

8

People often see the greed of Chinese-American parents as a negative and criticize it. But why don't we look at it a different way and reconsider the issue? The Chinese traditional view of supremacy of education is what drives parents' greed. But this doesn't come from a place of complete selfishness. Yes, it may be partly due to vanity and pride in one's children (one's own child is better than other children). But the parents may also worry about their children and want them to do better. Their greed, then, gives their children the impetus to study longer and harder. Without that inner driver of greed, human beings would be content with their lot and make no attempts toward progress. We might still live in caves and wear leaves if it wasn't for greed, the desire for something better. Chinese-American children have been making great achievements in their schools. But should we also give credit to the parents who are driving forces behind that achievement, who push and push without stopping?

Of course, too much of anything is never good, and, as such, pushing too hard isn't good for children. Once a certain limit is reached, parents' pushing might have the opposite effect than what's desired.

You may think of it however you want to, but I choose to consider the greed of Chinese-American parents from a positive perspective. It pushes Chinese-American children to continually make progress, driving them forward such that one achievement follows another.

If you agree with the young man's ideas about wealth in the story I told earlier, then you should consider his thoughts from the perspective of studying rather than money. Only by continually making progress are you able to succeed again and again. Think about it: if you're satisfied with a C, will you ever be motivated to try harder for a B, much less an A?

Now reconsider the old man's story, but replace the concept of fishing with that of studying and education.

> The old man smiled passively, "I *study* two hours a day. I dress warmly and can eat my fill each day. As for the rest of my time, I can greet the golden sunshine of an awakening day or enjoy a crimson sunset at eventide. I can feel the moist warmth of the earth as I snuggle a seed into its bowels. I can enjoy the subtle scent of flowering plants. Why should I gain *a higher score*?"

After reading this revised story, what reaction do you have? Has your opinion about greed for children's grades and scores changed at all?

9

There are some interesting differences in how parents deal with children's studying between Chinese and American parents:

Chinese	American
Greedy about scores.	Content with scores.
Never stop pushing—study harder!	Stop a child's studying if the child feels tired.
Studying is also the parent's business.	Studying is only the child's business.
Reward good grades and scores materially rather than orally.	Reward good grades and scores orally rather than materially.

I've repeated a survey many times in my classes, and in each one I receive the same results: all Asian-American parents are greedy and all American parents are content with their children's grades.

If we consider Asian-American parents as selfish because of their greed, does that mean that American parents are unselfish because they're content with their children's grades?

Is this view worth rethinking?

DIALOGUE

American parents: *Greed* doesn't sound like a very good word.

Huang: That's true, but greed is not a bad thing at all. It's a parent's expectations for their children, but it also asks for sacrifices from parents. As soon as you set a high goal or cultivate great ambition, you'll naturally become greedy.

American parents: The story about the old man and the fish is very thoughtful. If we use greed as a positive tool for our children's studying, what should we be aware of?

Huang: There are three different things you should take into account.

- Your greed must match your sacrifices. In other words, you can't be extremely greedy if you haven't sacrificed much for your children. You won't have authority in their minds, and thus, they won't listen to you.
- Your greed needs to match up with the goals, talents, and interests of your child. You can't expect your son to be a great singer if, like Yan, he has no singing talent.
- Greed puts pressure on your child, but you should consider it pressure on yourself first and foremost. Your greed has to be directly proportional to your sacrifice. Otherwise, you'll put unlimited pressure on your kids and have entirely too much greed. If you're putting the same amount of pressure on yourself, you'll understand how much greed is enough for you.

CHAPTER 5
THE LIFE UNION AS A MODEL FOR FAMILY

"The small streams rise when the main stream is high" versus
"the main stream is high when the small streams rise." Chinese
culture believes the former and views this as "viewing the
situation as a whole." So, each person in a family must make
supremacy of education their priority, to contribute and even
sacrifice whatever is needed for supporting kids' achievements.

A "ME" OR AN "I"?

1

One day while studying for my doctorate I addressed the fact that the Chinese often operate under a collectivist and sacrificial style of cooperation. Americans, in contrast, operate under an individualist and competitive form of self-reliance. At first, many were unconvinced. I even had a small argument with one of my classmates who didn't believe what I was saying.

"I have an example of a Chinese person achieving as an individual and not as part of a collective," one of my classmates said. "Last night, I watched a little sixteen-year-old Chinese girl win an Olympic gold medal in diving. You say that the Chinese achieve things mainly through cooperative and collective action, but diving is an individual sport! She had no teammates. She won all by herself! She climbed up that tall ladder to the ten-meter platform and she did seven or eight absolutely breathtaking and *perfect* dives on her own. Now she is an Olympic champion. Mr. Huang, can you explain that?"

"Sure. In fact," I said happily, "I should say 'thank you' because that is a great example of what I'm talking about! Even though diving is an individual sport, it is still easy to see how a collection of people produced this result."

"Okay, I'm listening."

"You say she was only sixteen, right? Do you think she was really able to stand up there on her own, at that age, in front of the entire world? Do you think her success was solely an individual effort? Whose goal do you think it was for her to win a gold medal? Was it her own goal? Did she decide on her own, when she was a toddler, to become an Olympic gold medalist diver as a teenager? Probably not. This was China's goal. This goal existed long before she was born, and it still exists outside of her. The little girl was not an individual athlete achieving for herself. She was a representative of China who was chosen and trained specifically to win this medal.

"If she is like any other Chinese Olympic athlete, she had a massive collection of people helping her along the way. Everyone involved had to make sacrifices to get her to where she ended up. She was most likely selected to become a diver at a very young age by a government coach, roughly comparable to an American scout. The coach, in many cases, had to travel far and wide, often thousands of miles into the countryside to find the kids with the most potential. That is the first sacrifice, the time and effort of the coach. After she was discovered, her parents had to make another sacrifice. Because child athletes are usually trained in centers far from home, her parents had to sacrifice their child! This is probably the biggest sacrifice overall from an American perspective.

"But it doesn't end with the parents. Who else had to sacrifice? Her coaches and trainers! How much time and effort do you think they put into this little girl's diving? How about her maids and her cooks? And, most of all, what about the little girl herself? Do you think this little girl would have chosen to be a diver if it was simply her individual choice? Between the little girl, her parents, her coaches and doctors, her maids and cooks, and the country of China itself, everyone's interests had to be *aligned together*. Everyone worked together to put that little girl on that platform, not just herself."

"But . . . isn't that unfair?" My classmate asked after some hesitation.

"Maybe," I answered. "But that is the Chinese way."

"No, no, I mean, isn't that unfair for us, for America," he clarified. "What I mean is, for American divers to compete against Chinese divers like this little girl, how could we ever win? In America, you can't force children to give up their education to go train in diving. Parents can say, 'No!' On top of that, most of our athletes are discovered in college. They are basically responsible for their own training. No one cooks for them or cleans up after them. Many of them may have to study and work other jobs. They can't devote every ounce of their effort to diving. Isn't it unfair that the Chinese athletes can simply focus on diving and have everything else provided for them while the American divers have to do it on their own?"

"I am listening." I said.

"As long as the collective holds together," he went on, "as long as it continues to function, the Chinese diver will have the advantage, won't she? Isn't it possible that this advantage is so great that no amount of talent and effort by any one person can ever overcome it?"

"Ah," said our professor, stepping in at just the right moment. "That is the question then, isn't it? What happens when you take away the collective?"

The professor's question resonated with me deeply. I thought about it for years to come. What does happen when the collective effort ends? Would Chinese divers still be able to perform as that sixteen-year-old champion had? If she were made to train on her own for the next Olympics, would she be able to come back and win again? If not, what does that tell us about her "education" as a diver? Was she truly better than the others, all those divers who didn't have the advantages provided by the Chinese collective effort?

2

Of course, when pursuing certain desirable ends, the Chinese often operate under a collectivist, sacrificial style of cooperation. Americans, by contrast, operate under an individualistic and competitive form of self-reliance. When something important is on the line, Chinese people will aggregate their talents and resources and dole out specific responsibilities to individual members of the collective. In order to fulfill their responsibilities, the individuals are expected to sacrifice their own ideals, desires, and goals. The goals of the collective come before those of the individual members.

In America, however, the pursuit of something as a true collective is difficult. In certain situations, it may even be impossible. This is because Americans believe strongly in inalienable individual rights, rights that cannot be violated by any other person or entity. Even the government cannot take an American's freedoms or property without due process or compensation. An American need not take any action he or she does not want to take. This emphasis on individual rights can often clash with the idea of a collective, where one or more members may need to sacrifice their ideals, desires, or goals for the good of the group. While *teamwork* is a popular term, when the rubber meets the road, Americans will rarely be comfortable forcing anyone to sacrifice their own rights.

In contrast, the Chinese have learned that the easiest and most efficient way to seek achievements (that is, to win something) is for everyone to work together toward that common goal. Working together means everyone's interests must be aligned. When an individual's interests differ from those of the collective in some way that is potentially harmful, those interests must fall into line. The divergent interests must be trimmed or adjusted. When necessary, they must be suppressed. The collective goal is far more important than any individual's ideals. The result is something that strikes many Americans as odd or "unfair."

My classmate asked another question during this exchange: "American divers need coaches and doctors as well, but why do Chinese divers need cooks?"

This is a puzzle for many Americans.

3

Professional Chinese athletes concentrate only on training. Excelling at their sport is the only thing that matters to them. As such, China provides professional cooks for their athletes. While my family had heard many stories about this phenomenon, we once experienced it firsthand.

In December 2009, the Tsinghai University Diving Team came to America for a competition. The coach, Yu Fen, who has probably fostered the most Olympic and world champions of anyone today, asked me whether, after the contest, her team could stay at my house for a few days. She asked, "Is your house big enough for my entire team?"

I asked, "Well, how many people are on your team?"

"Sixteen people altogether." she said.

I said, "Don't worry! We'll make room for the team."

I didn't even worry about where each team member would sleep— downstairs, upstairs, the basement—there were people everywhere! However, I neglected to consider one important problem: they might be excellent coaches, divers, and doctors but not a single one of them knew how to cook.

Have you ever tried cooking for almost twenty people (including ourselves) for two straight days? It kept me and my wife busy every second. For two days, all we did was cook and cook.

We were planning on seeing the team off at the airport very early on the morning of the third day, but we were so tired from all the cooking that we slept like logs. We didn't stir when they were leaving, and they didn't want to bother us, so they quietly left. When we woke up, it was to an empty house. The entire three-day period has become a joke among our friends.

4

A coin always has two sides. Chinese professional athletes don't know how to cook, and it seems ridiculous; on the other hand, when all members in a group contributes their unique and special talents, and a collectivist, sacrificial style of cooperation is implemented, can you see how powerful this group can be?

Here are some differences between the Chinese collectivist and sacrificial style of cooperation and the American individualistic and competitive form of self-reliance.

Chinese	American
The small streams rise when the main stream is high.	The main stream is high when the small streams rise.
Cooperation based on shared goals and member sacrifice.	Cooperation based on aligning or coordinating each person's individual goals or desires.
Compete collectively.	Compete individually against other individuals.
Your sport (study) is not only for yourself; it is also for your family, your organization, or even your country.	Your sport (study) is only for yourself.
Rely on a group.	Stand on your own.

At the opening ceremony of the Summer Olympics held in Beijing in 2008, a very adorable girl, Lin Miaoke, sang a beautiful song that moved many people. However, later it was revealed that this lovely little girl didn't really sing the song; she lip synched to another little girl's singing voice. To the Chinese, an adorable face combined with a beautiful voice resulted in the perfect outcome. Reporters and people around the world asked the girl who provided the recorded voice,

"Are you sad that you didn't get to be on television and sing the song to the world?" The seven-year-old girl, Yang Peiyi, said, "No, not at all. As long as we can gain a respectful 'face' for China, I am satisfied."[1]

If an entire group's strengths and talents combine to compete with others, that group has an advantage and will almost certainly win. The Chinese table tennis and badminton teams have won many, many world championships, both on an individual and collective basis. However, are you sure the person who wins is actually the best? Did you know that Chinese champions often climb atop others' shoulders on their way to the top? Did you know there might be many unknown stories behind what you see in front of you?

5

Here is an interesting story that is well known in China; however, it may bother Americans.

Ms. He Zhili, a former World Cup table tennis champion for China, beat all the Chinese players to win the championship of the 12th Asian Games in 1994, playing for Japan. This sweep shocked the Chinese people.

But the origin of the story goes back to when Ms. He played on the Chinese table tennis team. In 1987, her coach instructed her to intentionally lose a semifinal match in the world championships against Guan Jianhua, a fellow Chinese player who was considered more likely to win a potential finals matchup with a Korean player. However, despite the instructions to lose, she beat Guan (as well as her South Korean opponent in the final). However, she paid a high price for winning the championship.

For members of the Chinese delegation and coaching staff, the true shock wasn't Guan's loss; it was a player refusing to abide by the decision of her coaches. This had never happened among Chinese players, and all the members of China's delegation were shocked by Ms. He's behavior.

Chinese people are crazy about table tennis, which they call the national sport, and they were extremely anxious to win the gold medal in table tennis at the Olympic games in 1988 in Seoul, South Korea. Who would be selected to represent China? People began to worry about Ms. He's behavior, and, in the end, she didn't receive a single vote from any of the coaches to be on the team. The Table Tennis Association of China and coaches across China agreed with this decision. Although she had won the 1987 world championship, she was denied a chance to win a gold medal for China at the 1988 Summer Olympics.

She subsequently married a Japanese engineer and moved to Japan, for whom she continued to play table tennis.[2]

<h1 style="text-align:center">6</h1>

Many Americans may criticize the sacrificial style of cooperation espoused by the Chinese. But Chinese people will defend their methods fiercely. Let's use the table tennis team as an example.

First, while it may seem strange that individual players were asked to concede matches, you must remember that it's a table tennis *team*. Understood this way, one can see that the tactic of throwing matches to arrange favorable matchups in future encounters is very similar to changing players in football, basketball, volleyball, or soccer. Since each individual player has different strengths and weaknesses, determining where each player is at their strongest against different opponents is critical strategizing and decision making. Since the 1960s, many excellent table tennis players have conceded games or given up their individual gains in order to win collective honors. This is perhaps the most important tactic that China's table tennis teams have used to win so many championships at international competitions.

Second, without the help and sacrifices of others, how could Ms. He have been a champion? She would have a difficult time answering this question because so many people helped her along the way. This help came from her coaches, doctors, and cooks, but it also came from her fellow players. For instance, suppose Ms. Liang of South Korea was the main opponent of China's team. In preparation, the Table Tennis Association of China would take a hard look at all the players in China to find a player (male or female) who had a similar playing style to Ms. Liang. This player would forfeit his or her training and matches to help He Zhili practice to defeat Ms. Liang. If such a player could not be found, a special coach would imitate Ms. Liang's playing style to train with He Zhili. These special accompanying players are called "unknown heroes." It's the same as it is in boxing. We know Mike Tyson's name because of how majestic he looked in the boxing ring when he knocked down his opponents. We may never know the names of those he sparred with in training, the practice opponents who were beaten so badly they often had to look around for their teeth.

7

In 2002 my son was about to graduate from high school. It was around this time that we decided to visit some of the colleges he would be applying to. During the summer between his junior and senior years, we visited nearly a dozen colleges. On this trip I witnessed something that comes to mind any time someone brings up a similar question to the one my classmate raised about collective cooperation and sacrifice.

By the time we'd visited the fourth or fifth school, I believe it was Johns Hopkins, I noticed something. At Johns Hopkins (and each of the previous schools), we took a guided tour given by a current student. These were always group tours. In every single tour, there was at least one other Chinese family.

"Hey," I whispered to my son, "look at that kid." I pointed furtively to another Chinese boy in our tour group. Yan glanced over and then looked back at me. He frowned.

"I don't get it," he said. "What do you want me to look at?"

"Look at his hands," I whispered back.

"Baba, don't be weird," he said.

"Just look," I said. My son begrudgingly did as I requested.

"What are you talking about?" he asked. "I don't see anything."

"Exactly!"

Every single Chinese child that we saw on these tours walked around empty handed. Though the other kids all usually carried something—a camera, a book bag, or materials handed out by the school admissions offices, the Chinese kids all walked around holding nothing. Where did they keep their things? Without exception, each Chinese child was trailed by his or her parents, each of them carrying backpacks and bags, toting hats and umbrellas, pinching pamphlets and papers under their arms. The parents were loaded up like pack mules! I saw no less than three separate Chinese kids remove a jacket or sweatshirt and nonchalantly toss it to parents who carefully rolled it up and tucked it away into a bag or under their arm. The parents all seemed content to carry all of their children's belongings, allowing them to wander about entirely unburdened.

In contrast, the American kids generally all carried their own things. They carried their own backpacks, bags, and bottles of water. During one of the tours, while it was raining, I saw one American boy do an interesting balancing act while trying to retrieve his camera from his backpack while holding an umbrella. Using both hands, his teeth, and his armpits, he kept the umbrella up and open to block the rain while he dug his camera out of his bag to snap a quick picture. He never looked back for help from his parents, and they never looked at him.

While my son didn't really find this amusing, I certainly did.

"What a perfect illustration of the difference between American kids and Chinese kids," I said to him and his mother later that day. "Don't you agree?"

"I guess so," my son responded. "It's good news for me!" I watched as Yan removed his jacket and balled it up. He thrust it out at me, grinning.

"Thanks, Baba," he said. "My arms are really tired."

Why do Chinese kids and American kids act so differently? If you take a look at their states of mind, you can find an answer easily. Chinese and/or Chinese-American kids usually think that they study for their families or parents. As such, their main task is to study hard; with anything and everything else, their family members, particularly their parents, are responsible for taking care of things.

American kids, however, think that they study for themselves, so they must take care of everything related to their educations, from such small things as holding admissions materials to more important things such as applying for loans for college.

8

If individuals in an organization who give up their interests for collective interests are often unwilling, helpless, and without a choice, parents sacrificing themselves for their children are readily willing, in fact, perfectly happy to without any complaints or regrets. Family priority is given to children, and particularly to children's education. This is the essential principle of Chinese parenting and family education.

This can all be seen as the conflict between the concepts of one's *social role* and one's *self*. In Chinese culture, it is more important for people to fulfill their social role than it is for them to pursue the personal ends of the self. In America, while certain roles are important, the preservation and development of the self is paramount.

Let's look at a metaphor to help understand the difference. When the director of a play casts an actress for a particular role, it is expected that the actress will perform that part according to certain limits. These limits include the lines to be said, the character to be played, and the way those lines will be said to portray that particular character. In other words, even if she has her own strong beliefs about how the role should be performed or she personally despises the words and deeds of the character she is playing, the actress must submit her own views to those of the director. Few directors hate anything more than prima donna actresses who are resistant to direction. In order to put on the best play possible, it is often necessary for the individual actors and actresses to suppress their own ideas, beliefs, ideals, and goals and simply take direction.

Now let's expand that metaphor. Society itself can be seen as a type of "stage" for the play of life. As participants in society, we are subject to social "roles" much like an actress or actor in a stage play. Our roles may include "father" or "son" or "teacher" or "student." The direction we take is provided not by a single director, but by a variety of different cues, rules, and expectations that pressure us into behavior consistent with these social roles. The difference between these two situations, however, is that it isn't terribly difficult for actors and actresses to control themselves and perform their assigned roles in a play. A play is short, and such role-playing can often be an interesting diversion from one's true identity. Life, however, is quite a bit longer. Thus, it is much harder for people in society to consistently stay within the bounds of their social roles. There is a natural yearning to throw off the cowl, cast aside the mask, and act as one wants to act.

9

In America, this tension between one's social role and one's self is often resolved in favor of the self. What is it Americans are so fond of telling their children?

"Just be yourself!"

"Do what you feel is right."

"Find your own passion in life and stick to it."

"Follow your dreams."

These statements reject the idea that people should live their lives taking the direction of society and/or culture. While they don't call for outright rebellion against social expectations, they teach children to be wary of conflicts between their inner self and the roles that society and/or culture would have them play. Indeed, on the frontier, in that old unexplored American West, Americans grew up straddling the border between society and savagery. It took much effort to discern between the two, and it took a certain willingness to buck existing social conventions to settle that great wild land. As a people, Americans are suspicious of the virtue of constant unquestioning conformity to static social roles.

G. H. Mead, a famous American scholar, was, in a sense, similar to the Chinese sage Confucius. Neither directly wrote any philosophical works, but their students edited their class notes and conversations into academic works after they died. Mr. Mead had a famous idea. He argued that the "Self" consisted of two parts—an "I" and a "Me." In brief, the "I" was the subjective "Self" and the "Me" was the objective "Self."[3] While I'm not going to discuss the relationship between the I and the Me as Mead defined them, I am interested in how the social role and the self are differentiated in Western culture as opposed to Chinese culture.

In order to have a better understanding, an easier and a simpler comparison, we can simply think of the me as the social role, and the I is the subjective self.

Western culture prioritizes the I over the me. No matter where it is found in a sentence, the pronoun *I* is always capitalized, whereas the other personal pronouns (*you*, *he*, *she*, and so on, even *me*) are only capitalized when they are at the beginning of a sentence. In Western culture there is more attention paid to the I than to the me. In a similar way, the West also pays greater attention to the self than to the role one is expected to play in society.

In Henrik Ibsen's famous play, when Nora left the doll's house, Helmer said, "Remember—before all else you are a wife and a mother."

To which Nora replied, "I don't believe that anymore. I believe that before all else I am a human being."[4]

10

Many Chinese people, on the other hand, have never even realized that "Who am I?" is a question. The concept of a *subjective* self is largely an alien one in traditional Chinese culture. Chinese people think of themselves in terms of their social role first, such as "wife" or "mother," "husband" or "father."

Interestingly, like with I and me, we can see this relational definition of self reflected in the language. According to Chinese radicals, almost every personal pronoun relates to people, in contrast to items, materials, weapons, and so forth. Chinese pronouns all have some visible relationship to "people." For example, with 你 (you) and 他 (he and him), the character component 亻 means people. Even 她 (she and her) still relates to people because 女 means female person. Only one pronoun, 我 (I and me), does not mean people. Not only does it have no visible people symbol, the pronoun 我 has a negative connotation: it was originally derived from the symbol for an instrument of slaughter.[5]

Why does 我 (I and me) not mean people? Because traditional Chinese culture thought the self was equal to privacy or selfishness, two very negative characteristics devoid of virtue. Not only was it not virtuous, the self was considered the root of all evil. Thus, the self must be punished. It must be suppressed, contained, and even killed by the instrument of punishment. Confucius even famously said, "Restraining the self to follow the etiquette is benevolence."[6] What is benevolence? Its Chinese character is 仁 and includes two parts. As we know, 亻 means people, and 二 means two. It connotes a moral relationship between people.

The moral presuppositions of Chinese culture are to smother one's self for others, to throttle the individual for the collective and society. However, Chinese culture has not really been able to strangle the individual. It wisely separated the self and the social roles, then belittled the self and praised the social role with a whole set of role expectations and behavioral norms. This praising of the social role can be found in Confucius's maxim, "The monarch should have a monarch's manner; subjects should have subjects' behavior; a father should have a father's air; and a son should be a son."[7]

11

Western culture thinks of a person as containing two separate parts: the self and the social roles he or she plays. Traditional Chinese culture, however, attempts to treat people as solely their social roles. As people only have role mentalities, they're inclined to have cooperative relations with those in other roles—teachers and students, parents and children, and so on.

To sum up, Chinese culture utilizes a whole set of role expectations and behavioral norms to standardize people into various social roles without having to worry about the independent or antisocial acts of an individual.[8]

That is to say, the self is controlled in a Chinese family. Every individual plays his or her role, such as father, mother, and child. Because the Chinese celebrate the supremacy of education, the expectations and norms of each role must take this as their priority: children study hard and every member of the family sacrifices whatever is needed for ensuring their kids achieve their goals.

DIALOGUE

American parents: We don't know how you can discuss this topic with us as Americans because it has touched on essential differences between Chinese and American culture.

Huang: Yes, you're right. It's difficult to provide guidance for this topic because it's based on such a fundamental difference in cultures. Many Chinese people consider a family to be a "life union," from which individual elements cannot be separated. It is just like an ancient Chinese poem, which stated, "Making two clay figurines: one is me, the other is you. Then break them and mix the clay to make figurines again. Those would be made in which you fuse to me and I merge into you."

American parents: Very interesting!

Huang: Let me, instead, provide an example of the concept of social roles and the pressure they can hold. Liu Xiang won the gold medal in the 110-meter hurdles in the 2004 Olympics. He, however, failed to run in 2008 and 2012. I believe the reason he failed to succeed was the symbolism behind his number, 1356. Thirteen meant thirteen hundred million (1.3 billion) people in China; 56 meant the fifty-six nationalities of China. The Chinese Olympic Delegation chose this number for him in 2008 and 2012 after his success in 2004. The hopes of 1.3 billion people and fifty-six nationalities were on one individual's shoulders. Only Liu Xiang knew how heavy this number was.

American parents: On the other hand, Michael Phelps dropped out of two swimming events in the 2012 London Olympics. He told the world that it was more important to enjoy himself and have fun.

Huang: Chinese people always think they are representing their families, their organizations, and China itself. It's part of the life union, which I mentioned before. Some examples of this concept are a small band of soldiers who have penetrated deep behind enemy lines, runners on a relay team, and an airplane crew; they cannot leave anyone behind. If one loses, they all lose, and so they must band together. This is how the Chinese view the concept of collective. However, Americans think in terms of individualism; you wouldn't be able to beat it out of them!

American parents: On one hand, you're right. On the other hand, you're being a little pessimistic. Teamwork has been emphasized more and more in America.

Huang: Yes, I have heard the phrase "There is no 'I' in team" many times. Americans can learn something from the Chinese by concentrating the energy and capabilities of a family on one child's studying at certain times. For example, when your child is studying for a standardized test such as the PSAT or SAT, exempt him or her from chores and have a sibling take over (or you, as parents, can complete them). Allow the child to fully concentrate on studying. Or, if that's too difficult, perhaps create a quiet study environment and refrain from making noise and distracting him or her.

American parents: It's hard to apply these cultural views to American parenting.

Huang: I know, because both cultures are so different. Consider this topic as "homework." How can you incorporate social role versus the self into your parenting methods?

CARRYING GUILT VERSUS CARRYING LOANS

1

The external greed of parents can be transformed into the inner drive of a child.

What Chinese-American parents have done, or what they have sacrificed for their children's education, can place great mental or spiritual pressure on their children. When children realize how much parents have contributed to and sacrificed for them, this pressure can turn into their *guilty sense*.

In general, American children take on loans for their higher education. Some may even take a loan from their parents in order to finance their education. This is an aspect of American culture that Chinese parents joke about—children needing to borrow money from their parents for school. I do not understand or accept it at all. However, my students have explained the rationale behind this. Sometimes it isn't easy to get a loan from a bank or private lender, and parents don't force their children to pay them back within a certain time frame or charge interest. Therefore, children may prefer taking a loan from their parents.

On the contrary, Chinese parents, regardless of whether they're wealthy or poor, generally pay their children's academic expenses from start to finish, through the highest postgraduate degrees. Because of this, many Chinese children carry guilt about going to school, especially those from poorer families. The heaviest burden that American children must carry is loans to go to school. They're merely responsible to either their parents or the banks that loan them the funds for their education. As a result, they don't have any conception of the guilty sense carried by Chinese kids.

Carrying a loan versus carrying guilt: they are two very different cultural mechanisms, and they have resulted in two very different states of mind for children.

2

What is *guilty sense*? There is a saying: children innately owe their parents. Quite a few people believe that children should repay their parents for the love, care, and support they have provided since childhood. Regardless of whether you use the word *repay* or the phrase *carry guilt*, it implies that children should be conscious of their responsibilities toward their parents. When a child knows his or her behavior reflects on and affects others and society, he or she will not only be more disciplined, but will also have a stronger motivation to continue forward progress.

Of course, not every child can understand his or her parents' pains. There is a Chinese saying we've discussed previously, "the sad plight of all parents." It means that children cannot understand, or even misunderstand, their parents' pains, but parents are still duty bound to care for their children in every way possible. While this saying may make implications about parents' helplessness, it also references the immaturity of many children. Why do some children never mature? Why are they so self-centered? Because they refuse to understand, and thus don't realize how much others, including their parents, have done for them. Simply put, these children lack a sense of guilt.

Chinese people believe in the saying, "At the beginning, human nature was good and honest." Generally speaking, they do not believe in the concept of original sin. Therefore, Chinese people do not have a guilty sense that stems from early childhood. Their guilty sense comes from their developing consciousness of responsibility to their family, their clan, and even their society.

3

In recalling memories of my relationship with my father, I realize I've had a very deep sense of guilt ever since I was a young child. This guilty sense has driven me forward, continually inspiring me to make progress in all areas of my life. In 1996, I wrote an essay about my father for my hometown newspaper in which I addressed my sense of guilt toward my father.

The Deep Love of a Father

I addressed every letter I wrote during the first several years I was out of the country to every single person in my family. I always thought about writing specifically to my father but it was simply too difficult to put that pen to paper. I wrote my dissertation and even published two books in English, but I still never wrote to my father.

The very first night I was back in China in June of 1996, my sisters rather ceremoniously had me look at a piece in my hometown newspaper, the *Liuzhou Daily*. In a column headed "Unforgettable Teacher's Grace," there was an article written in remembrance of my father titled "A Bowl of Rice." The author had been a student from the poor countryside and, because of some difficulties, was considering dropping out of school. After my father had found out about it, he had the student over to his house and gave him a bowl of rice. The student cried as he ate the rice and listened to my father's advice. As he was leaving, my father slipped him ten Yuan (one-fourth my father's monthly salary) and a handful of meal tickets. Thus strengthened by my father's encouragement, the student had gone on to finish school and had since become the head of a brewery. I silently read this article in all of its bowl-of-rice simplicity. Over the following days I mentioned it every time I ran into anyone. Many people who had not even known my father recalled the essay. It was thus clear that it had not only touched me but many others as well. . . .

In 1960, China was in an extremely difficult situation. In order to unite as many people as possible to overcome the difficulties, one of the governmental measures was to remove the label of Rightist from most of those who had been branded as such, including my father. At that time, many people were poor and going hungry. The day my father was "liberated" from his spiritual shackles, he brought his four children to the fanciest local restaurant to celebrate his new freedom. Each of us had one piece of steamed sponge cake. I devoured it ravenously, raised my head, and asked, "Daddy, can you be a Rightist again?"

In 1979, there was a rumor that the Rightists would get their deducted salaries back. Father knew that the 10,000 Yuan the government owed him could make him a millionaire at that time. But after he learned that the government could not return his salary because of the difficult economic times, he was very generous and said, "Had we gotten the 10,000 Yuan, we would have already spent it all. My children have built character because of suffering without it, which is an invaluable asset to me."

This generosity on my father's part was very meaningful. My father always had to reluctantly borrow money from A to make up for B. I remember feeling so embarrassed on the days tuition payments were due. My siblings and I were always the last ones, paying with coins at the last possible second before the deadline. Though my father's love carried more weight than hundreds of mountains, he's never given me a cent. It was the first time I'd learned he'd given money and meal tickets to help a poor student.

Before I came to America, I detected that there was a trace of sadness that sometimes flashed in my father's eyes, which only a son could catch. Later, father said in a letter that he worried about my teaching at an American university. I believed him at that time, but now I realize that he had actually already known that he was ill.

There are two memories I have of my father that always make me feel very guilty. In 1959, my father (who was separated from our family) came to see us. Several of us were performing a song called "Socialism Is Good." When we sang the words "The Rightists tried to be against the Socialism, but they failed," we all pointed at my father. I didn't know why, at that moment, my father turned his face to the window. . . .

The other memory occurred during Chinese New Year's Eve of 1970, which was the scariest time in the Cultural Revolution. The head of school security informed me, "You have a phone call." At that time, there was only one phone in the entire school. I asked him, "Who's calling?" He was my father's former student but responded insidiously, "Don't know!" I went to the office and picked up the phone. A slight but excited voice rang out: "Do you know who I am?" My head was emptied by a "bang," and instead of responding I hung up the phone at the voice of a Rightist, the "State's enemy." I hesitated for a while and then picked it up again. There was only a slight electric buzz on the other end of the line. . . .

When I headed for the United States, father came to Nanning to see me off. As I was in the countryside, father secretly recommended me an article, *A View of Daddy's Back*, that was banned at the time. There was a scene in the essay that resonated with me: a father climbed onto the platform of a railway station to buy oranges for his son and the son sees his father's back. As I left for America, I gazed at my father's receding figure at the train station. I didn't realize that my father was bidding his final farewell to me as I gazed as his back from the train I was taking to a new world.

When my father was terminally ill, I was working on my dissertation. People asked him whether they should tell me. At that time, my father had been unable to speak. Two lines of tears came down from his eyes and he shook his head slightly. He worried others would not understand him and, with difficulty, he lifted a finger, closed his eyes, and firmly waved his finger once.

This was the deepest love my father could give me!

When I write here, I think, the letter to my father has not only been written but also sent. In fact, what I have written in my deep heart, only my father would be able to read and understand.

4

When my father passed away, I could not and did not see him off. I will never forgive myself for this; I will carry the guilt around for the rest of my life. Had I known my father was terminally ill, I would *certainly* have gone back to China. Because of my visa situation at the time, I likely would not have been able to return to the United States to complete my dissertation. I don't know how badly my father wanted to see me before he left this world, though I suspect he also badly wanted me to be the first recipient of a doctorate in the history of our family. Only God knows the struggle he faced between his hopes for my success and his wish to see his son one last time.

Father did not leave me any material riches but instead left me very rich spiritual wealth. His expectations for my success have deeply influenced my entire life. My relatives and friends, and even I myself do not understand: Why have I published so many papers, books, and dictionaries but still write until 2:00 a.m. almost every single day? So many of my classmates were much smarter than I was, but why haven't they been able to achieve similar academic success? While I'm sitting here writing, I suddenly realize that it turns out it's because of my guilty sense.

Why do so many sensible Asian-American children neglect their sleep and meals and bear hardship without complaint in order to study? Because in order to go to school without carrying the burden of a loan one must instead carry the burden of guilt! Therefore, external pressure can become internal motivation; guilty sense can become a sense of responsibility. If you think about your parents, who suffered untold hardship, you will feel pressure to fulfill your duty to your family. In fact, carrying guilt is to carry loans, too. The difference is that in carrying guilt you carry a psychological and spiritual loan that you will never be able to repay.

As you may know, Chinese culture does not allow soldiers to surrender in times of war. Prisoners of war are considered cowards in Chinese tradition. Therefore a POW is always burdened by shame. If you carry too heavy or too much of a sense of guilt, but cannot give up or surrender, then what might happen? You may resort to suicide as a way out.

I am afraid that this is one of the most important reasons that Asian-American children have a high rate of suicide.

5

Many people think that the pressure of carrying a loan is very heavy, but it likely isn't heavier than that which comes from guilt. Your state of mind is relatively independent when you have loans; you can have a loan and not feel guilt. If you're only studying for yourself, then the only pressure to make you feel you absolutely must win and cannot lose is from yourself. If you cannot win, then you can still be "the man" and surrender without shame. No wonder American POWs are always viewed and treated as heroes.

I was surprised to find that some of my American students who had taken out large loans for school gave up so easily when they faced difficulties. Just like shopping in a supermarket, you pick up something, give it a hard look, and then throw it away. That's it! Whether or not you give up depends *only* on yourself; there's no need to feel guilty on behalf of others.

With the term *guilty sense*, the key is not actually the word *guilt*, but the word *sense*. Guilty or not guilty; this is an objective fact. The sense, however, is subjective. It is invisible and intangible but follows you wherever you go and is constantly driving you forward day and night.

Of course, carrying guilt can be a double-edged sword. For example, if your parents paid for your education, you may adopt a dependent mentality toward them. You may feel guilt toward them, and thus you might study only for them. If this occurs, you will lose your independent and critical thinking; this may be one of the reasons why Chinese and Chinese-American children frequently obey their parents unconditionally.

6

After we got Yan settled down at his law school, we needed to return to Ohio. At the airport before we left, Yan very seriously said, "Mom and Dad, since you are spending so much on my law-school tuition, I promise to study three hours per day."

My heart jumped! Three hours? A very solemn commitment.

Later, almost every time we called him, Yan was studying at the library. Sometimes he wouldn't even eat dinner until midnight. He often studied more than thirteen hours per day.

Because of his hard work, each and every year he received a letter with the dean's signature commending him. Yan also won a medal at his graduation.

Behind this hard work, the letters from the dean, and the medal, I think there must be my son's very thick guilty sense.

Carrying a guilty sense may cause introspection and create new thoughts. Carrying a guilty sense can bring about consciousness of responsibilities. Carrying a guilty sense should cultivate sensible children. Carrying a guilty sense could produce ambition!

DIALOGUE

American parents: Is the guilty sense very critical in Chinese parenting?

Huang: The guilty sense makes people introspective; and self-questioning can bring about progress. The guilty sense of Chinese children comes from their self-examination regarding their parents' sacrifices.

American parents: Our culture breeds a guilty sense and introspection as well.

Huang: Yes, original sin is a guilty sense in Christianity. However, how do you translate that responsibility and guilty sense and channel it toward your children's education? And what about non-Christians? It's a big challenge for American parenting.

American parents: Do you have any suggestions?

Huang: That American kids borrow money from their parents is a complete cultural shock to Chinese and Chinese-American parents (including me). But another cultural shock I have found is that those among my students who have taken educational loans from their parents are more responsible than the students whose parents pay for their tuition, and they are more concerned about their families than the students who get their loans from banks. Parents providing educational loans to their children without interest, or with very low interest: Is this a way for the parents to take responsibility for their kids' education while also fostering the children's guilty sense?

American parents: Interesting!

Huang: I have talked to my students who have received loans from their parents. All of them expressed grateful acknowledgement of their parents for giving them interest-free loans, thereby helping them to avoid the complicated and painful loan-application process while also saving them from the difficulties of repaying the loans to faceless and uncompromising banks and debt collectors. Even though their parents did not set a deadline for repayment, I could tell that my students were nonetheless carrying a heavy guilty sense and intended to pay their parents back as soon as possible.

American parents: What happens if kids can't pay back their parents for the loan?

Huang: They'll find a way to pay it back one way or another eventually, assuming they want to. But the longer they carry the loan, the heavier their guilty sense will be.

American parents: And if they don't want to pay back the loan?

Huang: Well, only God knows how to answer this question.

INDEPENDENCE VERSUS FILIAL PIETY

1

While independent and critical thinking is at the core of American culture, filial piety (loyal obedience and respect paid to parents) is an extremely important Confucian concept and virtue in traditional Chinese culture. Therefore, many people believe that American and Chinese parenting styles are incongruous and in fact in opposition to one another. A hybrid style of parenting, however, can fuse Chinese and American parenting styles, melding the Orient and the Western in order to form unique characteristics. I long believed that this was impossible, but what I didn't realize was that it's not necessary to choose between American and Chinese parenting. These styles are not mutually exclusive. For example, a child who respects his or her parents can also develop independent and critical thinking. Just as Aristotle said, "Plato is dear to me, but dearer still is truth," cultivating a child with filial morality as well as independent and critical thinking is a vital goal of my parenting.

2

Historically, the Chinese character 孝 (filial piety) was inscribed on ancient bronze objects. The pictographic character depicted a child supporting an old man who is walking but cannot do so on his own.[9] This inscription illustrates the meaning of filial piety in Chinese culture; the English concept of filial piety is unable to encompass the true meaning of 孝. It emphasizes filial obedience, filial devotion, and a sense of responsibility for taking care of one's parents. This definition can be found in *The Standards for Being a Good Child/Student*, a book dating back to the Qing Dynasty that every child was required to read. For example, the book says of filial obedience, "Whenever your parents scold you, accept it with faithful compliance." Of filial devotion it says, "When your parents are calling, do not be slow to respond." And of caring for one's parents it says, "When your parents are ill, you will taste the medicine first before giving it to them."

I do not advocate filial obedience, which conflicts with a child's critical thinking, but I do endorse filial respect to parents. This does not go against a child's independent and critical thinking. In fact, *The Standards for Being a Good Child/Student* actually encourages independent and critical thinking. For instance, "If you recognize faults in your parents, exhort them to change for the better. Speak to them kindly and gently, with a pleasant smile on your face. If they cannot accept your advice, wait for an opportune time. You may even use tears to exhort them, but do not resent it if you are punished."[10] This makes it very clear that even in ancient Chinese culture filial piety, morality, and independent and critical thinking were thought to be compatible. The solution lies between filial piety and independent and critical thinking: the fostering of a *dongshi* child. I could not find a comparable English concept for this Chinese special virtue for children, so I approximate it with "sensible" here. *Dongshi* actually means "to be sensible/thoughtful" and "sensitive to the need/concerns of others."[11]

Blind filial piety, of course, is not good, but an independence that is merciless to parents is not good either. Too many American parents neglect to foster that crucial sense of responsibility for taking care of parents; it's my biggest issue with parenting in this country, and one that I cannot abide. Therefore, we need to find a medium between filial piety and independent and critical thinking; this happy middle is *dongshi*. If we can foster a *dongshi*, or sensible child, we will be able to cultivate a child who values and practice both filial piety and independent and critical thinking.

The following chart illustrates general differences between Chinese and American parenting.

Chinese	American
Filial piety is a vital topic of family education.	Independent and critical thinking is an important part of family education.
Be a sensible child.	Be an independent child.
Children never call their parents by their first names. This is considered frivolous behavior.	Children often call their parents by their first names. This is not frivolous behavior.
Parents maintain a very close relationship with their college-age children.	Allow college-age children their independence, letting them forge their own path.

3

When Yan was in elementary school, he drew a very big house, the house he imagined he would live in one day. He pointed to a window on the first floor and said, "This is yours, because when you are old it might be difficult for you to climb stairs." I was so deeply moved that I kept his picture and still have it today. When Yan went to high school, our most powerful and effective threat was, "Wherever you go to college, we will move there." "Wherever you find a job, we will move in next door," we'd say, enjoying watching him squirm! After he went to college, this threat didn't work anymore. "We will buy a house within a thirty-minute drive of yours," we teased. He said that he didn't mind. In fact, after Yan went to law school, he said that he wanted us to live close to him.

In fact, there is a Chinese saying, "Leaves will fall back to the roots." That is to say, no matter how high the leaves are, they will eventually fall back to the roots. Leaves get their nutrition from the roots, so, at the end, they will return to nurture the roots with their bodies. The Chinese use these words to describe the idea that no matter how far people go, they will eventually return to their hometown when they are old and be buried on the land where they grew up. Yan may not know that we might want to pass up that room on the first floor of his house to return to far away China as falling leaves.

4

Regardless of the cultural environment, children of certain ages model themselves after their parents. Once children become adolescents, they begin to seek new role models.

Two of the legs that make up my tripod theory—American school education and social education—go to great lengths to encourage independent and critical thinking. Unfamiliar with this culture of independence, Asian-American parents are often challenged by their children. These challenges can range from the life changing, such as choosing a major in college, to the minor, such as this little story.

One night, when I was still studying for my doctorate, we were watching television. It was almost 10:00 p.m., so I told Yan to go to bed. However, he neglected to comply and continued to dawdle in front of the TV for some time. I repeated to him, "Did you hear me? Go to bed!" Yan hesitated and then said, "Why can you watch TV, but I have to sleep?"

I was absolutely shocked by these words. Yan was supposed to be a good Chinese boy who obeyed everything his father directed him to do! My wife hastily interjected, "At your age, a child needs to sleep for at least ten hours. Now it's late, so you will wake up late."

After Yan finally went to bed, I could not concentrate on the TV. Instead, I reflected on the dueling impulses in my brain. Through Yan's small rebellion, I was one step closer to understanding independence. But I wasn't happy to see it in my son, and I wasn't sure I could accept it.

As Yan grew, his youthful rebellion became more and more pronounced.

One time I pointed out a problem with Yan's tennis. He said, "Baba, you don't know how to play tennis. How can you tell me what the problem is?"

Once I asked him to exercise and he responded, "You don't exercise. Why should I?"

When I wanted to discuss selecting a college major with him, he wouldn't hear of it. "I know! I know what I'm doing," he would exclaim.

No matter what I said, he would respond, "You don't understand what I'm talking about!"

I had a long conversation with Yan about this constant behavior. I told him, "There is no one who is perfect in the world. Therefore, criticism and self-criticism can help people to progress together. If a person who points out another's problems must be perfect, or a person with weaknesses cannot criticize others, no one would be able to criticize because everyone has defects. So, the key is not to consider who says it but whether what he or she says is correct. For instance, there are many children of Vietnamese and Kampuchean refugees in American schools. They study very hard and do well for themselves. They, however, would not tell their parents, 'You aren't educated, and you don't study, why do you ask me to study?' Why? Because they are sensible and know what's reasonable."

Yan listened to me. Indeed, he was a sensible teenager, made even more so because we tried to explain our hardships and sense of guilt to him. When I was a student at Miami University, Yan started learning to play the violin in elementary school. Most parents in the class also sent their children to have private lessons. As we knew, a child could learn only basic knowledge and skills in the school-provided violin classes. Therefore, if you wanted your child to learn more, you needed to pay for private lessons. These private lessons were very expensive, and with me being a dirt-poor student, there was no way we could come up with the kind of money needed to send Yan to private lessons. So Yan had to study in school and practice at home by himself.

Yan was so sensible; indeed, he never mentioned that his friends went to private lessons, and he never asked us to send him to private lessons, nor did he complain that we did not send him to learn from a private tutor. He, of course, also never said to us, "You don't know how to play the violin, so don't try to talk about it with me." Instead of this, he practiced violin very conscientiously and seriously after he came home every day.

As the school year finished, we attended the music presentation. The most exciting performance was when all the students stood up and played, accompanied by their teacher on piano. The teacher gradually sped up her rhythm, and more and more students had to sit down because they were unable to follow the teacher's speed. When she played more and more quickly, only three boys were able to follow her. One of them was Yan. However, one could see from their postures that Yan was the only one who hadn't had private lessons. I was sure this was obvious to everyone else in the audience as well.

As the boys matched the teacher's crazy playing speed, the audience burst into a violent storm of applause. While I clapped along, I felt so guilty inside that I really wanted to cry.

Chinese students compete fiercely to study longer and harder than their peers, regardless of their family's poverty or wealth, because the rewards of educational success are life changing. These children study outside where there is light and a stone wall for a makeshift desk. *Photo by Bo Wang.*

5

If you want to help build your child's base of sensibility, let your child know about your struggles. When you have a conflicted state of mind, share it with your child, but also make sure he or she understands your unconditional and unselfish love toward them. More often than not, lengthy speeches aren't what's required; even just a small reference to a topic is enough for a child to understand your meaning.

If this doesn't work, then encourage your child to have an open mind and put him- or herself in your shoes. Ask your child to think about the situation from your point of view. This is a give and take, so you must also think about the situation from your child's perspective. It's a great way to keep the lines of communication open and foster a discussion.

Keeping in constant communication with your children is the most important thing of all. In our family, Yan has our every confidence. Our difficulties, thoughts, perplexities, plans, ambitions, budgets—everything is open to Yan. Of course, everyone keeps small secrets, but as long as you're communicating on the larger issues, everything should be fine. During Yan's period of teenage rebellion, we knew he wasn't completely candid with us, but we still did our best to keep communication with him open and unblocked. As long as his secrets and sometimes rebellious behavior were not related to major issues, we strongly encouraged his independent thinking, even when he was exercising his imagination, particularly when it came to academic topics or arguments. Even when we didn't agree with his ideas, we supported him almost unconditionally.

6

Every child can't be a genius, but it isn't too much to expect every child to be sensible and show filial piety toward his or her parents. It is, however, still not good enough. A child with filial piety should not only be sensible, be reasonable, and consider others; he or she should also have his or her own unique set of characteristics, creativity, and independent and critical thinking. It's not necessary to sacrifice a child's ability to reason independently as the price for a sensible child.

Dialogue

American parents: We actually like the concept of filial piety, but we worry this idea might damage the independence and creativity of our children.

Huang: The older I get, the more I like the concept of filial piety and the more I understand it. Human beings are odd sorts of creatures. As children, they love their parents with some reservation, particularly after they get married. As parents, they love their children absolutely and unconditionally.

When you think about it, filial piety doesn't actually conflict with independence. Filial piety, as we use it here, means "filial respect to parents," not "filial obedience." The latter goes against the development and use of critical thinking, but the former, which I encourage, doesn't.

American parents: How should we educate kids in terms of filial respect to parents?

Huang: You've likely been fostering your kids' independence, creativity, and critical thinking since they were very young. Now, in addition to that, try to make sure that your kids:

- tell you before they leave the house,
- report to you when they come back,
- greet you before they go to bed,
- cook dinner for you once a week,
- clean your room (not just their own!) once a month,
- plan and host birthday parties for mom and dad,
- occasionally let you pick the TV show or movie the family watches,
- teach you about new technology, such as an iPad or how to do things on the computer,
- call you when they are out of town,
- take pictures of and *with* you, as well as teach you how to use your camera.

It's hard to imagine how happy you'll be when your children show filial respect to you while also retaining their independent and critical thinking.

ALL PROJECTS ARE FAMILY PROJECTS

1

Though the following story might not even raise eyebrows for those in American families, the incident described is shocking to Chinese-American parents' eyes.

A Chinese friend's son found a job in Los Angeles. He and his wife were very happy and drove their son to settle in, despite the fact that Los Angeles was a great distance from where they lived. On their way, they stopped at a sub shop for lunch. The boy stopped his mom, who was going to buy lunch for the three of them and instead bought a foot-long sandwich and paid just for himself. My friend and his wife looked at each other and then looked at their son, who was eating his sandwich by himself, like a stranger. A happy trip together became a depressing journey.

"I couldn't believe it!" my friend told me over the phone with great anger, "How could my son do this to us? He refused to let us buy lunch for him. What did that mean? He considers us as outsiders, strangers, not family members?"

Indeed, this is a very common situation in American culture: a son not wanting his parents to pay for his lunch. For a Chinese family, however, this is a big deal, a big issue, and a big problem. The boy's behavior could mean one of two things. First, that the son feels that he's completely independent and doesn't need his parents anymore, or second, that it's time for him to financially separate from his family.

The father talked over the phone, "If this was the first situation, why didn't he pay for us? He didn't want to spend $10 on us? If it was the second one, I simply want to cry. The gratitude for the love and care we've given to him for more than twenty years was that easy and simple to cut off and throw away? My parenting has failed!"

This is a conflict between the two cultures.

Children who grew up in America and as teenagers and young adults began to pay only for themselves can never imagine how strongly Chinese and Chinese-American parents might react to such behavior. This is because it's a normal expectation among American parents that their children will eventually declare financial independence. Doing so does not mean that American children do not love their parents.

Later, I had a chance to visit Los Angeles and talk to my friends' son about this "event." He was very surprised and said, "I have never thought about this at all. I don't even remember it."

I shared this story with an American friend of mine. He, too, was surprised. He asked, "What should the boy have done according to Chinese culture?"

I said that he would have been expected to do one of two things. Either he should have stayed in line, waited for everyone to order their meals, and allowed his parents pay, or he should have ordered and paid for everyone. Either of these actions would have indicated both that he considered himself a member of his family and that he cared for his family members. Family is the "root" no matter how old you are or how far you have traveled away from your family.

The American friend exclaimed, "Wow, an individual can never separate from family!"

2

There's a very interesting question that often strikes me: do you see individual trees or do you see a forest? In fact, this question addresses not just methodology, how you see the individuals versus the group, but also your values. Americans would likely see an individual tree first and then, moving from one tree to another, eventually see the entire forest formed by individual trees. A Chinese person, however, would see the forest first, and only then see the individual trees that form the forest. That is to say, Westerners pay attention to individual values, but Chinese people lay stress on collective values. The Chinese call their mode of thinking "viewing the situation as a whole," and it is embodied in many nuances of Chinese culture, including social relations, politics, fine art, traditional medicine, and so on.[12]

3

Should we see the entire forest first or individual trees first? Should we consider family first or the individuals first? This is a major difference between Chinese and American cultures.

Family is the root for individuals and the social foundation for countries. Since ancient times, Chinese people have stressed the concept of the family. Family not only nurses an individual's growth but also breeds the individual's spiritual sustenance. Therefore, many Chinese people use their family as their primary motivation for forward progress. The responsibilities to families and between family members form the primary foundation of the relationships between people in Chinese society. In Chinese family culture, the position and meaning of a family are always above those of the individuals. For most Chinese people, if there were no family in their lives, they would feel as though they had no definite spiritual residence. In this sense, Chinese-American parenting enhances the function of family.

Ambition is not just for individuals. The Chinese have family ambition as well. Chinese-American parents selflessly sacrifice themselves for their children and their family. Many Americans believe that Chinese people ask their children to repay them, but this isn't the case. Most Chinese parents don't ask their children to repay them. Instead they simply ask their children to fulfill their roles and responsibilities within and to the family, as their studying is for the family as whole, not just for a father or mother.

There are more differences between Chinese and American culture than just the conception of the family versus that of the individual. Before we can fully consider Co-Core Synergy Education, we have to consider these fundamental cultural differences.

4

If Chinese education was defined by the creation of the Imperial Examination System, what event or concept defines American education? Where do the values of American education come from? Why are the supreme ideals of American education (such as creativity, individualism, and independence) not emphasized in Chinese education?

For the answers to these questions, we have to venture to the American frontier.

By 1890, after so many decades of struggle and conquest, America hit a turning point. The vast western frontiers had finally been almost completely settled. The unexplored territories that had loomed just beyond the frontier for over a hundred years were no more. Further westward expansion was no longer possible.

In Frederick J. Turner's influential essay "The Significance of the Frontier in American History," he argues that the formative experience of all of America— the one thing that had the greatest hand in shaping the nation's character and values—was the exploration and conquest of the great western frontier.[13] But by the turn of the twentieth century, a nation defined by its frontier suddenly had no frontier. America had lost the most American part of America.

5

The ideals of the pioneer were so deeply entrenched in the American mindset that when the old frontier was no more, America simply established a new one. By the time Alaska became a state in 1959, Americans needed a new frontier. In 1960, John F. Kennedy stated, "We stand today on the edge of a New Frontier, ... the frontier of the 1960s, the frontier of unknown opportunities and perils, the frontier of unfilled hopes and unfilled threats."[14]

One of those hopes and threats was the uncharted area of space. Just three years prior, the Soviets had launched Sputnik, the first manmade satellite to be placed in orbit. A few years after that, they put the first man in orbit. The gauntlet had been thrown down. America, through Kennedy, vowed to be the first country to put a man on the moon. Thus, America's new frontier was outer space and the moon.

But the new American frontier of the 1960s was as much inward as it was outward. By challenging the American people to put a man on the moon by the end of the decade, Kennedy called not only for the outward physical exploration of space; he called also for an *inward* investigation of new sciences and technologies.

Education in America has traditionally been heavily influenced by this view. Pioneer ideals are prized above all. In order to ensure that the grit and resourcefulness of America's forbears—the unyielding independence and courage of the now-mythical frontiersman—lives on, American education must make sure that children absorb those ideals.

This involves a type of education that champions learning by discovery and exploration, developing independence and self-esteem, and cultivating ingenuity and creativity. In school, American kids are given responsibility over projects early and often. These are usually projects of which they must take some amount of ownership to complete. In order to do well on them, kids are required to figure things out, to plan, to organize, to prepare, and to generally make decisions, all on their own.

6

There are many factors that went into shaping American and Chinese characteristics; one of these, which makes for an interesting comparison, is the geographical features and conditions of each country.

What is China's geography like, and how has it shaped China's culture?

Geographically, much of China is closed off. To the northwest lies the endless desert; to the southwest is the dangerously steep Qinghai-Tibetan Plateau, which is called the roof of the world; to the north are boundless Mongolian grasslands; to the northeast are the vast Great Khingan and Lesser Khingan volcanic mountain ranges, and to the southeast is the sea. This closed-off geographic condition didn't encourage contact with other cultures. Ancient Chinese people didn't feel they needed to take a risk in reaching out to the outside world; they had huge amounts of fertile, richly endowed land, their own self-sustaining cradle of civilization. They could be content with their lot. If you consider *culture* as the suffix of *agriculture*, it's easy to see that the ancient Chinese agricultural economy and the self-contained characteristics of its geography influenced the closed, self-contained, moderate, and conservative Chinese culture. The Great Wall is an enduring symbol of this mentality and has become a metaphor for closing the country off from the outside world.

However, would you consider the sea to be open or closed geography? It could be viewed either way, but I believe this depends on whether the people want or need to venture out from the country's coast. The Chinese had no need to risk sailing into the unknown because they had, at their fingertips, the fertile Yellow River and Yangtze River Valleys, where people were happy and self-sufficient. In the case of the Chinese, the sea would be viewed as closed geography. If the land of China's interior had been poor and nutrient starved, and people needed to explore the outside world for survival, the ocean would have been considered open and inviting. To put it simply, it depends on whether the attraction of staying close to home is stronger than the attraction of exploring.

There are two very different ways a culture can react to expanding rival cultures. One is to retain traditions by means of resistance; another is to use warfare to protect or even extend one's own civilization.[15] The former was the Chinese way and the latter was the American way.

Because Chinese culture is conservative, the Chinese naturally began to rely on one another. Various collectives formed as a matter of course, such as families, clans, tribes, and the state.

How should one integrate two very different cultures, one collective and one individual, one moderate and one risk seeking? This is a question that Chinese-American parents must face.

7

We know that giving kids responsibility over their own projects is a good way to help children learn to figure things out on their own; that is, how to plan, organize, and make decisions. But how do we meld the individual and collective together? The answer is family projects, which are integral to Co-Core Synergy Education.

With our support and encouragement, Yan has undertaken many projects. One of them was particularly meaningful to me because I was able to help him with it.

In Yan's eighth-grade class, students were assigned a big project called "The Civil War Project." Every student was required to choose a topic of some relevance to the war. Yan decided to work on the Battle of Antietam.

At the time, Yan was crazy about an online computer game called MUD (Multi-User Dungeon). The basic gist of it was similar to an MMORPG—massively multiplayer online role-playing game—in which you create a character and interact with other people in the world. The game was set in a fantasy world created by MUD builders, and Yan had the software to build his own MUD world.

Was it possible to use MUD on such a big project? He had been playing with his MUD software for about a week when he finally got one of the most creative, unique, and ambitious school project ideas he ever had.

I really loved his crazy idea. At that time, however, Yan had just failed a project he'd worked very hard on and, in my opinion, had done very *well* on. I said to him, "Don't worry, if anything goes wrong, I'll support you, even if your project fails again."

Yan was very excited because I was showing strong support for his project idea, despite the fact that he'd just received a bad grade and I was usually very demanding about his scores.

I smiled, "I can only provide spiritual encouragement. When it comes to computer technology, I know nothing. You'll have to figure that out by yourself."

Yan laughed. "That's enough; I don't think I need any computer help from you."

So Yan had made his decision: he would use MUD to model the Battle of Antietam. He began by researching the battle—what the area looked like and the turn-by-turn events of the battle—so he could start building it on MUD. Then he researched the high-ranking generals and created characters for each, one by one. Finally, he programmed a personality into each using information he had gleaned from his research.

By the time he was halfway into the project, Yan was afraid he had bitten off more than he could chew. Error after error popped up. Every time he fixed one, it would cause another somewhere else. He spent weeks just fixing the errors! The last week before the project was due, he was still working like a maniac. Eventually, though, he managed to finish.

However, another major problem cropped up: he realized that his MUD would only be accessible from our home PC. He would need a direct connection from the school computer to our home computer to present it at school. Fortunately, after some searching, he found software that would allow him to do just that. But this created another problem: presenting the MUD at school meant that our computer at home had to be running the MUD at the same time. Who was going to keep the MUD working while Yan was at school?

You can imagine where this line of questioning was going. I was amused that, despite the fact that Yan had earlier said he wouldn't need anything from me, it had turned that he would need my help after all.

Here's what happened, in Yan's own words, quoted from one of his books:

> I used a page from Al Pacino's book and believed that I could teach my dad how to run the MUD in the four hours I had left that night.
>
> Usually my dad loves to fool around when you are trying to be serious. It seems to make him laugh so hard, you'd believe it was the funniest thing in the world if you saw the look on his face when he pretends to be stupid while you're trying to get him to cooperate. This would be the last thing I would expect from a Ph.D., but it was the first thing I expect from my dad.
>
> On this particular night, he saw that I was quite frustrated and serious about this project and the problem I was having, so he kept the fooling around to a minimum. He listened surprisingly intently and picked it up quite quickly, and around 11:30 I had him running the MUD as best as I could on such short notice. He promised to start it the next day and keep it going until I got home.[16]

I didn't hesitate; I canceled all my appointments (including a doctor's appointment) to stay at home to help Yan.

The next morning, Yan called me for our computer's IP address. He was amazed that I gave it to him immediately and accurately.

However, we hit a snag: Yan didn't realize that just as he was getting ready to present his project, our computer at home accidentally shut down!

I restarted the computer immediately and managed to find the MUD online, though Yan hadn't coached me on how to do that. I also found the new IP address, called the school office, and asked the secretary to give this new IP address to Yan's teacher.

After Yan came home, he vividly and enthusiastically described how breathtaking and stimulating his project presentation had been.

"Blank! 'Error connecting to remote computer.' My eyes nearly popped out of my face as I saw the error over and over. I tried as many things as I could think of to make sure it wasn't the computer's problem. Nothing! My Dad must have done something wrong at home."

But eventually, after I got things running again at home, Yan was able to successfully connect the two computers.

In the end, the project was very successful. When he was finally able to load the MUD, the script that he had so carefully devised took over. The MUD version of his teacher started to talk, "If you want to see history for yourselves, please take this key and open this door to walk into history." Everyone watched as the MUD teacher walked the class through a virtual battlefield. He walked among and spoke to the soldiers in the Confederate front line. After that he walked to the Union camp and spoke with the generals about their strategy to win the battle.

The entire project provided everything from background information to minute details of how the people looked. Yan had programmed in many of the students from his class as well. His teacher and his classmates, after seeing themselves inside the MUD, laughed and giggled extensively. The students were in awe as they watched one of the kids walk through the MUD. The kids, who had experience with MUDs were particularly crazy about it.

Yan said, "Dad, do you know what I recalled when the computer was down?"

"What?"

He smiled, not saying a word.

8

Yan's Battle-of-Antietam assignment was not a *simple* project, but it was meaningful for a father and son to work together. I met his teacher later. He said, "I can tell there must have been something lying behind the complicated project. Wow, without family, the project could not have been achieved. It should be considered a family project."

This small project that Yan and I worked on together fostered Yan's concept of family. This would repeat over and over again, culminating in a huge family project a few years later, the likes of which our family had never before seen. For more than four years, my family worked on a project together—creating a breakthrough Chinese-English dictionary.

The idea came to me in 2006, when one of my top students failed to turn in his homework. He told me that he had spent several hours searching for a Chinese character but had been unable to find it in the end. He checked through the vocabulary indexes in all of his textbooks. He even mobilized his girlfriend, who did not study Chinese, to help him.

This incident attracted my attention: Chinese dictionaries were useless for nonnative learners. I took a survey and found that only two out of over three hundred Chinese-language students at Miami University regularly used a Chinese dictionary. Only 0.7 percent!

Why don't American students use Chinese dictionaries?

I went on to discover that all Chinese dictionaries are designed for use by native Chinese speakers. An English dictionary is very simple; as long as you know the twenty-six letters of the alphabet, you can use it. However, Chinese dictionaries aren't so easy. In order to use a Chinese dictionary, one must know the more than two hundred radicals, count the Chinese strokes, and go through six strict steps without a single mistake to find the character; which is to say, one must have a very solid foundation in the Chinese language in order to seek out a Chinese character in a Chinese dictionary. This was the dilemma: because he was a beginner, he needed to use a Chinese dictionary very badly, but because he was a beginner he was unable to use a Chinese dictionary![17]

One night during dinner, I raised this issue with my wife and son. I told them I had created a way for my American students to search for Chinese characters.

My son, who has also had difficulties using a Chinese dictionary, asked, "How?"

I explained my method, and it made everyone excited.

"Should we make it a family project?" my wife proposed. "Why don't the three of us work together to compile a special Chinese-English dictionary?"

I had experience in teaching Chinese as a second language, my son had experience in learning Chinese as a second language, and my wife had computer-programming skills. Furthermore, my wife and I had a very solid foundation in Chinese, while Yan spoke pure English. The three of us decided to compile a Chinese-English dictionary directed solely at nonnative speakers. This dictionary would allow them to self-teach within one or two minutes and seek out and find an unknown character in less than sixty seconds.

While making the decision to compile the dictionary was easy, we didn't realize how *difficult* the process of doing so would be. For more than four years, none of us went to bed before 2:00 a.m. The hardships we went through for those years are something only the three of us can understand.

In order to work as efficiently as possible, we implemented goal management, in which everyone worked on his or her own subprojects. We three cooperated and competed with one another. After Yan went to law school, he was extremely busy. He not only needed to be diligent in his studies at law school, but he also had to finish his subprojects. Sometimes we would have to talk to him on his cell phone for hours until his cell phone burned so hot he couldn't hold it up to his ear anymore. Sometimes we'd argue until our faces were red over English definitions for Chinese words. For example, one time Yan thought that "this was a historically unfair treaty" could mean that it was unfair in history, but we didn't agree. We quarreled heatedly until we got angry, but finally we came around to his way of seeing things.

There are many Chinese concepts that don't have adequate English translations (filial piety, sensible child, and so forth), so these were the hardest part of compiling our dictionary. We'd argue back and forth for days, even weeks, about how to appropriately translate these abstract Chinese concepts. Sometimes we were so frustrated we didn't even want to pick up each other's phone calls. But there was a bright side to this, too: through our arguments, the three of us came to understand one another better and we found more optimal ways to communicate. Through our discussions, Yan deepened his understanding of Chinese culture. Indeed, this was another way of parenting.

Sometimes, when Yan was at home, the three of us worked in different rooms. At times we didn't want to bother one other with simple questions, so we would just make a phone call even though we were in the same house. When one person was tired and took a break or went to the kitchen to pour a drink, he or she would find that everyone else was quietly working hard. Though we were separated physically into different rooms, our spiritual motivation and goals were one, as a family. This sense of happiness was far beyond what language can describe.

Yan's creativity is very dynamic; he is able to seek solutions and creatively handle difficult cases. However, an outstanding lawyer also needs patience and meticulousness in order to pore over material (which is often very boring) to detect errors, such as unclosed loopholes, inexact definitions, and even stray punctuation marks. Patience and attention to minute details were weaknesses Yan needed to improve upon, which made this family project all the more meaningful to him.

Making Yan's Halloween costume at home was a shared project the entire family worked on. This family project taught Yan important lessons about family responsibility, the rewards of hard work, and the value of thriftiness. *Photo courtesy of the author.*

I have published a number of books, but this dictionary was the most valuable to me. After the dictionary was published, I looked at it again and again, turning each page with care. If it hadn't felt like a brick, I probably would have taken it to bed with me and curled up with it while I slept! Yan has also published books, but he seemed to value this dictionary more than the others as well. He couldn't wait for sample copies and instead ordered a copy online for himself. It was the fact that we accomplished this as a family that made the dictionary so hallowed in our eyes.

9

How can you combine the Chinese concepts of family and collective with American ideals of creativity and risk taking? I think this dictionary is a great example. Since the new method of searching Chinese characters was so revolutionary and innovative, we couldn't take the chance of disclosing our methods. This meant that the four years of extremely hard work were a huge risk because we had to compile the dictionary before seeking out a publisher. If no publishers appreciated our work, it would have been a tremendous loss for our family—every single day's effort over the course of more than four years. As such, it combined creativity (the new method) and risk taking (possibly not finding a publisher) with family (working together on the project). I hope this project, in itself, was a type of education for my son.

We really hope this unique tradition of conducting family projects can be continued and extended to Yan's new family in the future.

Western society makes the individual the center; the position and function of family are placed second. But emphasizing family doesn't mean you have to ignore individual rights and functions, nor do you have to sacrifice individual interests. Taking a look at how Chinese-American parenting uses the strength of the family in the education of children might be worth your time.

DIALOGUE

American parents: We don't have family projects like your dictionary; we're very much envious of it!

Huang: My American colleagues have said the same thing because they published many articles, essays, and books, but none were family projects. They believe this family project is priceless.

American parents: We've done many different family projects over the years, but none that lasted nearly as long as yours. Additionally, after our kids moved on to middle school, they were less willing to participate in family projects, yet Yan was still working on the dictionary when he was in law school.

Huang: These differences are cultural. We can't judge which culture is better or worse. Some people enjoy eating dinner as a family; others prefer to eat individually and quietly. Individual projects and family projects may be equally valuable, though for different goals. However, a good tactic for emphasizing familial acceptance is eating dinner together as a family. Many American families are used to eating dinner individually due to the busy and often conflicting schedules of various family members. However, we always greatly valued our family dinner time, during which we chatted, discussed family issues, argued over academic topics, and shared each other's problems and worries. In any event, our family dinner table was a forum that we used for communicating with Yan and also for giving and receiving understanding and support. After Yan went to college and then law school, we continued to save the vital and serious discussion topics for our family dinner table, and we still do so, even now. During Yan's junior year in high school, we found that he sometimes avoided eating dinner with us. However, we also knew that this was the time he needed us most. So we did the best thing we thought we could do as parents: no matter how late he said he would come home, we said we'd wait for him. When he told us he needed to leave early, we said we'd serve dinner as early as necessary. No matter what, he was stuck with us.

American parents: Let's say we want to try out a project for our family, what should we be aware of?

Huang: Family businesses are probably the most popular family projects in the United States, but there are others as well. Kids don't usually view school projects as family projects, but you can take the opportunity to work on things with them. This kind of family project, whether it involves the whole family or part of it, could be a beginning of *life union*, which will help the family to remain together mentally and spiritually. Try out some small projects with the idea of life union at the back of your mind.

Chinese parents: When we, as Chinese parents, engage in a family project, what should we be aware of?

Huang: Parents should not dominate the project. More importantly, do not use the family project as an excuse to suppress kids' independent and critical thinking. Let kids bring their creativity into play in a family project.

CHAPTER 6
OTHER INTERESTING PHENOMENA IN CHINESE-AMERICAN FAMILIES

Chinese "love" is like a powerful subsurface whirlpool, an underwater current hiding beneath a still and reticent surface. There is no visible bluff and bluster. It's hard to spot the movement of the water. There are few signifying ripples. Though it's not so much to look at, these underwater forces can be just as forceful and turbulent as a storm above the surface.

IN ORDER TO GAIN, IS IT NECESSARY TO GIVE UP FIRST?

1

A very interesting phenomenon in Asian-American education has attracted my attention.

Compared to Americans, Asian-American students generally wait *at least* four years longer than their peers to have friends of the opposite sex.

I asked my students to do an educational-comparison research survey for me. We collected about a hundred survey forms from Asian-American and Caucasian students and their parents.

One question asked students, "Do your parents allow you to have a girlfriend or boyfriend in high school?"

Among Asian-American students, 44 percent said yes.

Among Caucasian students, 100 percent said yes.

We also asked their parents the same question: "Do you allow your children to have a girlfriend or boyfriend in high school?"

Asian-American parents answered in the affirmative 38 percent of the time while 100 percent of Caucasian parents said yes.

As for whether or not Asian-American students were allowed to have a girlfriend or boyfriend in college, more than 10 percent said no.

Dating and having a girlfriend or boyfriend are important parts of growing up, just like bread and milk. Why do Asian-American children delay in dating and having friends of the opposite sex?

In traditional Chinese culture, people are not allowed to talk about sex to underage children. This is similar to children under twenty-one in the United States not being allowed to drink alcohol. In Chinese tradition, some believed *underage* meant fifteen years old for girls and eighteen for boys. In other words, talking about sex with girls who were under fifteen and boys under eighteen was thought to be offensive to public and social decency. Many people (including parents) considered the topic of sex to be a forbidden zone that they avoided addressing.

This father-daughter/mother-son dance practice, giving kids an opportunity to "rehearse" how to associate with the opposite sex, would be utterly foreign to Chinese parents, who consider associating with the opposite sex to be a distraction from children's duty to study hard. *Photo courtesy of Helaine Alessio.*

What is the implication of underage now in America? Well, it depends. From an Asian-American parenting perspective, in terms of the survey I mentioned above, underage is considered to be high school age for more than 62 percent parents.

2

Not long after I first came to America, I took up residence in a professor's house. When I heard Dr. Perterman's neighbor's children (who were in kindergarten) talk about how many girlfriends or boyfriends they had, I thought it was a joke. However, one day a neighbor pointed out a building to me that was under construction and said, "My daughter's boyfriend's father is building this one." I was surprised, but I was hesitant to even ask. His daughter was only in elementary school!

When Yan was in second grade, we found out that the school asked students to make cards for Valentine's Day. We did not really pay much attention to the matter, but on Valentine's Day we noticed that Yan brought home several cards. One of them was obviously made by a girl. The language was soft and touching, and there was also large red heart in it. Yan looked like he did not care much, so we decided to not mention it.

One day, when I answered the phone, I found that there was a little girl on the other end. She hesitated then finally said, "It's for Yan."

I was shocked but gave the phone to Yan.

Curious as to what little children talked about (and also knowing there was nowhere else in the small dorm I could go to give Yan privacy), I stood nearby and listened. However, Yan dismissed the girl after a few words.

Later, there was another call and it sounded like the same girl. Unfortunately, Yan was not at home.

Thereafter, she did not call again.

In any traditional Chinese family, sex is always a fierce flood and a savage beast. The idea of elementary-school children dating would simply be treason and heresy. In today's China, people's consciousness of sex is as open as in the West. Our generation, however, grew up in the time of asceticism during the 60s and 70s.

3

During the Cultural Revolution, the authorities restricted the people's entertainment and outside influences. Accordingly, there were only eight model operas and just a few movies that one billion people were allowed to watch. China became a cultural desert. As a direct consequence of this, the management of every company and factory tried very hard to recruit talent for their performing arts propaganda teams and sports teams. The idea of companies having sports and entertainment teams might be foreign, but their purpose was to enrich their enterprise culture. You can make an analogy comparing these companies and factories to American universities, which are crazy about recruiting sports players and other talent to enrich campus culture.

During this time, I was sent to the countryside as a peasant for three years. While there, I was recruited to be a member of the performing arts propaganda team for the Third Line for two of these years.

In any war, there are "lines" of defense, and the Third Line was just as its name implies. China was preparing for a potential war with the Soviet Union and/or the United States every day. As such, the front line was the first line, the rear area (behind that front line) was the second line, and behind that? That was the Third Line. The Chinese authority gathered countless peasants to build railways, power stations, and factories in the mountains; these were very far away from the borders. I was one of these peasants, and as I had nowhere else to go, I was happy to comply. That is, until late 1970, when the government allowed factories in the cities to recruit workers from those same students it had sent to the countryside, which made me uneasy. If I stayed with the Third Line, I would lose the chance to be recruited to return to city life. I decided to leave the Third Line and return to the village, called "Green," where I had previously been sent to labor as a peasant.

Upon my return, the village head said, "Little Huang, you have left the village for two years. Your skin is too fair and clear; you do not look like a peasant at all. You know what? You probably won't get the chance to leave the countryside until all your friends have already returned to the city. I think that you had better marry a *country girl* and stay here forever."

I said, "No, no, no! Chairman Mao's Red Guard would never date!"

The village head seemed to know something about my dating already. He gave me a strange look, did not say anything, and left.

One day three months later, the village head came barging into my room without knocking. It was a rainy day, so I was at home instead of laboring in the fields. I was lying on the bed reading a love poem about saying a very sad good-bye. I looked up when the village head entered my room. He was wearing an unnatural expression and quickly said, "Little Huang, an honored guest is looking for you. Did you know that?"

"Who?"

"A comrade, a Northerner from your hometown, Liuzhou City. He is a large man with a big beard. He is living in the guest house of our People's Commune." Upon hearing this, I pushed past the village head and tramped over hills and dales to our People's Commune, which was a large rural organization with governmental, political, and economic functions.

It turned out that our performing team (particularly myself and a few of my teammates) had left a very deep impression on managers and workers from a company that had built a power station in the Third Line. When the company was allowed to recruit new workers, the workers remembered us and the managers decided to send someone to meet with me at the People's Commune. As I've discussed, I had some family issues that might have prevented them from recruiting me. To avoid any barriers cropping up unexpectedly, the company sent the big Northerner with a big beard to put pressure on the People's Commune.

I was surprised to find that the big beard was very nice. He said, "We have investigated your situation. You work very hard, so we consider you to be a child who can be reeducated. You should not worry about your family and let their status burden you. You were unable to choose your class origin, but you are able to choose your future."

Children who were considered to be "reeducable" were those who could be taught to be "good" even though their origins—whether class, family, or something else entirely—were "bad" in the view of the Chinese authorities.

In those years, there were very few people who were as kind to me as this big-bearded man was. I tried to control my tears and just nodded my head.

Suddenly, the big-bearded man turned his face to me and spoke with a very serious tone. "Listen, you will be an apprentice for three years. During these three years, you will be strictly forbidden to date! Are you with me? If I hear anything, you'll be forced to return to the countryside. You should know what that means. Don't say that the Big Beard didn't warn you."

I said, "Just three years? You can make it four! Or five! I won't even look at a girl during these years!"

The Big Beard laughed heartily. "Hey, listen, don't think I don't know anything about *your*. . . ." He trailed off, looking at me for some time, but in the end he chose not to continue on this lethal topic of conversation.

Thank God! I screamed in my mind.

This happened when I had just turned twenty.

4

In 1977, I was almost twenty-six. All the friends I had made in the factory, in the countryside, in schools, and in the Cultural Revolution were already married and had children. Only I, a bachelor, still studied.

Fortunately, the nationwide College Entrance Exam (*Gaokao*) resumed in China that year. Before that, whether or not you could attend college depended not on your merit or grades but on your family origins. As a result, college students were basically workers, peasants, and soldiers. My family origin was bad; I absolutely could not go to college, though I wanted to very badly. I covertly carried my junior-high badge in my jacket pocket for three years, until I left the countryside. In those years, I had never imagined that I, a "child who could be reeducated," would ever be able to go to college. But now Deng Xiaoping had decided to reinstate the College Entrance Exam so that everyone had an equal right to take the exam and attend college. Now it would be your scores, and not your family origins, that determined admission. I was in one of the first groups of college students admitted after the Cultural Revolution. *The Modern Imperial Exam (Gaokao) rescued me!*

However, during my very first day at the university, the authorities made a very serious announcement: "No one is allowed to date during these four years."

Those who had already married were very fortunate, because they could talk with anyone. But when there were girls around, we bachelors would look like birds startled by the mere twang of a bowstring. Sometimes we had to beg the married students to help us pass on information. There is a Chinese saying: "Pretend to advance along one path while secretly going along another—do one thing under the cover of another." Who knew whose information those married ones delivered? They had the option of faithfully delivering your message or surreptitiously delivering any other message of their choosing. Who could you trust? Sometimes we had to discard these middlemen to conduct underground operations. For example, if I wanted to invite a girl to a movie, I would hold a book that had a movie ticket inside and pretend to be a well-behaved student. I'd then ask the girl, "Hey, so and so, I have a question for you on page 38, which I have thought about for a *long* time. Would you please kindly help me?" And then she would open the book to page 38.

If the girl did not want to go, she would say, "Sorry, I really don't know the answer."

If the girl hesitated and did not know whether she should or should not go, she might say, "Well, let me think about it. I will let you know when I have an answer."

Of course, if she wanted to go it would be very simple, "Sure, you're lucky. I'm probably the only one who knows the answer."

And even if the girl made it easy for you and immediately took the ticket, you couldn't arrive at the movie theater together. You had to wait until the movie started and the theater became very dark; only then could you go in, one after the other, just like the underground spies in the movie you might have gone to watch.

5

Traditional Chinese sex education begins with shame. A Chinese friend, Li Shuang, once said, "If you want a child to have a sense of shame about his toes, it's very simple. When the child touches his toes for the very first time, you must seriously scold him. If he touches them again, you must swear, 'That's disgraceful!' and order him to wear socks immediately. Tell him to not allow others to see them and also not to look at others'. You can tell him the names of any parts of his body except his toes. If he asks about his toes, either avoid the question or yell at him. Then congratulations! You have been successful in making your child be completely ashamed about his toes." It's not a healthy approach to sex, to be sure.

Let us look at the differences between how Chinese parents and American parents treat the issue of children dating.

Chinese	American
Education is the first priority; everything, including love, must make way for education.	Education is education; love is love. One should not yield to another.
In certain times, children must concentrate on study.	Love is love; as soon as it occurs, it must be nourished.
In this war of education, love should be postponed until after the war has been won.	Love is human nature; it should not be constrained.
Only when you win the war of education can you enjoy the sweetness of love.	Love is a "war," too. Losing the love war might also cause you to lose the war of education.

From this comparison we can see how Chinese parents handle their children's dating.

The very first strategy of the famous ancient Chinese art of war, as explained in *36 Strategies*, is "to release in order to catch." That is to say, "releasing" is a means, but "catching" is the goal and purpose. "Releasing" is temporary, but "catching" is final and permanent.

We didn't prohibit Yan from dating after he went to high school. In elementary school and junior high, Yan knew that dating was not allowed without us having to explicitly prohibit it. In the same way that the government prohibits children from drinking before reaching the age of twenty-one, driving before reaching the age of sixteen (at least in Ohio), and being admitted to theaters to watch certain explicit movies before reaching the age of seventeen, there must also be some rigid rules from parents when it comes to age. In elementary school and junior high, Yan associated with girls but did not go on dates. If he started to indulge in dating girls when he was in elementary school, how could he have concentrated on studying, built up ambition, and set goals for the future?

After Yan went to high school, we talked with him about our philosophy of love. A person's time and energy are limited; therefore, he or she must handle study and dating wisely. Proper timing is everything. For instance, when you take a test, you must concentrate on your test. The results of thinking about writing a love letter to a girl while taking a math exam would certainly be clear: your test results and the love letter would both be bad. The wise thing to do would be to concentrate on your test first and then think about and write your love letter later.

6

When I was in the countryside, some of my schoolmates couldn't handle the struggles we endured and ended up marrying local peasants. Because of this, they had to stay in the countryside forever. Later, when I was a worker in a city factory, others went to movies and on dates in the evening, but I studied in my dorm every day. An engineer was curious and asked me, "Why do you just stay in your room and study? Everyone else goes on dates."

I pretended to dance with a book and said, "I am dating. I date books!"

He was thoughtful for a moment and then laughed, remembering a meaningful ancient Chinese saying, "There must be golden houses in the books, there must be pretty girls in the books," the meaning of which referred to the rewards that come from careful and diligent studying.

Later, my friends at the factories also married and had children, which meant that they'd stay factory workers forever. I was the only one who went to college. Of course, after I graduated from college, it was finally my turn: I found love and established a happy family.

Sun Tzu, the author of *The Art of War*, is legendary for conceiving of effective but seemingly paradoxical routes to victory.[1] Thus, in order to ensure something is within your grasp, you sometimes have to temporarily let it go. Giving it up is not the end goal, merely a tactic to ensure you will gain it eventually. This, in the end, is the final goal!

There are very few parents who do not want love and a happy family for their children. Chinese parents are not unusually cruel or abstinent. Instead, they have concerns about what the most suitable time is for their children to date.

Picking fruit too early, when it's not ripe, isn't good; the fruits taste bitter and astringent. It's only fully mature fruits that are sweet and delicious.

Dialogue

American parents: This is a really interesting way of looking at things, but we're not sure we can follow the Chinese philosophy on dating.

Huang: The two cultural approaches are different, neither good nor bad. I have two thoughts about kids' dating. First, kids should focus on different things at different times; otherwise the competing interests in their brains will ensure that they don't accomplish anything well. For instance, when you are playing soccer, you should not think about your homework. When you're driving, you shouldn't send text messages with your cell phone. Second, sometimes it's good to restrict kids from doing things at too young an age. Perhaps dating is one of these things.

American parents: An eloquent argument, but we don't know whether our kids will buy it.

Huang: Interestingly enough, while there is not a concept of underage dating in English, there is not a concept of underage drinking in Chinese. This is because in America there's no age limit for dating and in China there's no age limit for drinking alcohol. Generally speaking, the standard age at which dating is considered acceptable by Chinese-American parents' standards is college age. When kids start dating too early, they may not mature properly.

Remember: in order to "gain" the fully mature fruits, you must "give up" the early ripened fruits first; that is, children should wait until they are more mature to date.

PHYSICAL OR PSYCHOLOGICAL PUNISHMENT?

1

As everyone knows, it's illegal to beat children in the United States. Because spanking is a part of Chinese parenting culture, Chinese-American parents are careful about this; nobody wants to cross the line. Interestingly enough, I was told that spanking is still allowed in schools in at least fifteen American states, despite the fact that parents are not legally allowed to beat their children. In China, parents, such as the Wolf Dad, can beat their children (as long as it does not consist of serious abuse), but teachers spanking students is illegal.

I talked about Chinese culture one day in class and mentioned spanking children as a part of Chinese parenting. My students were very excited. I seized this opportunity to do a small survey. All the Asian students in the class had been spanked when they were young. As for who would apologize? The children who were spanked were required to apologize for their bad behavior, not the parents who spanked their children.

2

In traditional Chinese culture there is a saying that parents love to throw around: "To beat is to love. To yell at is to care for." There is a genuine sense among Chinese parents that, in many situations, children will learn the most through suffering direct punishment. This is an idea that American parenting seems to have left behind long ago. Though so-called corporal punishment was the norm at one point in the American household, and even in many American schools, it has since earned a bad name. It's now equated by large numbers of Americans with child abuse. In China, however, there is a world of difference between physical abuse and appropriate and justifiable corporal punishment of a child for his or her betterment. The former is, of course, not acceptable. The latter, however, is widely seen as a necessity in educating a child properly. Using physical punishment to show parents' love—does this make any sense to

Americans? Probably not at all! It makes me think about how Chinese people show their love toward one another, which may confuse Americans even more. Chinese people never say "I love you" in public because traditional Chinese culture emphasizes connotation and subtlety rather than direct statements. Never saying, "I love you," and spanking as a way to show parental love for children: these are very unique and strange characteristics of Chinese culture.

A few years ago, I did an open survey of my students. I asked students in each one of my classes whether any of their family members ever said "I love you" to one other. I was not surprised by the results.

Out of the more than one hundred American students I had in my classes that year, each and every single one said that family members had said "I love you" either to them or to one another. Most of them admitted that they not only hear family members say it, they themselves say it routinely.

"My dad tells me he loves me every time we talk on the phone."

"My parents end all their e-mails with 'We love you,' unless I've done something bad."

"We say 'I love you' every time we say goodbye!"

"Oh my God, me too!"

"Who doesn't?" another asked.

They quickly found out who doesn't. When I asked my Asian-American (mostly Chinese- and Korean-American) students the same question, out of twenty-nine Asian-American students, only *one* had a parent who had ever said "I love you."

"And," she explained, "that was only when I left for college and my mom was already crying and emotional!"

None of the other Asian-American kids had ever had their parents say those words to them. And not a single one of them had ever heard their parents or any other Asian parents say "I love you" to each other.

My American students were absolutely floored.

"*Never*? Your mom has never said 'I love you' to you?" one particular flabbergasted American girl asked.

"No," her classmates responded.

"I don't even think I've ever heard my mom say the word *love*," one of my Chinese-American students said, drawing some laughs.

"Forget love," another Chinese student added, not to be outdone. "Mine have never even said they *like* me!"

After some back-and-forth discussion, one of my American students made a breakthrough.

"You know," she said. "One time a telemarketer called me—and I was so annoyed because I hate getting those calls—but for some reason I stayed on the phone and talked with him for a bit. Then at the end, when I said goodbye, I accidentally said 'I love you' because I say that all the time to my parents, and the man sounded a bit like my dad!" The whole class burst into laughter once more. After things quieted down, she continued explaining.

"Sometimes I say things, like, out of habit, you know? So I said it, but I didn't really mean it. Maybe that's just me."

"No," one of her male peers chimed in. "This morning I ran into a wall, and I actually said, 'Sorry.'"

3

I've repeated this survey in every one of my classes ever since, and the results hold true each and every single time. I realized that though these kids go to the same school, live in the same dorms, and spend large amounts of time with one another, there are small cultural nuggets such as this one that might otherwise remain obscured. I enjoy watching the students learn about the different aspects that are so integral to one another's cultures. Nowadays, I always end these surveys by saying, "I don't want you to answer the following question out loud, so please don't raise your hands. I just want you to think about it to yourselves. Do you think that those of us who don't say 'I love you' in our families actually feel differently about our parents, children, spouses, and siblings than those who do? Do you think they actually do not love one another? Are the words 'I love you' themselves what contain the power? Or are they just symbols of something that is already there? Have you ever said you love something that you didn't? Have you ever loved something or someone silently?"

As for my family, I, too, have never told my son that I love him. I know he doesn't doubt that I love him. However, my wife decided that she would start saying it after he left for college.

"I'm going to say it," she said. "I don't care what you think!"

She held true to her promise, but she doesn't say "I love you." She tells him, "We love you." Sometimes, when we're on the phone with Yan and we're about to hang up, she may forget.

During those times, I use various methods to give her a little reminder, such as a cough or a whistle. However, I never say the words myself.

Chinese love is like a powerful subsurface whirlpool, an underwater current hiding beneath a still and reticent surface. There is no visible bluff and bluster. It's hard to spot the movement of the water. There are few signifying ripples. Though it's not so much to look at, these underwater forces can be just as forceful and turbulent as a storm above the surface.

Of course, some parents may abuse children as a way to vent their anger when their kids misbehave. This is condemned by Chinese culture.

Spanking implies love without saying it outright. Not saying *love* directly also implies love. What a unique cultural phenomenon!

4

In fact, when children can feel, experience, and understand the love their parents have without having to be told—a love beyond the descriptive reach of language—that love will ingrain itself deep into the child's heart. Love that one can feel without any words is real love. This doesn't just apply to love between parents and children. When you love or don't love a certain food, it's not necessary for you to indicate your feelings toward it through words. It's evident by how you eat it. If someone is a guest in your home for dinner, he or she might say "Mmm, so delicious," while thinking, "My God! Salt must have been on sale yesterday!" It would be better not to say anything.

The low-praise, high-criticism style of Chinese parenting is rooted in a strong culture of emotional silence. For Chinese people in general, outward displays of positive emotion are incredibly rare. There are few situations in which Chinese people would feel comfortable verbally stating their love for or appreciation of someone else, even (perhaps especially) family members. Instead of outwardly expressing these emotions, the Chinese, as a people, rely on reserved and modest implicit expressions of love and appreciation. Even the love and appreciation of a parent for a child is not exempt from this rule. Chinese parents may not be able to sleep at night after yelling at or spanking their children, but they will not say it. They do not say "I love you" in public; they would also not apologize to their kids publicly even though they might have thought it a thousand times in their minds. This is the way Chinese parents do things.

This kind of Chinese love is deep and implicit; children need time to gradually feel, experience, and understand it.

5

I was very naughty when I was a kid. My father spanked me several times as a form of discipline, once very hard. Despite this, I have never doubted my father's deep love for me.

I was competitive by nature as a child. I wanted to be better than everyone else at everything; I wanted to be a leader rather than a follower, and I often got into fights. After my father was labeled a Rightist, this character trait became even more pronounced. Because my father was so downtrodden by the authorities and everyone else around us, I wanted to be a king among the children and lead the sons whose fathers led my father. I was popular both off and on campus and my grades were good. Singing, dancing, and sports—you name it, I did it well. My father, however, kept one eye open to my naughtiness. I was beaten hard by father on one occasion.

The middle school at which my mother taught was a new school that was far away from the heart of the city, and there were no elementary schools nearby. Because of this, my mother had to leave me to stay with my father while I was in elementary school.

Though father was not a teacher, he, as a janitor, had a close relationship with the librarians. He often quietly borrowed books for me. Starting in third grade, I began reading adult-level books. Because I was so tiny and the books were so thick, my father would say, "An ant is carrying a big bone."

One day, I read a book that talked about how capitalists cruelly exploited workers and how workers fought with capitalists. I loved books about wars. This book was a little boring, but it inspired me to think up some questions.

On that day, father was not in a good mood, but a question had been bothering me for quite a while. So I asked, "Daddy, this book said that the capitalists cruelly exploited workers. Why did the workers go on strike, willing to die rather than have the factory closed? Isn't it ideal for workers to not be exploited by capitalists? Why were the workers willing to die so they could be exploited and work more?"

I was looking down at the book while I asked the question. I did not hear any responses from my father, so I raised my head.

My God! My father's eyes were wide open, as was his mouth.

I was stupefied!

Suddenly, father roared, "Scoundrel! What impudent words did you say? You want to die?" And then he turned around to look for something.

I knew what my dad was looking for! There was a feather duster with a bamboo stick whose function was to "implement" my family's regulations, just as batons were sometimes used for maintaining public order. I did not know what I had done wrong, but I instantly turned around and ran. I wanted to run to my mother, but she lived too far away. My mother often quarreled with my father; she would protect me, I was sure.

I ran and ran, and after some time, I didn't see my father following me. I continued to run awhile longer. I knew my father. I had run, and the farther I ran, the more sternly I would be punished. The only other option was to run away forever, perhaps to my mother, but I knew she wouldn't agree to me giving up elementary school. As I was pondering my circumstances, I began to slow down, to my own peril. Suddenly, I heard my father's roaring behind me: "STOP!"

I stopped in my tracks, frozen just like a picture in so many movies.

I turned around to look: father was flustered and exasperated but did not have the feather duster. I immediately realized that this punishment would be conducted in private rather than out in the open; it would be more serious!

6

Many years later, after I had come to America, I had my first opportunity to listen to the presidential candidates' debate before the November 1988 US election. One candidate said, "We should create more capitalists to provide more jobs for workers."

I was shocked! This candidate had answered the question that my father had answered with a stick thirty years earlier—according to Marxism, it was capitalists who cruelly exploited workers. *My questions had gone against Marxism*!

There is a Chinese saying, "Misfortune comes from mouth," and, indeed, my father's misfortune of being labeled a Rightist had come from his mouth. It struck me that by administering that heavy beating my father had actually been trying to protect me from my own mouth when I was a kid.

Over the years that passed, my father and I never mentioned my questions or the punishment that followed, even after I left China. But it didn't matter whether I was a child without sense or a middle-aged man with gray hair, whether in China or here in America, I always feel my father's deepest love for me.

Of course, some Chinese children may not feel the true extent of their parents' love because it can only be sensed and cannot be explained in words. It's only after their parents pass away that many begin to realize how deeply they were loved. The problem is that when children cannot experience their parents' love, it's almost impossible to understand that there is love that exists behind the punishments and that the punishments come from a place of love. When children think that their parents' punishments come from a place of hurt and maliciousness, they will resist in their minds the lessons their parents mean to teach by administering the punishments. Consequently, education through punishment will lose its positive meaning.

These can be considered downsides of Chinese parenting: first, physical punishment is improper, and second, there are no kind words to follow up physical punishment that show the true depths of the parents' love for their children.

7

Here, we are going to touch a very difficult, very interesting, and very different cultural comparison and analysis.

The purposes of punishment in Chinese culture is very different from the purpose of punishment in American culture.

The American way (particularly in schools) is to modify or correct the student's misbehavior. In other words, the American way is to draw lines in the form of classroom rules or school regulations and then discipline or punish the person who broke or crossed the lines. In essence, Americans punish transgressions against laws and/or regulations.

The Chinese way (family, school, and social education in general) is to find, to dig out, and to clean the roots of misbehavior. That is to say, the Chinese way is to figure it out the root causes of misbehavior, demonstrate for the person why the behavior is wrong, and then try to educate the person to be moral. It is similar to rehabilitation, to some extent. It is so called *ruling by benevolence/morality*.

Where does a child's misbehavior come from? The Chinese believe that it comes from ego that is located in the person's mind. Ego is seen as a terrible thing in the human mind. Ego is an evil built upon selfishness that makes people become cold blooded and self-centered. Therefore, an extremely important goal of education is to control and punish the ego. Laws, school regulations, and family norms all set their purposes toward controlling and punishing the ego. We have discussed this in the section "A Me or an I?" While physical punishment is necessary, the essential goal of punishment is to aim a person's mind, not just his or her body.

However, I have argued in my book *Quality Education in America* that the primary reason why there have not been any Nobel-prize winners in sciences at

Chinese universities is because Chinese culture has controlled and punished the ego *too much*. My argument has caused a lot of questions and debates in China.

American punishments, while not of the physical variety, have their own unique and difficult characteristics. In fact, if some American punishments were implemented in Chinese schools, many tragedies would occur; Chinese children would simply be unable to bear them. For example, a common American school punishment for young kids consists of a teacher drawing a circle on the blackboard and asking a child to use his or her nose to touch the circle until the teacher releases him or her. American children who are punished through this method might make funny faces during the exercise. After the punishment, it seems as though nothing has happened; the child waves to his or her friends like a little hero. Why? One of the reasons is that his or her ego is not damaged by the punishment. However, this type of punishment would destroy the self-esteem and mental health of Chinese children, increasing their suicide risk as teenagers. Why? Chinese kids have more fragile egos.

8

When Yan was young, he went to school in the morning and was home by around 2:00 or 3:00 p.m. Since the kids in his class were young and did not go to school for a full day, it was customary for parents to provide early afternoon snacks for the children.

One day, Yan asked his mother to take him to a supermarket as soon as he came home. When they got to the store, he pulled his mother into the frozen foods aisle and carefully searched behind the glass doors. Suddenly, he said, "I want Popsicles, can we get them?"

All he wanted was a normal Popsicle. My wife was surprised because he didn't like Popsicles all that much, so one box would last him a long time. This time was different. As soon as he got home, he was incredibly impatient. Tearing open the box, he began to eat one Popsicle after another. He ended up eating three in a row, which was very odd. My wife and I looked at each other and wondered what had happened to him.

I asked him, "Could you let me have one bite?"

Yan hesitated for a while and then said, "No!"

He was enjoying his Popsicle so much, so I asked, "Why do you love Popsicles now, when you never liked them much before?"

"Today, Jessica's mom brought Popsicles to school and everyone ate one," Yan cried. "But I couldn't."

I was shocked. "Why?"

Yan hesitated to tell us, but finally he confessed: he talked to his friends during class, so his teacher punished them by not allowing them to eat the Popsicles.

It's been said that the most effective way to make a dog mad is not to prevent it from eating, but rather to make it watch other dogs eat. I could see that Yan had not coped well with this punishment. Watching your friends and fellow students eat while you're prevented from doing so; it's too cruel for a little kid.

Yan was very sensitive and saw my face change. He tried to pretend he didn't really care about it and said, "Some of the other kids tried to use the Popsicles to make us angry, but we pretended we didn't see them." And then he added, "I don't care at all!"

He had eaten three Popsicles in a row, a snack that he hadn't even previously liked. How could he not care at all?

A few weeks later, when we attended a parent's conference, I saw Yan's teacher. We talked about the Popsicle event. I expressed my concerns: I didn't think this was a healthy way to punish children.

The teacher looked like she didn't think my concerns were even worth a thought. She believed that not allowing a child to eat a treat would result in a lasting memory that would condition the child to refrain in the future from repeating the behavior for which he or she had been punished.

I felt that the teacher had given short shrift to locating the root causes of the misbehavior and explaining why the behavior was wrong and how Yan and his classmates should have behaved. Instead, she gave too much emphasis to punishment.

9

The idea of human nature being pure in Chinese culture has impacted how people view mistakes as well. People start out as completely good; if they gradually become selfish and evil, it must result from the negative impacts of social conditions and education. Thus, many Chinese believe that the Chinese style of punishment is to give a physical warning to the person. Even though a physical punishment appears to be more serious, it's an external punishment intended to avoid hurting the person inside.

Chinese parents and teachers, more often than not, punish physically; the American method of punishment, for the most part, has been trending toward psychological rather than physical intervention.

Darshak Sanghavi, healthcare columnist for Slate.com, reports that according to nationwide data from the National Institutes of Mental Health gathered by a Gallup telephone poll, "almost every parent regularly tries to reason with a wayward child, and nearly three-quarters redirect misbehaving kinds into another activity or use time-outs." However, the same data showed that "roughly half of all respondents admitted to 'spanking on the bottom with a bare hand.'" Other, more serious types of physical punishment were reported at considerably lower rates. Still, this data marks a trend toward reduced reliance on corporal punishment, since "94 percent of parents [in the United States] endorsed hitting kids" as recently as 1968.[2] What, then, accounts for this trend?

Some factors include tougher laws prohibiting child abuse, the employment of no-spanking nannies and daycare centers, and beliefs that spanking can lead to long-term psychological harm. Sanghavi argues that the explanation may be that parents have simply come to the practical conclusion that there are "more effective ways of disciplining children." He points out that "modern practices of child discipline are conveyed through books, television shows, and other forms of popular culture that have shifted parenting norms." Beginning with the mid-twentieth-century publication of pediatrician Benjamin Spock's *The Common Sense Book of Baby and Child Care*, American parents have increasingly had access to "owner's manuals" for caring for and raising children, such as the more recent bestseller *How To Talk so Kids Will Listen and Listen so Kids Will Talk* by Adele Faber and Elaine Mazlish. And the ideas conveyed in these mass-market childcare guides have informed popular television shows such ABC's *Supernanny*, offering "an immersive curriculum on disciplining children without hitting them."[3]

"Without realizing it," says Sanghavi, "we zeroed in on a style of parenting that sociologist Annette Lareau calls 'concerted cultivation.'" Lareau's conclusions have been popularized in Malcolm Gladwell's *Outliers*, which we touched on earlier. Sanghavi argues that concerted cultivation is "what separates those who hit kids from those who don't," and this difference "divides largely along socioeconomic fault lines." "Middle-and upper-class parents," he says, "tended to treat children as peers, with the pint-sized ability to make choices, respond to reason, and have valid emotions. It's not a huge leap then to see children as having nascent civil rights that conflict with regular corporal punishment." And, in fact, nationwide, all but fifteen states now prohibit the use of spanking to discipline children in schools, with the outliers mostly concentrated among conservative Southern states.[4]

Concerted cultivation describes a parental approach in which "parents make behavior charts or create token economies for rewards, answer questions with explanations, and encourage kids to accept and express their feelings." And according to Lareau, "such discipline tends to be self-reinforcing, and part of a broader ecology of parenting" in which children "develop an 'emerging sense of entitlement'—a trait that may carry some negative connotations but generally correlates with better verbal skills, school performance, and a sense that they can actively shape the world around them."[5] Concerted cultivation, however, requires "enormous effort," according to Lareau, "and there may be hidden costs of a parenting style that relies purely on non-physical modes of discipline." Deprived of physical outlets for punishing children, some parents "may inflict equally hurtful emotional pain."[6]

The contradictions in the National Institutes of Mental Health data, showing that "almost every parent regularly tries to reason with a wayward child" while at the same time revealing that about half of parents admitted to spanking their children, may indicate that the enormous effort required by concerted cultivation may be too much for many parents. In other words, it may be the case that American parents have been generally influenced by the ethos of concerted cultivation, as conveyed by experts in the field and the behavior of peer parents who have adopted the strategies advocated by the experts, without fully developing the skills and commitment needed to successfully implement the particulars. Many such parents discard corporal punishment but do not compensate by using other nonpunitive techniques to support a disciplined environment for their children, resulting in parental overindulgence, which, in turn, can result in children having an overdeveloped sense of entitlement and an underdeveloped ability to negotiate structured social environments involving authority figures such as schoolteachers and job supervisors.

Because the parenting ethos in American society has evolved into one that discourages physical punishment, many parents who do not know how to use the methods described by concerted cultivation, and have found that nonpunitive techniques such as time-outs and grounding no longer work, reflexively turn to psychological punishment techniques to enforce discipline. However, psychological punishment techniques such as criticism, name calling, discouragement, blaming, shaming, and using sarcastic or cruel humor can result in negative short- and long-term emotional consequences, such as "low self-esteem, becoming a permanent part of the child's personality."[7]

We all make mistakes; no one is perfect. If grown people and parents make mistakes, how can immature children not do so? Consequently, should children be punished? If so, how should they be punished? These are the questions every family in the world has to consider.

Whether you're the punisher or the punished, punishment in general is not fun. However, it's very difficult to parent successfully without punishing your children, but on the flip side, improper punishment is absolutely unacceptable.

Finding this balance is difficult; punishment can be an art.

Let's summarize the differences between Chinese and American punishments.

Chinese	American
Physical punishment.	Nonpunitive techniques or psychological punishment.
Who was punished must apologize.	Who was wrong must apologize.
Silent love exists everywhere, including within physical punishment.	Love is love; punishment is punishment.

DIALOGUE

American parents: We're uncomfortable with physical punishments, but you don't favor psychological punishments. Can you explain your reasoning?

Huang: Let's take Amy Chua as an example. She detailed in her book how she destroyed her daughter's toys one by one in front of her. This was incredibly cruel. There's a saying: "Kids treat toys as their friends; adults treat their friends as toys." Children often sleep with their toys; they talk to them as friends. As a result, destroying these toys in front of your child is a brutal spiritual punishment. If Chua had let her daughter choose between spanking and destroying her toys, I'm certain she would have chosen to be spanked. This is an example of negative psychological punishment.

American parents: Well, physical punishments are out of the realm of possibility for us, and psychological punishments are too painful. What should we do?

Huang: Rather than punishment, I prefer positive psychological stimulation and education. There is a Chinese story about the King of Chu. One night, the king hosted a banquet for his generals. Suddenly, a gust of wind blew out the candles. While the room was dark, a brazen general, Jiang Xiong, touched the queen's hip. On impulse, the queen grabbed his hat tassel and then asked the king to relight the candles to find out who was missing a hat tassel so that the offender could be punished. The king complied, but he first ordered all of the officials to remove their hat tassels before the candles were lit so no one could determine who the guilty party was.

Years later, the king was surrounded by enemies. Many officials surrendered, but the guilty general fought desperately and rescued the king.[8]

American parents: An interesting example, to be sure! What are the differences between psychological punishment and positive psychological stimulation/education?

Huang: The king could have chosen from among a thousand different ways of physically and psychologically punishing and humiliating Jiang Xiong. However, the king instead used silence to positively stimulate and educate Jiang Xiong; instead of punishing Jiang Xiong, the king stimulated his *guilty sense*, which we discussed earlier. If you really want to say this was a psychological punishment (I prefer psychological "education"), we can define it as a *positive* psychological punishment. The intent of *negative* psychological punishment is to humiliate. However, a precondition of this positive method of education/ punishment is that the person on the receiving end must understand his or her mistake; otherwise, it won't work.

We discussed authority and power previously. The king built his authority in Jiang Xiong's mind through positive psychological stimulation/education. Obviously, if the king had used his power to punish Jiang Xiong, the result would have been very different. American school, social, and family education often uses only power to punish people, but neglects to use authority to educate people.

It's easy to tell a story but difficult to figure out how its lesson applies to your own children, much less how to implement the lesson. Nevertheless, it is possible to use a form of "punishment" that is neither physical not psychological.

FISH OR FISHING?

1

Asian-American children achieve very good grades and some may think that it is because they are good at tests. Of course, Chinese-American students, in particular, may be influenced, to some extent, by the exam culture that is a legacy of the Chinese Imperial Examination System. Nevertheless, they are in American schools and experience the same education as American children. My question is, in addition to the impact from exam culture, are there any other reasons for why they are consistently superior academically?

When it comes to poor grades, some parents blame their children's IQs, some complain about teachers' pedagogy, and some blame the school environment. When Chinese-American parents face this problem, they approach it from a perspective of further increasing and heightening their children's abilities, particularly their abilities to self-teach and apply knowledge (solving problems by drawing inferences using previous knowledge).

2

There is an ancient Chinese proverb that most Americans are likely familiar with, one I've mentioned previously: "Give a man a fish and you feed him for a day. Teach a man to fish and you feed him for a lifetime."

Rather than focusing on the noun (fish) this saying focuses on the verb (to fish). As an educational philosophy, it emphasizes that there are three ways students may approach academics. The first is to passively take the fish that teachers hand out. The second is to engage with teachers on one's own initiative and procure more fish from them. And the third is to teach oneself to fish, or cultivate the ability of self-teaching. Self-teaching is more complicated than it appears, though. It's not only about teaching oneself facts ("what") and procedures ("how"). It's also about the "whys"; that is, understanding why a procedure or methodology yields a correct answer and why a certain assertion is true, not false, and therefore factual. This is the basis of self-teaching.

In comparison to simply receiving knowledge imparted from one's teachers, teaching oneself or studying by oneself creates a deeper and more intimate understanding of the knowledge one has acquired. To fish for yourself and then dine on your catch will make your dinner much more delicious and meaningful than dining on a "fish" caught at the grocery store. More importantly, while gaining knowledge, you are also fostering your various *abilities*. Therefore, Chinese-American parenting actively encourages children to teach themselves.

3

I really enjoyed cultivating Yan's self-teaching ability through the math textbooks I bought him, encouraging him to learn the material on his own rather than wait for his teachers to teach it to him.

Many teachers focus solely on teaching children how to do things and are interested primarily in pulling the correct answer from the children. To produce correct answers, students need only understand the what (established facts) and the how (procedures, as in the case of arithmetic, for solving problems). Such teachers often neglect to stress the *why* behind what they're teaching. This method makes things easier and faster for the teacher, but it isn't beneficial for fostering students' ability to self-teach. This is why I focused on making sure Yan understood the why. If Yan could comprehend the why behind the math problems (the patterns of logic that underlie the mathematical operations), he would have no difficulty with the procedures for actually solving them.

More importantly, understanding the why through self-teaching is *essentially* different from understanding the why by passively learning from a teacher. Self-teaching and goal management help to increase children's learning capacity. Yan taught himself eighth-grade math when he was in the second grade. He's not a math genius at all, but we didn't have to teach it to him. Because we fostered his self-teaching abilities, he was able to accomplish this on his own.

4

In educating Yan, we put emphasis on the idea that "all roads lead to Rome," that there are *a variety of ways* to arrive at the same solution. American education was generally helpful with this, as it often encourages children to solve problems using different methods. However, Yan also benefited from a math game called 24. Chinese children can solve math problems very quickly, and it looks impressive on paper, but they are only interested in the quickest way to solve problems. They aren't interested in finding different or more creative methods to solve problems. I decided to use the game 24 to cultivate creative problem solving in Yan starting when he was about five years old. Here's a rundown of how the game works:

Participants: Unlimited. In our case, the participants were usually just my wife, Yan, and me.

Materials: One or more set of playing cards. Remove all of the face cards (jack, queen, and king), keeping only the number cards and the jokers. The aces stand in for the number 1.

Methods and Rules: Pick out four cards from a facedown deck and place them face up on the table. Using the numbers from the four cards on the table, each player tries to calculate 24 using addition, subtraction, multiplication, and division. Each number can only be used once. The two jokers are wild cards and can be used as any number. Whoever is fastest and reaches 24 first wins the four cards.

For example, let's say the following four cards are drawn: 6, 4, 8, 6.
Here are three possible solutions to reach 24.
Solution 1: $6 \times 6 - 4 - 8$
$(6 \times 6 = 36, 36 - 4 = 32, 32 - 8 = 24)$
Solution 2: $6 + 4 + 8 + 6$
$(6 + 4 + 8 + 6 = 24)$
Solution 3: $(8 \times 6) - (6 \times 4)$
$([8 \times 6] = 48, [6 \times 4] = 24, 48 - 24 = 24)$

In general, you may be able to calculate 24 through several different methods, but there is usually at least one solution.

Sometimes you may be unable to calculate 24 from the numbers on the cards, but patience is key. Someone might eventually figure out a way, as creative methods are sometimes required. Only when all players agree to give up on a certain group of cards can you temporarily put the cards aside. The person who wins on the next set of cards also gets to take the previous set, so there's added incentive to win the next round.

It's always exciting when a joker is one of the four cards. Because the Joker is a wild card, everyone becomes so excited and flustered that no one can reach an answer quickly! If you have a heart problem, you had better walk away when a joker appears.

Because we started playing 24 with Yan when he was so young, he wasn't really good enough to play against us in the beginning. To get around this, I played the game with my wife and let him choose which of us he would help. Thus, he gradually became interested in the game. By the time he reached first grade, he really loved the game and often challenged us to play on his own initiative. He could barely play and lost much more often than he won. As is the case with most skills children learn from parents, early struggles gradually give way until the child becomes competent; before long the child's skill has exceeded the parent's. By the time Yan reached the third grade, he disdained playing with us (it didn't mean he was better than us, but he was tired of playing with us); it was only when other adults participated and there was "fresh blood" at the table that he was still interested.

Playing 24 with Yan fulfilled multiple goals for us. First, it taught him to think quickly and skillfully. Second, it exercised and enhanced his basic math skills. And third, it encouraged him to become more flexible in his thinking, teaching him that there are usually multiple ways to reach one's goals.

5

Yan came to the United States in 1990, and he didn't return to China until 1997, when he was almost thirteen years old. Everyone in China wanted to see how Yan had changed academically as a result of having studied in America. Many people we knew would try to test him surreptitiously, but our relatives didn't disguise their intentions; they tested him openly. My sister's husband and my wife's brother, who were both engineers, asked Yan to solve some math problems. They discovered that while Yan didn't always immediately know the answers, he was able to reach the answers using different methods, some of which were very strange and odd. This amazed our Chinese friends and relatives but didn't necessarily impress them. They thought Yan's methods were silly and unwise. They believed that the smartest way to solve any problem is the fastest, easiest, and clearest.

6

Here's an amusing story I first heard a long time ago:

A professor named Alexander Calandra was called into a colleague's office to deliver a verdict on a student's physics exam. The professor wanted to give the student a zero, but the student claimed he deserved a perfect score.

Calandra looked over the exam question, which asked students to demonstrate how to determine the height of a building using a barometer. The student had answered the question correctly, in Calandra's opinion, but not according to the principles of physics that the students had been taught in class. Specifically, the student said that one could tie the barometer to a rope, lower the barometer from the roof of the building, and then measure the length of the rope, which would correspond to the height of the building. That would, indeed, provide the height of the building, but his answer did not use the methods the physics professor required. Giving the student a high grade on the exam would imply a level of proficiency with physics that his answer did not demonstrate.

Calandra suggested that the student be allowed to answer the question again, with the caveat that the answer must include physics, a condition to which both the student and professor agreed. Again, the student did not answer in a conventional way, but this time he used physics equations in his answers. At this point, Calandra's colleague gave up and gave the student an almost perfect score.

As Calandra left the office with the student, the student disclosed additional ways that the barometer could be used to find the building's height, the easiest of which was to offer the barometer to the building manager in exchange for the building's height. In the end, the student told Calandra that he did know the "proper" way to answer the question, but that he was tired of his instructors trying to control how he thought while valuing the scientific method above all else.[9]

7

As a teacher, I can divide my students into categories according to the following criteria:

1. After I show them examples, they're able to apply the technique to similar problems.
2. Based on the examples and explanation I've provided, they're able to tease out the basic principles and apply them to other, more varied problems.
3. I give them a textbook when the semester starts, and by the end of the semester they'll have taught themselves the entire book.

As parents, we can divide our children into categories using similar criteria:

1. They need to preview lessons before class.
2. They need to review lessons after class.

3. They need to preview lessons before class and review lessons after the class.
4. They need not preview before class or review after class.

However, these categories can be misleading. For instance, many people may think that the children who need neither to preview nor to review are the best students. In many cases, this assumption is wrong, since these students may only be able to complete problems similar to the examples provided by the teacher. It's the child who previews the lesson and teaches it to him or herself who is actually the best student, similar to the students who teach themselves the textbook. As I've discussed, this ability to self-teach is very valuable.

DIALOGUE

American parents: You have detailed the "hows" and "whats" in this section, but not the "whys." *Why* should children understand the "whys"?

Huang: I am glad we are approaching the core of the delegates' story.

American parents: So, we would have to return to your question: Why is it that Chinese middle-school students win the Academic Olympiad competitions every single year while, at the same time, since the first Nobel Prizes in the sciences were awarded in 1901, not a single adult in a Chinese university has ever won? Furthermore, why is it that, in terms of primary education, Chinese kids so easily beat American kids out of the gate, but Americans have, in the end, won the most Nobel Prizes in the world? In short, why is it that the delegates' conundrum has continued to puzzle both the Chinese and Americans for so many years?

Huang: These are the questions that I've been pondering for years. Here is my answer:

There are two kinds of knowledge: that which we, as human beings, know and that which we don't.

Chinese education creates excellent exam takers while American education cultivates learning explorers. This is an essential difference between Chinese and American education.

The purpose of the Academic Olympiad, PISA, and every other standardized test is to evaluate students' ability to recapitulate already-established knowledge. The Nobel Prizes in scientific disciplines encourage scientists to explore and discover new knowledge.

American parents: It seems as though you're trying to say that American education has been producing the top talent in the world. If that's the case, how can you explain the delegates' story? What do we need to work on to improve American education if it's already producing the top talent?

Huang: America does have the best universities in the world. Yet, at the same time, it took an entire semester to have the driveway outside my office paved, something Chinese civilian workers, most of whom were educated as farmers in rural outlying communities, would have been able to do in two days. American culture, identity, and education produced Steve Jobs, but for many different reasons, Apple's products are made in China.

Whereas students in the United States are encouraged to learn by exploration, which unleashes the extraordinary talents of the nation's most creative thinkers while leaving behind the majority of students who lack such extraordinary creativity, the Chinese method of educating students for mastery of the details and methods of established knowledge, so as to ensure success on exams, produces widespread competence throughout the culture at the expense of fostering the creativity needed to innovate toward the end of producing new knowledge. In short, American educational strategies tend to benefit the best and brightest while fostering mediocrity among average students; Chinese educational strategies cultivate widespread competence and even excellence for the majority of students while constraining the creativity of the brightest students by focusing their efforts too narrowly on exam success.

American/Chinese parents: Can you explain the answers to the problems from the delegates' story that have been bothering both cultures for so many years?

Huang: As we know, Chinese kids "have to win" the game, while, as the frontiersmen's descendants, too many American kids are *only* interested in changing the game itself, in the manner of a Bill Gates or Steve Jobs. On the other side, Chinese kids *only* want to win within the game; they never think about designing or changing the game.

American parents: Dr. Huang, you've indicated that Chinese farmers are able to do math in their heads; but too many American college students can't do basic math without a calculator. You're breaking our hearts! What can we do to fix the problem?

Huang: Unfortunately, too many Americans (including parents, teachers, and even professors) think that math is unnecessary for students who do not plan to pursue careers that specifically require a high level of mathematical competence. The number of American adults and children who have to rely on a calculator to do simple math is astounding. What these people don't realize is that math is a sort of "brain gymnastics," good for exercising logical thinking. Learning by analogy and inferring principles from single facts, which I've touched on in this section, is a good way to combine the Chinese method of building basic knowledge and the American way of fostering creativity.

In other words, while we keep working on identifying the *whys*, we must simultaneously improve our ability to understand the *hows* and practice the *whats* without a "calculator."

WHAT IS THE MAIN RESPONSIBILITY OF A STUDENT IN THE FAMILY?

1

The American media learned in 2001 that Yan had published a bestseller in China at a young age. As a result, he received many interview requests. One time, the host of a Fox News program asked Yan, "Can you tell me why you wanted to write a book?"

Yan smiled and said, "When my mom asked me to cut grass or do chores, I could say: 'Mom, I'm writing a book!' She wouldn't ask again."

His answer made the host laugh heartily.

The host said, "Well, I'd rather mow the lawn or do chores than write a book."

The host thought Yan was making a joke because, in many people's minds (and particularly children's), writing a book is much more difficult than doing chores.

Of course, Yan's answer was intended to lighten the atmosphere of the interview and make him more comfortable, but it wasn't actually a joke.

Because writing a book or studying is much more difficult than working around the house, when a child chooses a more difficult task, Chinese-American parents will strongly encourage them. Many Chinese or Chinese-American parents think that not every child wants to study, but every child can mow the lawn. Therefore, when their children choose to write a book or study, why wouldn't parents support and encourage them?

2

Here is a comparison of chores in Chinese parenting and American parenting.

Chinese	American
Doing chores is a punishment (from the child's point of view).	Doing chores will be rewarded (often with money).
Doing chores is a child's responsibility; there's no reason to pay them for it.	Doing chores is only partially the child's responsibility, so you should pay them for doing it.
The primary responsibility of a child is to study; he or she may choose to not do chores or have a job if these interfere with studying.	The responsibilities of a child may include chores and getting a job, along with studying.
Doing chores without money removes the reward; as a result, doing chores might not become a habit.	At the beginning, a child does chores for money, but doing chores may later become a habit.
Money is a very complicated and subtle topic in family education.	Money is a very clear and simple issue in family education.
If money is a real problem for the family, the child may get a job. Otherwise children should focus on important matters, such as studying.	Children want to be independent, therefore they may get a job regardless of whether they need money.
The only thing for which money is used as a reward is achieving good grades.	Parents often reward children for completing their chores with money.

3

Many American children start doing chores when they are very young. Often, their parents will pay them to do their chores. I've asked American parents what the logic is behind this practice. Children are members of the family; why should you pay them to do what is their responsibility? Some said they used chores as a method of educating their children that you must work in order to make money. Others told me that they wanted their children to have their own money so that they would have an opportunity to learn how to save or spend it responsibly.

Some Asian-American families are influenced by American culture; they also use money as a reward when their children complete their chores. However, many Chinese-American families that I know do not follow this practice. To be honest, I've never liked this custom. Why should children be paid to fulfill their duties? Aren't the children also part of the family? Why use this method to teach them to be responsible with money when the tradeoff is deemphasizing their responsibilities as a family member? For this reason, I believe children shouldn't be paid when they complete chores. No one pays a father after he has mowed the lawn, therefore no one should pay the child for doing the same chore. If we don't foster a sense of family responsibility in our children, we're teaching them to be preoccupied with their own personal gains and losses and to be intent on nothing but profit. When such preoccupations are encouraged, parents may even find themselves haggling with children about how much they should be paid for doing their chores. It's not good for money to become children's primary motivation.

However, if you don't have money as an incentive, it's difficult to convince children to complete their chores. Many times when we needed Yan to mow the lawn, we would have to lecture him about the principles behind why we were asking, talking about family members' responsibilities and duties. Since this didn't usually work, we often had to force him to do it. I once thought that if we paid him to mow the lawn every time, we probably wouldn't have to go through this process of explaining and forcing. In fact, he might even ask to mow the lawn on his own initiative. However, money is money and responsibility is responsibility; these two should never be confused. As such, we decided that we would rather have the headache of educating Yan every time instead of just paying him money, which would have sent a message that would have encouraged him to be solely focused on profit. In the end, we never paid Yan to complete his chores, but neither did he do his chores of his own initiative.

4

I have never regretted my stance on not paying for chores, though I did rethink my methods based on a casual observation after Yan went to high school. One day, he missed the school bus after school because of his extracurricular activities. I went to school to pick him up and also gave rides to three of his friends who'd also missed the bus. When I pulled up to the last boy's house, I noticed garbage cans in many yards because it was trash day. As soon as the boy jumped out of the car, he immediately picked up his family's garbage cans and pulled them back into his garage.

I said to Yan with deep feeling, "Look how sensible he is. He noticed the garbage cans and put them back of his own initiative. Would you do that?"

Yan responded, "Probably not."

I wanted to say something else but didn't exactly know how to phrase it.

We were both silent for some time, and then Yan said, "It's a chore that many American children do when they're young. If their parents ask them to pull the garbage can back to the house, they get five cents. If they do it without being asked, they receive ten cents."

I said, "But he's in high school now. Does he still get ten cents for doing it? Is that why he does it?"

Yan answered, "Probably not. He's just gotten used to it by now and considers it his responsibility."

I was lost in thought.

5

We hadn't ever set up a bank account for Yan before he went to college. We told him, "The money in our accounts is yours too." We had also never paid Yan for doing his chores or given him an allowance. Consequently, Yan didn't really understand what money meant before he went to college. When he received money as a gift or from somewhere else, he just gave it to us to put into our accounts.

Theoretically, I believed my approach was correct. It's important to teach children that they're part of and have responsibilities within the family, just as it's good to educate people that they're part of and have responsibilities within their community and country. However, I had to wonder why we often fail to do what's best for the community or country on our own initiative. Why couldn't Yan *see* that the garbage can was out and pull it back of his own accord, simply because it was best for the family to which he belonged?

Bad habits flourish in the absence of human consciousness or will. And in many cases, the strength of individual initiative is inversely proportional to the size of the organization, community, or country to which one belongs. Therefore, individual initiative would be weaker in a larger organization and stronger in a smaller one. This has been demonstrated in China's experiments with communism.

Children are too young to understand their family responsibilities when they first start doing chores. Should we bind those chores to money so that the theoretical and intangible responsibilities can be transformed into clear figures for the child? How many rights (or in this case, how much money) one had would be directly tied to how many responsibilities one took on.

This makes me think that the American method is a double-edged sword; it could help children, but it could also hurt them.

Chinese culture and traditions emphasize that family members are mutually dependent. American family education encourages individual independence. How can we master this weapon and not be hurt by it? This is an issue that needs some serious work. When it came to Yan, I knew that I'd failed in educating him in his family responsibility to do chores, but I was never willing to face this failure because, theoretically, I should have been correct.

6

Money is a very complicated and subtle issue in Chinese parenting, particularly in Chinese-American parenting and family education.

"Gentlemen stress righteousness; mediocre men seek profits."[10] These Confucian words made money a shameful subject in China for more than two thousand years. But in 1992, when China started conducting a market economy, people realized they had to face the issue of money. Before that year, the economic differences between most people were very small, but that changed quickly. Your friends, relatives, and neighbors might have become very wealthy, but you were still poor, subsisting only on your regular salary. This wealth gap, the conflict between realistic attractions and traditional values, makes Chinese people love but also fear money.

When my generation was in its prime, we experienced the change from traditional to modern society in China firsthand. Our conflicted ideas about money were reflected in the torturous ups and downs of the quickly changing Chinese social economy.

When I was sent to the countryside as a teenager, I was very poor, and so was everyone around me. We worked from sunrise to sunset and only made 32 Chinese cents per day for our labors. Those in our neighboring village were even worse off; they made just 8 cents per day, not even enough for a bowl of noodles. However, I never thought I was poor at the time. Of course, I didn't believe I was rich either, but the point is that I didn't really think in those terms. Everyone claimed that the head was the richest man in the village, but his house, food, and clothing were no different from anyone else's. Since no one was rich, no one was poor. Even if you had the inclination to steal, there was barely anything to take. When people went out into the fields during the day, no one locked their doors (not even the village head!) because there was nothing to protect within the homes; the doors simply didn't need to be locked.

After I graduated from college, I became a professor at a university and made about 50 Yuan per month. I, of course, was not rich, but my salary was enough to provide for my basic needs (housing, water, and utilities cost around 1 Yuan). At that time, China was starting to see its first rich men. It was then that we started to feel there was a gap between rich and poor people, and it made us realize that money was actually important.

7

The ultimate aim of traditional Chinese family education in regard to money is not to waste or be frivolous with it but at the same time to not pay too much attention to it.

I was deeply influenced by this kind of family education.

After my father was demoted to janitor, his monthly salary was reduced substantially; my mother became the primary breadwinner for the family.

I'm not sure what her reasons were, but when I was in the fifth grade, my mother started sewing large amounts of money into my clothes. I'm not exactly sure how much, but I could feel that there was a lot in there.

One day, my mother came by my school and spent a few minutes whispering with my teacher, who was her friend. My teacher let me out of class and my mother took me to a private place, away from prying eyes, and explained that she needed money very badly. She had come to her "bank" to withdraw 15 Yuan of her savings.

She removed the money and then I went back to my classroom.

After class, my teacher held me back. She patted me on the head and said, "Your mom came to you. . . . Good boy. . . ." She was overcome with emotion and couldn't continue to speak her thoughts aloud.

During that time in China, many people were starving to death. Though I was just a boy, my mother had entrusted me with a large sum of money, which I could have spent on various very enticing snacks and sweets.

I have thought about this for a long time and now realize that there are two reasons why my mother stitched money into my clothes when I was a boy. First, she wanted to give me a sense of how to be responsible with money. She wanted to set an example of saving money rather than spending it wastefully. Second, she wanted me to feel responsible and foster a sense of trust. If someone trusts you, you have a responsibility to reward his or her faith in you. What a great mother she was to me. By stitching that money into my clothes and making me "rich" as a child, she's enriched me for a lifetime.

Money is, unfortunately, a topic that you can't avoid, and because of that, it's also an educational issue that no culture can ignore.

Regardless of whether you're raising your child using Chinese or American parenting methods, allow them to work and manage money. By working hard, they will understand the value of money, have new experiences in society, gain some independence, become more responsible, and become more able to survive in society on their own. This is proper parenting.

Chinese and Chinese-American parenting methods put too much emphasis on studying as the primary responsibility of a child, which neglects the importance of doing chores and working. On the other hand, American parenting might overemphasize chores and working to the detriment of studying. A balance between the two approaches is necessary.

8

A business friend of mine from North Carolina had dinner at my house one evening. He brought along his son, who was working for him as his assistant at the time.

He asked, "Did your wife ever stitch money into Yan's clothes when he was a child, to promote the idea of saving?"

I looked at my wife and said, "There's a little boy in our neighborhood who just turned six. His parents collected all the money he'd received as gifts (around $200) and opened a bank account in his name. After they came home from the bank, the boy was so excited that he put on his dad's suit and walked around with his checkbook, yelling, 'Who wants to borrow money from me?'"

I added, "A Chinese boy, as I was all those decades ago, might try to save money and be rich, but this American boy was trying to use his money to make more money!"

My friend and his son laughed!

Whether we're talking about 15 Yuan or 200 dollars, I understand that parental education is intangible but priceless.

9

Which parenting style should we use? The Chinese style? The American style? Or perhaps we should use Chinese-American Co-Core Synergy Education?

We'll still be debating these issues when our Chinese-American son develops his own parenting style in the near future.

DIALOGUE

Chinese parents: What's wrong with emphasizing the "student" role under Chinese parenting?

Huang: It's not good to emphasize that your child should *only* be a student to the detriment of everything else. A child who *only* studies but doesn't do chores, work, and socialize with other children, and ignores extracurricular activities that aren't directly tied to academics, isn't a well-rounded, healthy child. In fact, many Chinese-American parents have abandoned this single-emphasis view; they realize that "street smarts" is even more important than "book smarts."

Chinese parents: How can Chinese parents in China incorporate your Co-Core Synergy Education into our parenting styles? Chinese-American parents have no way of avoiding American schooling and society, so it comes more naturally for them.

Huang: I have written a series of books to answer your questions. In summary, the roots of parenting must be planted in society, and education shouldn't only focus on training exam takers. Chinese parenting and education must forget the delegates' story about American education and instead pay particular attention to how Americans emphasize creativity, critical thinking, independence, and other traits that make children well-rounded and healthy individuals.

Chinese and American parents: Are you talking about Co-Core Synergy Education?

Huang: Yes! But with the theory comes more questions. For example, how do we create a reality in which Asian Americans, who currently occupy 20 percent of the seats in the top twenty universities, also occupy 20 percent of the positions as top lawyers, doctors, scientists, and Nobel-Prize winners? There is always room for improvement, and as a Chinese-American father and professor, I am greedy for more!

EPILOGUE

Chinese Parenting + *American* School Education + *American* Social Education
= *Chinese-American* Education

When you convert the above formula into a graph, a very interesting phenomenon appears: while the core strengths of Chinese education and American education *appear* to be separate, as illustrated below, Chinese-American students benefit from a combination of the core strengths of each.

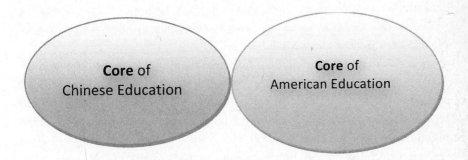

Chinese-American parents and children don't have a choice; they must adapt to the changes resulting from their necessary participation in American school and social education. Therefore, these two *cores* of education have combined into what I call Co-Core Synergy Education. Sometimes, having no choice can be a good thing. Because Chinese Americans have no say in this matter, similar to other Asian Americans, Chinese-American children have achieved extraordinary successes by combining the essentials of two different cultures and their associated educational styles.

However, American families aren't forced to face this same dilemma. As a result, they often ignore or are unaware of the benefits of educational styles practiced in other cultures. American parents may therefore be completely ignorant of the potential benefits of trying the strategies that are at the core of Chinese education.

If we want to get ahead, whether as an individual or a country, we must face challenge and competition from others. In the competitive modern world, the best way to get ahead is to identify superior techniques used by others so that you can put those techniques to work to improve your own performance.

Asian-American parenting and education are now firmly planted within the American educational environment, providing competition and balance to the system. Looking at things from a political point of view, think of Asian-American education as an opposition party. Just as Republicans scrambled to adopt the social-networking techniques that were used so effectively by Democrats to mobilize voters during the 2008 presidential campaign, American parents and educators should identify and incorporate the most effective strategies used in Asian-American parenting and education. Likewise, education in China could benefit from a careful exploration of the strengths of American parenting and education in a search for strategies that might help Chinese education produce not only successful exam takers, but also knowledge creators who might vie for Nobel Prizes and the Fields Medal.

For Chinese-American families, Chinese family education *must* accommodate American school and social education to produce Chinese-American education. That causes the two cores to overlap, producing *synergy*. With regards to the overlapping portion, which represents educational synergy, how big should it be? It will vary with each individual. However, it isn't good when there is a complete overlap because a bigger overlap signifies less competition between opposing educational philosophies, and competition is what produces innovation.

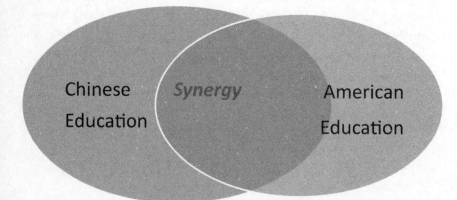

Synergy education can make kids—not just Asian-American kids, but American kids as well—stronger.

As for how you should implement Co-Core Synergy Education and how big the synergy portion should be for your own individual kids? You, an explorer, must answer that question for yourself.

NOTES

INTRODUCTION: THE BESIEGED CITY

1. Zhongshu Qian, *Besieged City* (Beijing: People's Literature Publishing House, 1980), p. 89.

2. Sun Tzu, "Sun Tzu," *Concise Edition of the Chinese Philosophy* (Beijing: Beijing Publishing House, 1973), p. 177.

3. National Commission on Excellence in Education, "A Nation at Risk: The Imperative for Educational Reform," April 1983, http://datacenter.spps.org/uploads/SOTW_A_Nation_at_Risk_1983.pdf (accessed October 8, 2013).

4. "No Child Left Behind Act," *Wikipedia*, http://en.wikipedia.org/wiki/No_Child_Left_Behind_Act (accessed October 8, 2013).

5. Barack Obama, "Remarks by the President in State of Union Address," United States Capitol, Washington, DC, January 25, 2011, http://www.whitehouse.gov/the-press-office/2011/01/25/remarks-president-state-union-address (accessed October 13, 2013).

6. Organization for Economic Cooperation and Development, *PISA 2009 Results: Executive Summary*, 2010, p. 8, http://www.oecd.org/pisa/pisaproducts/46619703.pdf (accessed October 8, 2013).

7. Since the College Board and other testing institutions only track testers by broad racial groups (such as "Asian and Pacific Islander" or "non-Hispanic white"), there are no reliable statistics for Chinese students only. However, one can infer from the fact that Chinese Americans account for a majority of Asian Americans that many of these statistics are reflections of the influence of Chinese education.

8. "America's Asian Population Demographic patterns & Trends," Proximity One, http://proximityone.com/cen2010_asian.htm (accessed October 8, 2013).

9. "America's Best Colleges: How to Find the Right School for You," *U.S. New & World Report* (2010 Edition): 137–91.

10. About 49 percent of all Asians in the United States have earned a bachelor's degree or higher, compared with 31 percent of non-Hispanic whites, 18 percent of non-Hispanic blacks, and 13 percent of Hispanics. See Pew Research Center, "The Rise of Asian Americans," Pew Research Social & Demographic Trends, June 19, 2012, http://www.pewsocialtrends.org/2012/06/19/the-rise-of-asian-americans/ (accessed October 8, 2013).

11. As of 2008, the Council of Graduate Studies estimated that Asians were overrepresented in every major area of graduate studies except "humanities and arts" (5 percent) and "public administration and services" (3 percent). See COGS, "Graduate Enrollment and Degrees 1997–2007 (Revised November 2008)," Council of Graduate Studies, http://www.cgsnet.org/ckfinder/userfiles/files/R_ED2007.pdf (accessed October 9, 2013).

12. Ibid. Areas of overrepresentation include business (23 percent), education (13 percent), engineering (13 percent), health sciences (12 percent) and physical sciences (9 percent).

13. Pew research Center, "The Rise of Asian Americans."

14. This refers to the Nobel Memorial Prize in Economic Sciences, not one of the original prizes associated with Alfred Nobel, but nowadays largely synonymous with "Nobel Prize."

15. John Bardeen won twice in physics and Linus Pauling won once in chemistry and peace. See "United States Nobel Prize Winners," Jinfo.org, 2012, http://www.jinfo.org/US_Nobel_Prizes.html (accessed October 8, 2013).

16. http://en.wikipedia.org/wiki/List_of_Chinese_Nobel_laureates

This list includes Tsung-Dao Lee, Frank Chen Ning Yang, Samuel Chao Chung Ting, Yuan Tseh Lee, Steven Chu, Daniel Chee Tsui, and Roger Yonchien Tsien. See "List of Chinese Nobel Laureates," *Wikipedia*, http://en.wikipedia.org/wiki/List_of_Chinese_Nobel_laureates (accessed October 8, 2013).

17. Quanyu Huang, *Educational Selections from Quanyu Huang: Quality Education in America* (Beijing: People's University Publishing House, 2010), p. 5.

18. Qian, *Besieged City*, p. 89.

19. *China Book Business Report*, February 27, 2001, p. 11.

CHAPTER 1. "CHINESE-AMERICAN" EDUCATION

1. Yan Tzu, "Yan Tzu Visited Chu State" in *Chinese Proverbs & Allusions* (Shanghai: Fine Art Publishing House, 1984), pp. 1452–63.

2. Amy Chua, *Battle Hymn of the Tiger Mother* (New York: Penguin, 2011), pp. 3–4.

3. "Battle Hymn of the Tiger Mom," *demeter clarc* (blog), February 16, 2011, http://www.demeterclarc.com/tag/amy-chua/ (accessed October 10, 2013).

4. Emphasis added. Amy Chua, *Battle Hymn of the Tiger Mother* (New York: Penguin, 2011), p. 53.

5. "America's Best Colleges: How to Find the Right School for You," *U.S. New & World Report* (2010 Edition): 137–91.

6. "The Rise of Asian Americans," Pew Research Social & Demographic Trends, June 19, 2012, http://www.pewsocialtrends.org/2012/06/19/the-rise-of-asian-americans/ (accessed October 8, 2013).

7. Yan Tzu, "Yan Tzu Visited Chu State," pp. 1452–63.

8. Quanyu Huang, *Educational Selections from Quanyu Huang: Gifted Education in America* (Beijing: People's University Publishing House, 2010), pp. 195–96.

CHAPTER 2. EDUCATION CAN CHANGE GOD'S WILL

1. Quanyu Huang, Tong Chen, "Sino-American Kids' Leisure Time Comparison," unpublished student project, Miami University, September 28, 1993.

2. Lan Yu, Hoi K. Suen, "Historical and Contemporary Exam-Driven Education Fever in China," *KEDI Journal of Educational Policy* 2, no. 1 (2005): 17–33, http://suen.educ.psu .edu/~hsuen/pubs/KEDI%20Yu.pdf (accessed October 21, 2013).

3. He Gan, "Chinese Education Tradition: The Imperial Examination System in Feudal China," *Journal of Management and Social Sciences* 4, no. 2 (2008): 115–33, http://www.biztek .edu.pk/downloads/research/jmss_v4_n2/5%20chiness%20Education%20Tradition%201.pdf (accessed October 21, 2013).

4. Quanyu Huang, R. Quantz, and T. Chen, "Marxism and Christianity within the Great Wall," *Asian Philosophy* 4, no. 1 (1994): 44–45.

5. Rui Wang, *The Chinese Imperial Examination System: An Annotated Bibliography* (Lanham, MD: Scarecrow Press, 2013), pp. 18–19.

6. "Chinese Students Are Good at Math, It May Be because of Chinese Characters," Global Network for Chinese Professionals, http://www.networkchinese.com/region/spore/ mahua.html (accessed October 21, 2013).

7. Malcom Gladwell, *Outliers* (New York: Little, Brown and Company, 2008), p. 231.

8. Ibid., p. 233.

9. Ibid., pp. 247–49.

10. "Fields Medal," *Wikipedia*, http://en.wikipedia.org/wiki/Fields_Medal (accessed October 14, 2013).

11. Gladwell, *Outliers*, pp. 227–31

12. Quanyu Huang, *Educational Selections from Quanyu Huang: Gifted Education in America* (Beijing: People's University Publishing House, 2010), pp. 403–404.

13. Mencius, "Mencius," in *Concise Edition of the Chinese Philosophy* (Beijing: Beijing Publishing House, 1973), p. 187.

14. Gladwell, *Outliers*, p. 233.

CHAPTER 3. DEVELOPING KIDS' AMBITIONS
BEFORE DISCOVERING
THEIR INTERESTS

1. Confucius, "Confucius," in *Concise Edition of the Chinese Philosophy* (Beijing: Beijing Publishing House, 1973), p. 42.

2. Lao Tzu, "Lao Tzu," in ibid., p. 235.

3. Pius Ephenus, "Goal Setting—The Power of Writing Down Your Goal," Articlesphere. com, http://www.articlesphere.com/Article/Goal-Setting---The-Power-Of-Writing-Down-Your -Goal/98032 (accessed October 15, 2013); Tom Bay, *Look Within or Do Without: 13 Qualities Winners All Share* (Pompton Plains, NJ: Career Press, 2000).

4. Maureen Dowd, "'I'm President,' So No More Broccoli!" *New York Times*, March 23, 1990, http://www.nytimes.com/1990/03/23/us/i-m-president-so-no-more-broccoli.html (accessed October 16, 2013).

5. Tim Teeman, "Lang Lang: The Piano Man," *News* (*Australian*), December 1, 2012, http://www.theaustralian.com.au/news/world/lang-lang-the-piano-man/story-fnb64oi6-1226 526459089#sthash.oYheHgMQ.dpuf (accessed October 21, 2013).

6. Paul Richter, "Chinese-Born Pianist Denies He Played Song to Insult U.S." Los Angeles Times, January 25, 2011, http://www.huffingtonpost.com/2011/01/25/lang-lang-chineseborn -pia_n_813860.html (accessed October 21, 2013).

7. Confucius, "Confucius," p. 42.

8. Yan Tzu, "Lao Tzu," p. 235.

9. K. Huang, *My Seven American Teachers* (Taipei, Taiwan: Tienwei Press, 2001), pp. 154–58.

CHAPTER 4. WHAT DOES "PARENTING" MEAN
IN A CHINESE-AMERICAN FAMILY?

1. Xu Fang, "A Chinese Professor becomes a Nanny in the U.S.," People.com, September 4, 2006, http://scitech.people.com.cn/GB/4774853.html (accessed October 21, 2013).

2. Ariel Tung, "Big Apple Tempts Chinese Buyers," *China Daily*, October 8, 2012. http:// www.chinadaily.com.cn/china/2012-10/08/content_15799223.htm (accessed October 17, 2013).

3. Peng Xia, "How to Prepare Educational Funds for Your Children?" Xiangrikui.com, May 25, 2012, http://quick.xiangrikui.com/blog/420681.html (accessed October 21, 2013).

4. K. Huang, *New Heights in America* (Beijing: Jieli Publishing House, 2001), pp. 8–16.

5. Quanyu Huang, J. Leonard, and T. Chen, *Business Decision Making in China* (Binghamton, NY: International Business Press, 1997), pp. 261–62.

6. Guihua Wu, "How Many Christians Are in China?" Mzb.com, April 2, 2012, http://www.mzb.com.cn/html/Home/report/289230-1.htm (accessed October 21, 2013).

7. Florrie Fei-Yin Ng, Eva M. Pomerantz, and Shui-fong Lam, "European American and Chinese Parents' Responses to Children's Success and Failure: Implications for Children's Responses," *Developmental Psychology* 43, no. 5 (2007): 1239–55.

8. Runsheng Wang, Lei Wang, *Tendency of Ethic in China* (Guiyang, Guizhou: Guizhou People's Publishing House, 1986), pp. 18–19.

CHAPTER 5. THE LIFE UNION AS A MODEL FOR FAMILY

1. Zheng Xu, "Yang Peiyi Doesn't Feel Wronged for Lip Synching for Lin Miaoke," December 19, 2008, 163.com, http://sports.163.com/08/1219/10/4TH3UIHJ00051KMJ .html (accessed October 18, 2013)

2. Cindy Blumenthal, "From He Zhili to Yu Wang: Two Generations, Same 'Match-Fixing' Victims," August 7, 2012, examiner.com, http://www.examiner.com/article/from-he-zhili-to-yu -yang-two-generations-same-match-fixing-victims (accessed October 18, 2013); Quanyu Huang, J. Leonard, and T. Chen, *Business Decision Making in China* (Binghamton, NY: International Business Press, 1997), pp. 238–40.

3. Paul E. Pfuetze, *Social Self* (New York: Record Press, 1954), p. 91.

4. Henrik Ibsen, *A Doll's House*, in *Six Plays by Henrik Ibsen*, trans. Eva Le Gallienne (New York: Random House, 1978), p. 77.

5. Xiegang Gu, *A Simple Explanation to the Origin and Development of Characters* (Beijing: Rong Bao Publishing House, 1979), p. 408.

6. Confucius, "Confucius," in *Concise Edition of the Chinese Philosophy* (Beijing: Beijing Publishing House, 1973), p. 49.

7. Ibid., p. 46.

8. Quanyu Huang, R. Andrulis, and T. Chen, *Opening the Great Wall's Gate* (Binghamton, NY: Haworth Press, 1994), pp. 70–71.

9. Xiegang, *Simple Explanation*, p. 39.

10. "Ti Tzu Kui," (Yuxiu Li, *The Standards for Being a Good Child/Student*), *Wikipedia*, http://en.wikipedia.org/wiki/Ti_Tzu_Kui, (accessed October 27, 2013).

11. Quanyu Huang, T. Chen, and K. Huang, *McGraw-Hill's Chinese Dictionary* (New York: McGraw-Hill Company, 2011), p. 1818.

12. Huang, Andrulis, and Chen, *Opening the Great Wall's Gate*, pp. 69–70.

13. Frederick Jackson Turner, "The Significance of the Frontier in American History," in *The Frontier in American History* (New York: Holt, 1921), http://xroads.virginia.edu/~HYPER/ TURNER/ (accessed October 22, 2013).

14. John F. Kennedy, "The New Frontier," Democratic National Convention nomination acceptance address, Memorial Coliseum, Los Angeles, CA, July 15, 1960, American Rhetoric, http://www.americanrhetoric.com/speeches/jfk1960dnc.htm (accessed October 22, 2013).

15. Huang, Andrulis, and Chen, *Opening the Great Wall's Gate*, pp. 6–7.

16. K. Huang, *My Seven American Teachers* (Taipei, Taiwan: Tienwei Press, 2001), pp. 192–93.

17. Huang, Chen, and Huang, *McGraw-Hill's Chinese Dictionary*, p. vii.

CHAPTER 6. OTHER INTERESTING PHENOMENA IN CHINESE-AMERICAN FAMILIES

1. Sun Tzu, "Sun Tzu," in *Concise Edition of the Chinese Philosophy* (Beijing: Beijing Publishing House, 1973), p. 161.

2. Darshak Sanghavi, "Spank No More: Why Are Fewer Parents Hitting Their Kids?" Slate.com, http://www.slate.com/articles/health_and_science/medical_examiner/2011/12/spanking_is_on_the_decline_why_.html (accessed October 25, 2013).

3. Ibid.

4. "Study Finds 15 States Still Legally Allowed to Spank Students in School," CBS Atlanta, March 16, 2012, http://atlanta.cbslocal.com/2012/03/16/study-finds-15-states-still-legally-allowed-to-spank-students-in-school/ (accessed October 23, 2013).

5. Sanghavi, "Spank No More."

6. Ibid.

7. "Child Discipline," *Wikipedia*, http://www.en/wikipedia.org/wiki/Child_discipline (accessed October 25, 2013).

8. "Don't Manifest Others' Problems," cd.org, http://www.cd.org.tw/becute/big5/tai/tai_27.htm (accessed October 27, 2013).

9. Alexander Calandra, "The Barometer Story," Reading for Philosophical Inquiry: A Brief Introduction to Philosophical Thinking, http://philosophy.lander.edu/intro/introbook2.1/x874.html (accessed October 23, 2013).

10. Confucius, "Confucius," in *Concise Edition of the Chinese Philosophy* (Beijing: Beijing Publishing House, 1973), p. 50.

INDEX

"able to do," 87, 106, 117, 118, 120, 121.
    See also "love to do"
Academic Olympiad, 236. *See also* PISA
    (Program for International Student
    Assessment); TIMSS(Trends in Interna-
    tional Mathematics and Science Study)
accompany one's child in studying, 137.
    See also Peidu; one family one child
ACT, 21. *See also* AP; PSAT; SAT
American Dream, 36–40, 54, 66, 152. *See
    also* New World
American Idol, 117, 118, 120
American Imperialism, 50
American imperialists, 16
Anti-Rightist Movement, 49
    Rightist, 49, 50, 182, 183, 222, 223
AP, 83, 85. *See also* SAT; PSAT
Aristotle, 187
Art of War, The (Sun Tzu), 14, 216, 217
asceticism, 211
at the beginning, human nature was
    good, 181. *See also* human nature is
    pure; original sin
authority, 16, 44, 47, 52, 145, 146–54,
    165, 228, 230. *See also* power; tran-
    scendent influence

Battle Hymn of the Tiger Mother (Chua),
    29, 33
battle of elimination, 54, 64. *See also* life-
    or-death struggle

Besieged City (Qian Zhongshu), 9, 24,
    27, 88
"Big 14," 110, 113
Bill Gates, 47, 237
brain gymnastics, 238
Bush, Barbara, 121

capitalists, 222, 223
career selection, 47, 115, 116, 119, 120,
    127, 128. *See also* great ambitions
carry guilt, 180, 181. *See also* carry loans;
    guilty sense
carry loans, 184. *See also* carry guilt
census data, 18
China's geography, 198. *See also* frontier;
    frontiersmen
Chinese Bridge Competition, 107, 108.
    See also Confucius Institute; HSK
Chinese family culture, 196
    carry guilt, 180, 181
    dongshi (sensible child), 188
    filial devotion, 188
    filial obedience, 188, 194
    filial piety, 34, 187, 188, 189, 193,
        194, 204
    filial respect, 134, 188, 194
    life union, 167, 179, 207
    sacrifice, 34, 39, 43, 47, 51, 69, 103,
        117, 131, 132, 137, 140, 144, 145,
        150, 151, 152, 135, 165, 167, 168,
        169, 170, 171, 173, 174, 178, 180,
        186, 193, 197, 206